Voices from the Vietnam War

VOICES FROM THE
VIETNAM WAR

Stories from
American, Asian,
and Russian Veterans

XIAOBING LI

THE UNIVERSITY PRESS OF KENTUCKY

Scholarly publisher for the Commonwealth,
serving Bellarmine University, Berea College, Centre College of Kentucky,
Eastern Kentucky University, The Filson Historical Society, Georgetown
College, Kentucky Historical Society, Kentucky State University, Morehead State
University, Murray State University, Northern Kentucky University, Transylvania
University, University of Kentucky, University of Louisville, and Western
Kentucky University.

Editorial and Sales Offices: The University Press of Kentucky
663 South Limestone Street, Lexington, Kentucky 40508-4008
www.kentuckypress.com

14 13 12 11 10   5 4 3 2 1

Maps by Dick Gilbreath, Stephanie Shaw, and Ted Smith
at the University of Kentucky Cartography Lab.

Library of Congress Cataloging-in-Publication Data

Li, Xiaobing, 1954-
  Voices from the Vietnam War : stories from American, Asian, and Russian
veterans / Xiaobing Li.
      p. cm.
  Includes bibliographical references and index.
  ISBN 978-0-8131-2592-3 (hardcover : acid-free paper)
  1. Vietnam War, 1961-1975—Personal narratives. I. Title.
  DS559.5.L518 2010
  959.704'30922—dc22   2010007779

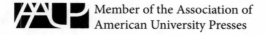 Member of the Association of
American University Presses

For Tran, Kevin, and Christina

Contents

List of Maps   ix
List of Photographs   x
Abbreviations   xi
Note on Transliteration   xiii
Acknowledgments   xv

Introduction: The Long War   1

Part One. *A Country Divided*

1. A Buddhist Soldier Defends a Catholic Government   15
2. Surviving the Bloody Jungle   23
3. Electronic Reconnaissance vs. Guerrillas   31
4. Communist Regulars from the North   39
5. People's War against Americans   47
6. No Final Victory, No Family Life   55

Part Two. *Hanoi's Comrades*

7. Russian Missile Officers in Vietnam   65
8. The Dragon's Tale: Chinese Troops in the Jungle   73
9. Chinese Response to the U.S. Rolling Thunder Campaign   85
10. Russian Spies in Hanoi   93

Part Three. *Saigon's Allies*

11. Long Days and Endless Nights: An Artillery Story   101
12. And Then They're Gone . . . Just Like That   111

13. No John Wayne Movie: Real Bullets, Real Blood   123
14. More Than Meets the Eye: Supporting the Intelligence Effort   131

Part Four. *Doctors and Nurses*
15. Medevac and Medcap Missions and More   143
16. Drowning Tears with Laughter   153
17. Life and Death of an ARVN Doctor   165
18. A Korean Captain and His Hospital   177

Part Five. *Logistics Support*
19. "Loggie's" War: Napalm, Fuel, Bombs, and Sweat   191
20. Support and Survival in Thailand   199
21. Three Great Escapes   205
22. Chinese Railroad Engineering Operations   215

Conclusion: Perspectives on the War   223

Notes   229
Selected Bibliography   251
Index   269

Maps

 1. Vietnam and Asia   4
 2. Vietnam, 1955–1975   18
 3. Saigon and Surrounding River Bases, 1964–1975   34
 4. Ho Chi Minh Trail, 1963–1975   50
 5. Viet Minh's Dien Bien Phu Campaign, March–May 1954   58
 6. Chinese AAA Divisions in Vietnam, 1965–1968   80
 7. Da Nang, South Vietnam   146
 8. ARVN Fourth Tactical Zone and the Mekong Delta, 1964–1975   169
 9. Gih Dinh Province, South Vietnam, 1955–1975   208
10. Major Railroads in North Vietnam, 1965–1973   219

Photographs

1. S.Sgt. Huynh Van No and the author in Ho Chi Minh City in 2006 21
2. Memorial service of the Airborne Division in Oklahoma City in 2003 28
3. Lt. Nguyen Nhieu in the United States in 1998 37
4. Capt. Ta Duc Hao and the author in Longxuyen in 2006 53
5. Lt. Gen. Huynh Thu Truong in Saigon in 1975 61
6. Lt. Gen. Huynh Thu Truong (PLAF, ret.) in My Thanh in 2006 62
7. Russian SAM-2 missile in North Vietnam 69
8. Capt. Zhao Shunfen (PLA, ret.) in Beijing, China, in 2005 83
9. Chinese AAA troops in Yen Bai in 1966 89
10. Sgt. David E. McCray and Battery E in 1971 103
11. Sgt. David E. McCray in 2004 109
12. Maj. Curt Munson at the Khe Sanh Mountains in 1970 114
13. Maj. Curt Munson in 2008 120
14. Lt. Gary Doss and the "Ugly Angel" at Ky Ha in 1967 126
15. Lt. Gary Doss and one of the graduate research assistants in 2003 129
16. Lt. Col. Terry Lynn May in 2003 138
17. 2nd Lt. Judy Crausbay Hamilton and her aero-medical evac team in 1966 155
18. 2nd Lt. Judy Crausbay Hamilton receives her medal in 1967 161
19. Dr. Nguyen Canh Minh and other physicians at the prisoner camp in 1976 173
20. Dr. Nguyen Canh Minh in 2007 175
21. Dr. Walter B. Jung in 2001 187
22. M.Sgt. David Graves in 2004 202

Abbreviations

AAA	antiaircraft artillery
AIT	advanced individual training
ARCOM	Army Commendation Combat Medal (U.S. Army)
ARVN	Army of the Republic of Vietnam (South Vietnam)
BITS	Basic Infantry Training School (U.S. Marines)
CCP	Chinese Communist Party
CIA	Central Intelligence Agency (U.S. government)
CMC	Central Military Commission (Chinese Communist Party)
CPVEF	Chinese People's Volunteer Engineering Force (PLA)
CSF	Chinese Supporting Forces (PLA)
DEROS	rotation to the States (U.S. armed forces)
DIA	Defense Intelligence Agency (U.S.)
DMZ	Demilitarized Zone
DRV	Democratic Republic of Vietnam (North Vietnam)
ETS	estimated time of separation (U.S. Army)
FAA	Federal Aviation Administration (U.S. government)
FAC	forward air controller (U.S. Air Force)
FDC	Fire Direction Center (U.S. Army)
FO	forward observer
GRU	Intelligence Directorate of the General Staff (Soviet Union)
H&S	headquarters and support (U.S. Marines)
IRT	infantry regiment training (U.S. Marines)
KGB	Security and Intelligence Service (Soviet Union)
KIA	killed in action
LARC	lighter, amphibious, resupply, cargo

LCU	large, military cargo water craft
LZ	landing zone
MACV	Military Assistance Command, South Vietnam (U.S.)
MAG	Marine Air Group (U.S. Marines)
MARS	Military Affiliate Radio System (U.S.)
MASH	Mobile Army Surgical Hospital
MAW	Marine Air Wing (U.S. Marine)
MCRD	Marine Corps Recruit Depot
Medcap	medical civic action program (U.S. armed forces)
NATTC	National Aviation Technology Training Center (Memphis, U.S.)
NLF	National Liberation Front (Viet Cong)
NCO	non-commissioned officer
NCOCS	Non-Commissioned Officer Candidate School (U.S. Army)
NVA	North Vietnamese Army (or PAVN)
PAC	Pacific Alaska Columbia (U.S. company)
PACEX	Pacific Exchange System (U.S.)
PAVN	People's Army of Vietnam (or NVA, North Vietnamese Army)
PLA	People's Liberation Army (China)
PLAF	People's Liberation Armed Forces (Viet Cong, South Vietnam)
POW	prisoner of war
PRC	People's Republic of China
PTSD	post-traumatic stress disorder
PX	post exchange (U.S. armed forces)
R&R	rest and recuperation
ROK	Republic of Korea (South Korea)
ROTC	Reserve Officers' Training Corps (U.S. armed forces)
RVN	Republic of Vietnam (South Vietnam)
SAM	surface-to-air missile
SNIE	Special National Intelligence Estimate (U.S. government)
USMC	U.S. Marine Corps
USO	United Service Organization (U.S.)
VA	Veterans Administration (U.S. government)
VC	Viet Cong (Vietnamese Communist, South Vietnam)
VNA	Vietnamese National Army (Bao Dai Vietnamese government)
VVAW	Vietnam Veterans Against the War

Note on Transliteration

The Vietnamese names follow the traditional East Asian practice that the surname is written first, then middle name, and then first name, as in Ngo Dinh Diem and Vo Nguyen Giap. Most people in Vietnam are referred to by their given names, therefore President Diem and General Giap. The exceptions are for a very few particularly illustrious persons, such as Ho Chi Minh, who was called President Ho (or Uncle Ho).

The Vietnamese names of places follow the spellings in two atlases: Tap Ban Do Hanh Chinh, *Viet Nam* (Vietnam Administrative Atlas) and Michael P. Kelley, *Where We Were in Vietnam: A Comprehensive Guide to the Firebases, Military Installations and Naval Vessels of the Vietnam War, 1945–75*. For some popular names of places, traditional well-known spellings appear in parentheses after the current spelling, such as Ho Chi Minh City (Saigon).

The *hanyu pinyin* Romanization system is applied to Chinese names of persons, places, and terms. The transliteration is also used for the titles of Chinese publications. Names of individuals are written in the Chinese way, the surname first, such as Mao Zedong. Some popular names have traditional Wade-Giles spellings appearing in parentheses after the first use of the *hanyu pinyin*, such as Zhou Enlai (Chou En-lai), as do popular names of places like Guangzhou (Canton).

Acknowledgments

Many people at the University of Central Oklahoma (UCO), where I have been teaching for the past seventeen years, have contributed to this book and deserve recognition. First, I would like to thank Provost William (Bill) J. Radke, Vice Provost Patricia A. LaGrow, Dean of the College of Liberal Arts Pamela Washington, Dean of the Jackson College of Graduate Studies Richard Bernard, and Associate Dean of the College of Liberal Arts Gary Steward. They have been very supportive of the project over the past eight years. The faculty merit-credit program sponsored by the Office of Academic Affairs and the Liberal Arts College research grant at UCO provided funding for my research and student assistants.

Special thanks to Stanley J. Adamiak, who proofread most of the chapters. Chen Jian, Richard Peters, Zhang Shuguang, and Xiaoming Zhang made important comments on the early draft. Lt. Col. Terry May worked with me on a couple of chapters before he passed away in 2003. Clary James reproduced all of the photos for the book. Dick Gilbreath, Stephanie Shaw, and Ted Smith at the University of Kentucky Cartography Lab produced the maps. Candace Carollo provided secretarial assistance. Lacey D. Bryant helped with documents processing. Several graduate and undergraduate students at UCO contributed to the book. They traveled with me to meet the veterans, transcribed the interviews, read parts of the manuscript, and sometimes worked on the bibliography. They are Lynn Brown, Maj. Phredd Evans (U.S. Army, ret.), Jonathan Freeman, Sharon Kelting, Hugh Long, Michael Molina, Senior Airman Oliver Pettry (U.S. Air Force), Xiaowei Wang, and Yang Yu.

I also wish to thank the two anonymous readers for the University Press of Kentucky, who offered many valuable suggestions and criticism. Several other reviewers at the early stage of this project, such as John Prados, also provided important suggestions. At the University Press of Kentucky, Stephen M. Wrinn, executive director, and Anne Dean Watkins, acquisitions editor, patiently guided the production of the book. Any remaining errors of facts, language usage, and interpretation are my own.

During the research and writing period over the past eight years, my wife, Tran, encouraged my interest and helped me with the contacts, interviews, and translations in Vietnam. Our two children, Kevin and Christina, got used to my working weekends, and shared with me the burden of overseas travel. I dedicate this book to them.

Introduction

The Long War

Huynh Van No was sweating as he showed us the War Remnants Museum on one of the comfortable spring days in Vietnam. Over sixty and reticent, Mr. No was not a typical tour guide in Ho Chi Minh City (formerly Saigon). We worried about him after we scrambled into the underground Cu Chi tunnels. "I'm OK," he said, "I have this problem for years."[1] As a Southerner, Huynh served as a staff sergeant in the Army of the Republic of Vietnam (ARVN) during the Vietnam War. After the Northern victory, the Communist government sent all the former ARVN soldiers and officers to prison or labor camps. Huynh survived seven castigating years, from 1975 to 1982, and lost his health and most everything else: his parents, three brothers, his wife, and two of his three children.[2] One thing good came out of the war, Huynh joked with a complacent smile: he had learned how to speak English during his three-month training in the United States as a Battalion Maintenance Officer. With workable English, he could now make $3 a day as a guide to foreign tourists to support his handicapped daughter at home.

The lengthy war claimed 3 million Vietnamese lives. For the Vietnamese veterans like Staff Sergeant No, the war lasted for thirty years, starting with the French Indochina War, 1946 to 1954; then an insurgent rebellion supported by the North against the South from 1955 to 1963; then the conflict known as the American War in 1963–1973; and finally, the civil war ending in the Communist takeover in 1975. Other ARVN veterans we met in the southern provinces had similar stories. They grew up with the war, fought in it, and then lost almost everything to it. Lt. Nguyen Yen Xuan described the war not as an event, but as his life and family history.[3] This is also true for Vietnam War veterans from other parts of the world, including more than 2 million Americans. They became part of the war and it changed them in a multitude of ways. Numerous personal memoirs have been published in the United States, including many excellent oral histories.[4]

This book, as an oral history collection, tells twenty-two personal stories of American, Vietnamese, Chinese, Russian, and Korean soldiers and officers. It shares the lives of international veterans, whether a U.S. Marine or a Chinese major, a Korean captain or a Russian spy, and reveals ironic similarities and differences. In their own words, they share firsthand accounts of their war experiences in Vietnam as well as their family life before and after the war. The book provides Communist stories from "the other side of the hill," including those of a general of the People's Liberation Armed Forces (PLAF, or Viet Cong), officers of the North Vietnamese Army (NVA, or officially the People's Army of Vietnam, PAVN), Chinese soldiers of the People's Liberation Army (PLA, China's armed forces), and a Russian officer. These stories bring fresh insights from Communist veterans, examining their motivations, operations, and perceptions. Their narratives humanize and contextualize the war's events while shedding light on aspects of the war previously unknown to Western scholars, and provide an international perspective for readers to have a better understanding of America's longest war.

The Bear vs. the Dragon

For the first time in English, this book provides personal accounts of Russian and Chinese Communist veterans, including three Chinese PLA officers and two Russians, a missile training instructor and a KGB spy. Western strategists and historians have long speculated about the international Communist role in Vietnam, but these stories indicate the extent of outside involvements. Between 1964 and 1974, Vietnam became a battlefield, a testing ground, and even a training site for two of the largest Communist forces in the world. The international Communist support to North Vietnam, including troops, equipment, finance, and technology, provided a decisive edge that enabled the NVA and Viet Cong to resist American forces and eventually subjugate South Vietnam. The Soviet and Chinese support prolonged the Vietnam War and made it very difficult, if not impossible, for South Vietnam and the United States to win.

After Nikita Khrushchev's fall from power in 1964 and Leonid Brezhnev's succession, the Soviet Union shifted its Vietnam policy from "staying away" to "lending a hand." In February 1965, Soviet premier Alekei Kosygin visited Hanoi and signed an agreement with the North Vietnamese to increase Russian aid to 148,500 tons, including 55,000 tons of military aid, by year's end. North Vietnam also requested a Soviet missile combat brigade, comprised of four thousand Soviet troops, to arrive that spring.[5] After 1965, the Soviet Union continuously increased its aid to Vietnam, particularly intensifying its military assistance. Chinese historian Li Danhui describes Moscow's primary goal as being to "infiltrate politically and win control over the strategically important Southeast Asian region, and Vietnam presented the best avenue whereby this objective might be achieved."[6] In 1967, Russia increased its military aid to Vietnam to over $550 million, exceeding that provided by the Chinese.[7] From 1965 to 1972, the Soviet Union provided a total of $3 billion in aid to Vietnam, including $2 billion in military support.[8]

The Soviet Union felt compelled to use all means possible to win Vietnam over as a political ally against the People's Republic of China (PRC) in the international Communist movement. Beginning in 1958–1959, because of complicated domestic and international factors (the most important of these being whether Moscow or Beijing should be the center of the international Communist movement), the Sino-Soviet alliance, the cornerstone of the Communist international alliance system, collapsed.[9] The great Sino-Soviet polemic debate in 1960–1962 undermined the ideological foundation of the Communist revolution. Historian Chen Jian states that, in retrospect, few events played so important a role in shaping the orientation and essence of the cold war as the Sino-Soviet split.[10] Moscow lost its total control of the international Communist movement. The conflicts between the two Communist parties extended to their strategic issues in the 1960s. The 1964 transition in the Soviet leadership from Khrushchev to Brezhnev did not improve Sino-Soviet relations. China's bellicose rhetoric in the early 1960s and the Great Proletarian Cultural Revolution sweeping across China beginning in 1966 completely destroyed any hope that Beijing and Moscow might continuously regard each other as "comrades in arms."[11] As the Sino-Soviet relationship worsened, it gradually moved from hostility to outright confrontation during a border war in the late 1960s.

China did not want to see Soviet influence increase in Southeast Asia. To keep the Soviets out and North Vietnam on its side, China was willing, at first, to provide more military assistance to North Vietnam. In 1963, China provided about $660 million in military and economic aid to Vietnam, nearly 30 percent of its total foreign aid.[12] This valuable support included enough weapons and ammunition to arm 230 infantry battalions. The massive contributions to North Vietnam enabled North Vietnamese

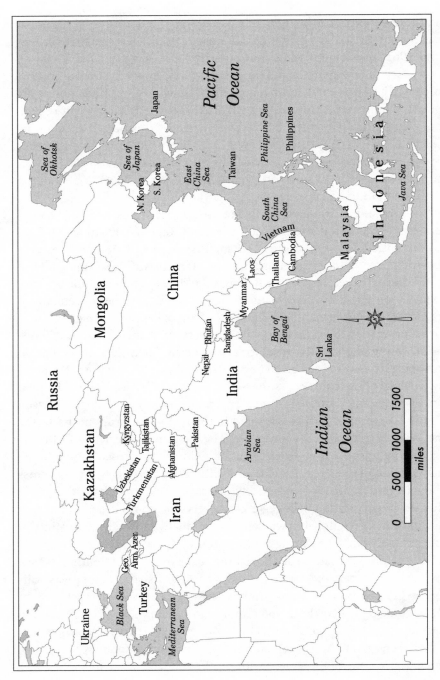

Vietnam and Asia

leader Ho Chi Minh to send more NVA troops to the South. After 1964, China increased its aid to Vietnam. From 1964 to 1973, China provided about $20 billion in aid to Vietnam, and it remained the largest supplier of war materials to North Vietnam among the Communist states until 1967, providing about 44.8 percent of the total military aid that year.[13] Historian Shuguang Zhang determined that between 1965 and 1970, aid to North Vietnam made up 57.6 percent of China's total foreign aid.[14] China's massive aid certainly helped North Vietnam survive a protracted war of attrition with the United States. Beijing did not want to see a U.S. success or North Vietnam softness when the Johnson administration escalated American involvement. China's interest was best served by backing up the North and keeping the ground war in the South.

Meanwhile, China began to send its troops to the Vietnam War. On April 17, 1965, the first PLA troops entered North Vietnam.[15] By March 1966, China had dispatched 130,000 troops to Vietnam, including surface-to-air missiles, antiaircraft artillery (AAA), railroad, combat engineering, mine-sweeping, and logistics units. Three years later, according to Gen. Zhang Aiping, former defense minister of the PRC, China had rotated in twenty-three divisions, including ninety-five regiments plus eighty-three battalions, totaling 320,000 troops.[16] The Chinese forces in North Vietnam enabled Ho Chi Minh to send more NVA troops to the South to fight American ground forces and to intensify warfare in the region.[17] China's military involvement may have also restrained the Johnson administration from further U.S. military escalation, which could have triggered a large-scale Chinese intervention like that in the Korean War in 1950–1953. Jung Chang and Jon Halliday point out, "It was having China as a secure rear and supply depot that made it possible for the Vietnamese to fight twenty-five years and beat first the French and then the Americans."[18]

Soviet and Chinese military aid to North Vietnam between 1965 and 1973 did not improve Sino-Soviet relations, but rather created a new front and new competition as each attempted to gain leadership of the Southeast Asian Communist movements. North Vietnam knew that the Soviet Union and China were rivals in the Communist camp, competing for the leadership of the Asian Communist movement, including Vietnam. Each claimed itself a key supporter of the Vietnamese Communists' struggle against the American invasion. Military historian Spencer C. Tucker states that therefore the Vietnamese brought both Communist nations' troops into North Vietnam, increasing the competition between the Chinese and

Soviet Communists.[19] The Chinese high command ordered its AAA troops to intensify their training in order to shoot down more American airplanes than the Soviets could. Maj. Guo Haiyun recalled that the Chinese AAA troops had two enemies in North Vietnam: "the American imperialists in the sky, and the Soviet revisionists on the ground."[20]

The Vietnamese government and the NVA officially deny any foreign involvement in the Vietnam War. Other Communist and former Communist countries, like Russia, Romania, Yugoslavia, and Poland, have maintained a similar position. The Russian government has concealed the participation of the former Soviet Union's military in the war. Soviet official records are closed to the public and scholars. Most Russian veterans do not want to talk about their experience in Vietnam, and those who are willing are difficult to reach. Because of the unavailability of sources and language barriers, there is an absence of an oral history that provides voices directly from these Communist veterans. Even though a few historians have covered Soviet and Chinese policies and involvement in the Vietnam War, no personal accounts of the Russian and Chinese veterans are available in published books in the West.[21]

Interviewing Communist Veterans

Between 2001 and 2008, I interviewed more than ninety Communist veterans in Vietnam, China, Russia, Ukraine, Kazakhstan, Hong Kong, and the United States. The accounts from Russian veterans came from my four interviews in Kazakhstan, three in Russia, three in Ukraine, two in America, and two in China. Five of the Russian veterans were officers, six of them soldiers, and three former KGB agents. All of them agreed to be interviewed only on the condition that their names would not be used. During the interviews of Russian veterans, the same questions were asked from a standard list concerning their training, service experience, most vivid memories, worst thing, and scariest moment in their war experiences. The standard questions also included how much they knew about the American and ARVN forces, what they thought of their combat effectiveness, and the biggest lesson they may have learned from their war experience.

Before each trip, my contact persons made arrangements with the Russian veterans who had agreed to be interviewed. I flew from Urumqi, the capital city of China's western border province Xinjiang Uygur Autonomous Region, either to Astana, capital city of Kazakhstan; to Moscow, Russia; or to Kyiv, Ukraine, in separate trips. Most of these Russian veterans answered the questions in their own languages with a translator. Two interviews in America were in English and conducted in Maryland and Texas.[22] These interviews offer an important source of information from the former Soviet Union and different viewpoints for interested readers in America. To check the accuracy of the Russian recollections, I consulted with primary and secondary sources in Moscow and Hanoi. Since the collapse of the Soviet Union in 1991, the Communist governmental and diplomatic documents in Moscow have gradually opened up, especially since 1995, filling in some gaps in the cold war historiography.[23] We can now present some of the firsthand accounts of Russian veterans to fill part of the gap in the Vietnam War history.

Among the Communist countries, only China has acknowledged its intervention in 1965–1970. In the spring of 1979, after China lost its brief war with Vietnam and withdrew its 200,000 troops, Beijing published many details about its military aid and engagements in the Vietnam War between 1965 and 1970. The government tried to prove in the 1980s that China had been friendly, generous, exacting, and sacrificing, only to be betrayed by an odious, aggressive, and greedy Vietnam. Continuing quarrels between Beijing and Hanoi brought a considerable number of war memoirs to Chinese readers in the 1990s. Some are books, others appeared as journal and magazine articles, or as reference studies for restricted circulation only. With official permission, I conducted individual and group interviews with forty-eight Chinese veterans in nine provinces, including Guangxi and Yunnan, which border Vietnam. I also visited some of the headquarters of the engaged AAA divisions during my four research trips to China between 2001 and 2008. Since I am a native Chinese and served in the PLA in the early 1970s, the interviews went very well and contain new information on the Chinese role, previously unavailable to an English-language audience.

Since the normalization of relations between Washington and Hanoi in 1997, scholars have had opportunities to visit the battlefields and libraries in the Socialist Republic of Vietnam and write on the war. Although the declassification process of the war archives in Vietnam has not yet started, a few publications became available, including stories from the generals, officials, and diplomats.[24] After 2002, the NVA and PLAF veterans began to talk about their personal experiences in the Vietnam War and to publish their memoirs, recollections, and war stories, adding a new perspective on the subject.[25] The NVA and PLAF veterans were also more willing to share their wartime memories. No matter how politically indoctrinated they might be, the Communist veterans were culturally bound to cherish the past. More importantly, they felt comfortable in talking about their experiences and allowing their recollections to be recorded, written, and published in America.[26]

More than thirty interviews of Vietnamese Communist veterans were conducted in seven provinces both in the South and the North during my three research trips in 2002–2006. My wife helped with oral translations from Vietnamese to English if an official translator was not available. Although these stories offer direct testimony from the soldiers themselves, their personal stories often followed the official accounts that glorify the Communist victory in Vietnam. To ensure the accuracy of these personal recollections, I consulted with primary and secondary sources in Hanoi and Ho Chi Minh City. I also noted any contradicting accounts, such as the number of casualties, whenever it occurred. Although the Vietnamese government still has a long way to go before free academic inquiry becomes a reality, the value of the NVA and Viet Cong veterans sharing their wartime experiences cannot be underestimated in our research and teaching of the Vietnam War.

The collection of the Russian, Chinese, and Vietnamese stories has outlined a way of war that is different from that of the West.[27] For example, the Western way of war has a propensity to exclude political party control over the military, while the Communist leaders had a tendency to view the military aspect as one part of their revolutionary organization, the military as a subordinate branch of the whole party. The Soviet military brought Vietnam the Red Army tradition of the Communist Party's being in command, political propaganda, and ideological education. The long war allowed the Vietnamese Communists to make progress and successfully adopt the Soviet military system and technology. The Vietnamese Communist force transformed from an irregular peasant army to a professional modern army. The Soviet training, mobility, technology, and professionalism were a major difference between the Russian and the Chinese forces. The Chinese military brought Vietnam their asymmetric combat experience in guerrilla warfare, in which a weak Third World army could fight against a strong Western force in their country. The NVA employed some Chinese guerrilla tactics, such as engaging in mobile operations, avoiding the usually superior enemy firepower, achieving surprise whenever possible, fighting in close combat, and using ambush tactics, tunnel networks, and night attack.[28] Thus, the NVA could function on both conventional and unconventional levels, which the American military, in many ways, was not fully prepared to face. The advantages of the American forces were neutralized by this resourceful foe.

Vietnam Revisited

Teaching Vietnam War history has been the most challenging class in my twenty-year college teaching career in the United States. No matter if I taught it at private universities, state universities, online graduate classes for Norwich University, or the Summer Seminar in Military History at West Point, the U.S. Military Academy, I always felt underprepared for the students and their questions. Our students have changed. They are the grandchildren of American veterans, to whom the war seems far away in the past; the second generation of the Southern refugees, who still attend ongoing anti-Communist Vietnamese rallies at local churches or temples; and international students who were born and grew up in Vietnam, Russia, and China. They had different questions in the class. What thematic topic can reach them all? How can I put all the veterans on the same page to compare and explain?

One day, I was surprised by the students' reaction to my wife's visit. Tran shared her refugee story with the class. As one of the "boat people" at twenty-two, she escaped from South Vietnam and survived a pirate attack, a long sea voyage, and hardship at the refugee camps in other Southeast Asian countries. For nine months, she could not stop, traveling from one place to another. She could not die, since she had to take care of her little cousin, Sunny, a twelve-year-old boy. Sunny lost his father in the war after his mother left Saigon to go overseas. After the war, Tran's family sold everything for these kids to get out of the country on a fishing boat and look for Sunny's mother.[29] Her story was simple, but compelling. It was not only about the bloody battle and military technology, but also about family, survival, and hope for the future, which touched many students in the class. Responsibility, technology, and training can transform a citizen into a warrior; passion, patriotism, and belief can also turn an ordinary individual into a soldier. An examination of each veteran's background, education, and family life before and after the war provides a workable approach to understanding and comparing the international veterans. Therefore, I have chosen social history topics for my class and discussed the war events as human experience.

This book's focus moves away from the conventional combat-centered war history and instead looks into the relatively neglected subject of men and women's lives beyond the battleground. By examining topics such as their religion, marriage, education, and occupation in their home countries, the work details veteran backgrounds before the war and their civilian life after. It puts each veteran in the context of the society, culture, and politics. By introducing these young soldiers and junior officers and telling their stories, this work employs a social history methodology and provides an impetus to larger issues. It shows from the bottom up that each society has its own way to transform its civilians into soldiers, and that the people viewed and responded to similar problems differently. Oral history, of course, has its own weaknesses. The book does not intend to present a comprehensive coverage of the war, but a "limited" presentation of the voices of the international soldiers from all sides. Their stories may not be the bloodiest, but they will broaden our perspective on the war. Some of them are the noncombat stories of people who served in logistics, intelligence, medicine, and engineering, soldiers whose roles and contributions are often overlooked by historians.

The selected chapters present a life story and show the feelings and perceptions of the war by the men and women who lived it. The chapters follow the participants' lives before, during, and after their service, to put each individual soldier in a common, broader context. To connect each man and woman with his or her social and political environment, a vignette is included as a background introduction to each personal account. Besides the Communist stories, there are fourteen stories of American, South Vietnamese, and Korean veterans.

It was difficult to select only eight American veterans from my interviews of fifty-three in fifteen states. I regret that time and space has not allowed me to include the stories of other veterans, who performed their duties in Vietnam heroically. Their stories have certainly provided a solid historical background for comparisons with the others and an analytical framework for the discussions of important issues. They also provided a large amount of wartime memorabilia, such as diaries, letters, photographs, newspapers, recommendation letters, and official documents.

The selection of South Vietnamese stories was based on interviews with ARVN veterans both in the United States and in Vietnam. Among the seventy-two South Vietnamese soldiers interviewed, sixty-one veterans and their families were in the United States. These ARVN veterans either fled the country after the war in the late 1970s or came to the United States later through humanitarian organizations and other American programs in the 1980s and 1990s. Some interviews were conducted in English, but most were done in their own native language through an interpreter, since I did not trust my Vietnamese. Certain words were changed during the translation and editing process for clarity. Between 2002 and 2006, I made three research trips to Vietnam and interviewed eleven ARVN veterans in four southern provinces. My wife helped with translations since the veterans did not feel comfortable with any official translator or other people knowing about the interview and their anti-Communist past. Reluctant and hesitant, they often avoided details about the lost war that sent them to jail for up to seven years. They did not keep many photos, records, and letters from their ARVN service. Some of them only started talking after my third visit or a dinner at a local restaurant. Some believed that the Communist government and local authorities still watched them.

The chapters are organized in both geopolitical and thematic ways. Part One begins with the narratives of six Vietnamese veterans from both sides. The second part focuses on the Russian and Chinese Communist veterans, North Vietnam's allies. Part Three examines Saigon's allies through four Americans' stories. Then, the next part organizes the stories to show the efforts of medical personnel, including a doctor, nurse, medic, and hospital security captain. The last segment examines several different logistical support persons, including a U.S. Army lieutenant, a U.S. Air Force sergeant, a South Vietnamese official, and a Chinese colonel. The conclusion summarizes the perspectives on the war and provides a unique way of understanding Vietnam. In their own words, these former warriors put the readers in the midst of wartime life.

Part One

A Country Divided

Chapter 1

A Buddhist Soldier Defends a Catholic Government

S.Sgt. Huynh Van No was very affable and gregarious, even though he had a tough time during the war and a fatigued life thereafter. Before each interview in Ho Chi Minh City, he usually started a conversation with me and my wife on an interesting topic like the difference between traditional Mahayana Buddhism in Vietnam and Westernized Buddhism in America. Sometimes they were so engaged that I had to step in by offering them a cup of "caphe sua" (Vietnamese ice coffee) before they got carried away with their enlightening and serious discussions.

Staff Sergeant No was serious about the common Western assumption that the ARVN failed to defend its own country even with American direct intervention in the Vietnam War.[1] He argued that this supposition is not fair to the ARVN, which he entered in 1962 at eighteen. His testimony suggests that the ARVN departed from traditional values and lost popular support only after the Americans transformed it into a modern army.[2] Its modernization or Westernization detached the ARVN from Vietnamese society. In other words, while providing advanced technology, military training, democratic ideas, and even Christianity to the ARVN, the United States should also have promoted nationalistic pride as a reason for the South Vietnamese soldiers to fight for their own country's independence and sovereignty. Ignoring and overlooking Vietnamese nationalism made the ARVN a hotbed of apathy. Staff Sergeant No felt like he was fighting for his Catholic commanders, President Diem, and American advisers, not for himself, his family, and the Vietnamese people.

In retrospect, the U.S. Vietnam policy was originally aimed at supporting *the government and people of South Vietnam in their efforts against Communist aggression. From the beginning, Pres. John F. Kennedy emphasized that the South Vietnamese should fight this war "by themselves, for themselves, win or lose, it is their war, the people of Vietnam against the Communists."[3] He authorized $41 million to improve the ARVN and the civil guards in 1961. According to Staff Sergeant No, his unit and other ARVN troops had made some progress in carrying out some of President Diem's policies, like the "Strategic Hamlet Program" in 1962–1963.[4] The program was designed to protect the rural population and neutralize Viet Cong insurgents. However, the battlefield failure in 1963–1964 convinced American leaders that the ARVN could not protect its government and South Vietnam from further attacks by the PLAF and NVA. Their assumed failure and incompetence influenced the Johnson administration's military escalation of the Vietnam War in order to help the hopeless South Vietnamese in an American way.*

Approximately 3.6 million South Vietnamese served in the ARVN from 1963 to 1975. During that time, most of the adult males between seventeen and forty-five years old were drafted into the war and stayed in the army until the end.[5] Staff Sergeant No was wounded during the Viet Cong's Tet Offensive campaign in 1968, but was lucky enough to live to see the end of the war.

S.Sgt. Huynh Van No

First Battalion, Third Regiment, An Giang Provincial Command, ARVN (South Vietnam)

I was born in 1944 into a peasant's family in Long Hung, a small village near Long Xuyen, An Giang Province, South Vietnam. As the youngest in the family, I had seven brothers and sisters. Their hard work in family farming helped me through elementary and secondary education in the town of Long Xuyen. I enjoyed riding my bicycle along the river to my school every morning, waving good-bye to my father and brothers who already worked in the rice field. Our teachers talked about the First Indochina War all the time, but it seemed far away from our classroom in the late 1950s.

My favorite subject was drawing and painting, both in watercolor and oil colors. I had painted a lot of pictures of the rivers, rice paddies, and people in my hometown. The life was so quiet and peaceful at Long Xuyen that sometimes I was even bored to death. I dreamed of leaving our village and traveling all over the country.

I liked visiting the Buddhist temples with my parents and grandparents either in our village or in the city. I met many people there, including my relatives, friends, neighbors, teachers, and those whom I didn't even know. It seemed natural for the Vietnamese families to carry on their religion from one generation to the next as a family tradition. Like in my family, my ancestors were Buddhists, so my grandparents, my parents, and my generation just kept it going on and on as the Buddhists forever.[6] One of the most exciting things during my childhood was riding in the boat (for a whole day) down the river and climbing to the top of the Ba Den Mountain to see the Buddha statue in the Ba Den temple.

At the beginning of the 1960s, some troops of the Army of the Republic of Vietnam [ARVN] moved into Long Xuyen and were stationed in several camps along the country roads. They were Buddhist soldiers, since I saw them quite often at the Buddhist temples in the city.[7] They protected the villagers from being harassed by the South Vietnamese Communist guerrilla troops, or the Viet Cong [VC]. Since we lived nearby the city, I didn't see any Viet Cong during my school years. Also I didn't know much difference between the antigovernment Viet Cong and Pres. Ngo Dinh Diem's government. At that time, I really admired the young ARVN soldiers who carried their rifles in uniform, walked around with a lot of attention in the town, and shopped at the market with cash.

In 1961, President Diem called up the young Vietnamese for service in the ARVN to fight against the Communist insurgents in South Vietnam. I answered the call and joined the army in 1962. Reluctant and unhappy, my parents had to make a tough decision: either letting me go or losing one of my older brothers as their field hands. What made them feel better was that I joined the ARVN provincial forces, which stayed in each province under its military regional command.[8] My training camp wasn't too far away from my hometown, even though I couldn't go home and visit my family at all. My brothers told me later that my parents prayed a lot for me in the village temple when I served in the army.

During my three-month training, I remember that everyone was so happy when we got paid about $20 per month. It was the first time in my life to see so much money in my own hands. We would spend money in the market and eat lavishly with our money. At the time, I didn't know that we got only one half of our pay since the corrupt training officers kept the other half for themselves. Later I was told that some soldiers might leave the army if they had made and saved a lot of money. In fact, my monthly

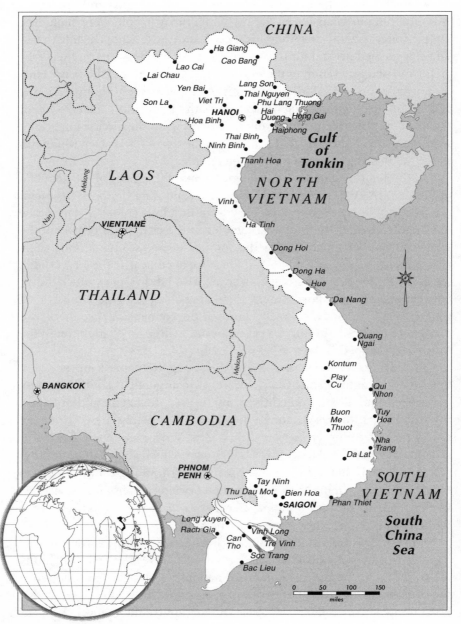

CHINA

Ha Giang
Lao Cai
Cao Bang
Lai Chau
Yen Bai
Lang Son
Son La
Viet Tri
Thai Nguyen
Phu Lang Thuong
HANOI
Hai
Duong
Hong Gai
Hoa Binh
Haiphong
Thai Binh
Gulf
Ninh Binh
of
Thanh Hoa
Tonkin

LAOS

NORTH
VIETNAM

Vinh

VIENTIANE
Ha Tinh

Dong Hoi

THAILAND
Dong Ha
Hue

Da Nang

Quang
Ngai

Kontum
Play
Cu
Qui
BANGKOK
Nhon

Buon
Tuy
Me
Hoa
CAMBODIA
Thuot

Nha
Trang

Da Lat

PHNOM
PENH
Tay Ninh
SOUTH
Thu Dau Mot
Bien Hoa
VIETNAM
SAIGON
Phan Thiet

Long Xuyen
South
Rach Gia
Vinh Long
China
Can
Tre Vinh
Sea
Tho
Soc Trang
Bac Lieu

0   50   100   150
miles

Vietnam, 1955–1975

pay of $20 wasn't enough for me to survive outside the camp for one week since the cost of living in our area was $100 per month, or $25 a week. Anyway, I was happy with the little money I got at the moment. I am a Buddhist, and always satisfied with what I have.

Many new recruits were Buddhists just like me. I enjoyed meeting so many young men from all of the country. I had never traveled that far in my life to know the people from cities like Can Tho and Ca Mau. Friendly and kind, they were as scared as I was to go into the war against Viet Cong and North Vietnamese Communists. I made some friends at the camp.

During our training, the training sergeants told us that nobody was allowed to eat outside the base. We had been warned not to go out into the nearby town in our uniform. The sergeants and the American advisers were paranoid that the food outside the base could be poisoned. I didn't understand why we, as Vietnamese soldiers, were afraid of our own people. Anyway, I was not afraid. One day I snuck out with a couple of my friends into the town. My friends and I saw corn on the cob and other food sold by peddlers in the street. We bought lots of corn and hid it in our tents. The training sergeants would come in and lift our blankets and yell at us.

Most of the training officers were Catholic. I knew that our president was Catholic, too. Loyal to him, I liked President Diem and wanted to fight for him, even though I didn't know much about Christianity. In Long Xuyen, there were two small Catholic churches among a couple dozen Buddhist temples. It seemed to me that the rich kids and wealthy families went to the Catholic churches every Sunday. They had to dress up or wore something very nice to go in there. They had to know how to read French or English. We didn't have to worry about our dress or shoes when we stopped by at the Buddhist temples. Anybody can go in there anytime.

At the training camp, I received a copy of the Bible for the first time. Of course, it was in Vietnamese. I could read it, but I didn't. These Catholic officers were very mean people, who yelled to us every day, beat some of the new recruits, and even spit in our soup and then asked us to drink it up. They were not nice to us at all. They only wanted to please their superior officers and the American advisers in the camp. They worked for the Americans and got paid by the Americans anyway.

After the training, I was assigned to the First Battalion, Third Infantry Regiment of An Giang Command, Fourth Tactical Zone. My battalion stationed around Cai Dau to protect Route 9, one of the major provincial roads. It was a little far away from my hometown. From 1962 to 1964, we worked on President Diem's "Strategic Hamlet Program" in the villages around Cai Dau. Our company moved into a village and worked with village armed teams, or the Popular Force, to build up their defense work. The "Strategic Hamlet Program" was aimed at separating the Viet Cong's guerrilla troops from the South Vietnamese farmers in order to cut off their supply and recruitment and reduce their harassment.[9] After we finished the defense work construction and trained the local farmers in one village, we moved on to another village. It seemed to be working and we felt very good by helping the farmers just like us. I liked the policy and enjoyed what we were doing for their safety and protection against Viet Cong insurgents. I felt that we had accomplished our mission each time leaving a village. I became a corporal in 1963. Unfortunately, President Diem was killed later that year and then the "Strategic Hamlet Program" was winding down in the next year.

In 1965–1966, we began to engage in the battles. Many of these fights took place in the hills, forest, or along the river. I had no idea why we were sent out in the middle of nowhere. The country became ugly because of this long war. We saw some forest burned down to the ground, some hills turned black because of heavy bombing, and many shell holes all over the rice field. I was scared every time we were sent out in the woods or on the hills. Our battalion took heavy casualties and some of the men just deserted during the operations. I also saw many civilian casualties, including women and children who were just like my neighbors and friends in my hometown. I prayed every day for Buddha's mercy through my faith for the end of this endless killing and destruction.

More American advisers came to our battalion. They commanded many of the battles. We were asked to learn how to speak and read English. I started my English study by taking some conversation and reading classes offered in our camp. Because of my educational background, I made a good progress in my English learning and soon became a teaching assistant to our American language instructors.

The year of 1967 was the best year in my service since I was selected to receive further training as Battalion Maintenance Officer in the United States. For the first time in my life, I took a military airplane and flew out of the country. There were five other ARVN officers in this training group. We studied the curriculum in military technology, communication, and management at a U.S. Army base. Then we took some hands-on training

S.Sgt. Huynh Van No (left) and the author in Ho Chi Minh City in 2006.

courses. We learned a lot of new things in three months. We had a good time during our training in the U.S.

After my return, I got promoted to a master sergeant. The year of 1968, however, was the worst in my service. We had more casualties and deserters than ever before. I tried to take care of my unit during each operation. But the battle got tougher and tougher, since we were then fighting against the well-trained regular forces from the North Vietnam Army [NVA] rather than the guerrilla troops of the Viet Cong [NLF]. My friend got shot in the back and I got injured in my arm in a battle. The bullet was aimed for me because I was the one with the machine gun. The bullet's casing chafed my arm. I still have a big scar. I remember my friend. He was lying down on his stomach right before he got shot in the back. When he was hit, his whole body rose almost two feet into the air and he ended up on his back. It was so sad to see your friend die.

The wound prevented my return to the combat unit after my hospitalization. In 1969, I was so happy to know that I was reassigned to a training base near Long Xuyen, my hometown. Since I knew how to speak and teach English, I became an instructor of English language and small arms in the training programs from 1970 to 1975. My family was happy to see me back alive and working as an officer in the city. I also taught English as a part-time teacher at a local middle school, which I enjoyed the most, in 1972–1975. I visited the Buddhist temples with my students and traveled to the Ba Den Mountain with my family. You know what happened to me after 1975.[10] As a Buddhist, I am always happy.

Chapter 2

Surviving the Bloody Jungle

Rose always prepared the green tea in the traditional way before each interview. As a sophomore at University of California–Los Angeles (UCLA), she took the Vietnamese language class and History of Modern Southeast Asia. She learned a lot about the country her parents came from, and tried to understand why they could not go back. "I will get a job at LA after my college," Rose told me behind her father. "I want to move my parents from the Twin Cities to California. The weather is much warmer there." Her voice was low but adamant. She continued, "I will save some money and take my parents back to Vietnam for a visit. You can tell they really miss their hometown. It has been twenty-eight years." What a wonderful daughter for the ARVN veteran! Lt. Nguyen Yen Xuan is so lucky!

Lieutenant Xuan is certainly proud of his daughter and two sons. But he did not feel lucky at all, just like so many ARVN soldiers who went through the Vietnam War.[1] "We could have won the war." He said it many times. His story contradicts some Western assumptions that internal reasons caused the weaknesses of the ARVN. Lieutenant Xuan explained that external factors played a major role in the ARVN's failure. Among these external problems was the attempt, on the part of the United States and ARVN high command, to Americanize the ARVN troops through U.S. aid and training. Thus, U.S. aid came with many conditions demanding the Vietnamese fight the war in an American way. In the meantime, the ARVN became more dependent on the Americans. Moreover, the White House and Pentagon did not design or expect an ARVN victory for the Vietnamese people, but an American victory for South Vietnam's government.

As a soldier in the Airborne Division, the elite forces of the ARVN, Lieutenant Xuan felt like he was fighting the war for the Americans in 1968–1973.

After the United States withdrew its troops from South Vietnam in 1973, the incomplete Americanization led to the total defeat of the ARVN. He believed that the ARVN soldiers should have fought their own war, not the American War. In 1968, South Vietnam's government called up every available man for service. By 1969, the ARVN totaled 1 million strong, including 400,000 national troops in thirteen infantry divisions, 250,000 men as regional or provincial troops, and 350,000 local or Popular Troops.[2] Among the three forces, the national troops were the best combat troops. They received better weapons and equipment and had American advisers top down to the battalion levels. The national troops, however, suffered the heaviest casualties since they engaged in more battles than other forces. From 1969 to 1971, the ARVN averaged combat deaths of 22,000 men per year, and by 1974 it had a total of 254,256 dead and 783,602 wounded in action.[3] Besides the heavy casualties, all of the ARVN units also suffered low morale, poor combat effectiveness, and high desertion rates.[4]

Lt. Nguyen Yen Xuan

C Company, Second Battalion, Airborne Division, ARVN (South Vietnam)

When the war began, I didn't know anything about it since I was very young. I became aware of the war when my oldest brother enlisted in the ARVN, and then another elder brother. They wanted to protect their hometown from Viet Cong harassment.[5] I think they did a pretty good job and our family business was growing. I helped my parents' small shop to sell food and goods.

In the late 1960s, however, my brothers and their unit were transferred somewhere far away from our town. According to my parents, the war situation seemed to be turning bad. I was drafted into the ARVN in 1969 and stayed until 1975, when the South lost the war to the North. During the first three years, I was trained and served in the Infantry Division, and then was transferred to the Airborne Division, one of the strongest units in South Vietnam.

In 1969, I received three-month training, including how to fire a gun, operate small arms, and other techniques on how to fight. After our basic training, we were sent to an ARVN advanced [technical] training base. We learned how to ride on helicopters, drive a light truck, and operate some machines. I found that learning experience fun and interesting. One day, we were told that the Viet Congs were going to attack our base, and we had to be prepared. I was so nervous at that time since it was my first battle. For weeks, there was no attack.

I never forget my first battle, which was a surprise attack on our technical training base. That evening, after dinner, we were lying in our tent and talking to two other guys from my hometown. One of them had shopped in our family store before he joined the army. They came to visit me and shared some of their survival experiences. It seemed to me they were so smart, like big brothers, and not scared of anything, like a role model to me. I hoped I could go home together with these new friends.

Not too long after their leaving my tent, enemy mortars began falling at our base. The Viet Cong launched a night attack. I got ready and followed the others to the defensive trench positions. I couldn't see anything in the dark outside the base, and I fired only twice. That was probably the reason I didn't get killed that night. I learned later that the Viet Cong snipers looked for targets by spotting the gun firing points. The more you fired, the better chance you could get shot. The Viet Cong didn't take over our base that night. After their withdrawal, next morning, we cleared up and gathered the men who died last night. The two men from my hometown were killed when their tent was hit by mortars. I couldn't believed that a night before we were just talking about our families and were looking forward to returning to our hometown together. And now they both died. It was really sad.

After the technical training, I was assigned to the Third Company, Second Battalion, Twenty-third Infantry Division. I made some new friends in the company. Since the company was stationed close to the Viet Cong-occupied areas, we frequently engaged with the Viet Cong troops.

One day, when we patrolled along the road, we were ambushed by the Viet Cong. We took cover and fired back. For fifteen minutes, we couldn't see the enemy, but kept shooting randomly. One of my friends, who was just behind me, got shot and fell down. Everyone thought he was dead. About twenty minutes later, we received air support, which pointed out the enemy positions. The captain reorganized us into small groups to target different enemy positions. Soon the Viet Cong disappeared into the bushes. And, to everyone's surprise, my friend somehow sat up from the ground and waved to us. He had returned to life! I was so happy and helped him get up. He was lucky. Our company lost nineteen men in this thirty-minute battle. We also had thirty-seven men wounded.

There were more American advisers who came to our battalion in 1970. I liked the American advisers. Smart and funny, they were curious to almost everything in Vietnam. I really appreciate their sacrificing their own lives for the freedom and democracy of the Vietnamese people. During the battle, we felt like friends working together. We covered each other, helped each other, and shared food and water with each other. But, after each operation, they went back to their camp and their life, and we returned back to our camp and our life. That was the reality. We realized that the Vietnamese and American soldiers were different people.

The American advisers were very young, younger than average Vietnamese soldiers. In some cases, they didn't have enough experience in the jungle. But they were very bossy and always demanded us to do things their way, the American way. If we didn't follow their instructions, they always threatened us by cutting our supplies, or reducing our rations. They provided us with weapons, ammunition, and aid with so many conditions to make sure we did everything in their way.

Many of our operations were commanded by the American officers. And in an operation, we usually were ordered to "follow the Marines!" or to "cover the Americans!" or something like that. We felt like we were working for the Americans. The Vietnamese officers in our battalion and division commands didn't question the American advisers' decisions because they needed ammunition, new equipment, and supplies for their troops. They used Americans like their supply officers or warehouse keepers. I can tell you that some of the Vietnamese officers were interested only in how to get money and supplies and tried to avoid the battles. Many ARVN soldiers also lost their interest in the war and left the service. Many of us felt that the war was designed by the American leaders in the White House for us not to win. They were only interested in America's victory, not the Vietnamese victory. We were fighting the American War in Vietnam.

Because of the large casualties and desertions, we received new replacements after each battle. You fought with different men next time. It was hard to know each other and form some sort of brotherhood. We offered cigarettes and candy bars to each other, and talked about our hometown a little bit. Usually, those who were in the army longer played a big brother role since we were pretty much the same age. The officers, medics, and cooks were the older guys in our company. They took good care of us. I remember one day, when they were cooking rice, we received an order to move out. The cooks didn't want to stop cooking and throw away the rice.

They had four guys carry the rice cookers to continue their cooking during our march. It was really funny. As soon as we got to the new location, they served us a hot meal. They were nice and hard-working guys. They always cooked some special dishes to celebrate when no one from our company got killed or hurt after a battle. It was the best time.

Then, in early 1972, a group of the experienced soldiers in the Twenty-third Division was transferred to the Airborne Division. I was one of them. We were so happy because the Airborne was the best division of all the ARVN forces.[6]

I was assigned to C Company, Second Battalion. We were sent to Saigon for advanced training for three months. We learned how to ride on the helicopters, engage after landing, conduct night operations, and surprise attack behind the enemy lines. We also learned some new technologies.

We were trained and equipped in the image of our U.S. counterpart. We learned how to do things in the American way. We dressed like American soldiers, operated like Americans, and were treated as an American unit. That was the first time I had to learn English, since some of the equipment instructions and manuals were in English. We moved frequently from one base to another, but most of them in the cities, such as Da Nang, Thuong Duc, Tung Son, Hue, Deo Phu Da, and Phu Tuc.[7] In many cases, our unit served as a rescue force to save or safeguard the other ARVN infantry troops. We usually stayed at one base for a few weeks, and then we were transported to another base. At Phu Tuc, we engaged against the NVA, the North Vietnamese infantry regiments.

The battle at Phu Tuc was a hard one. The NVA proved a better fighting force than the Viet Cong. We suffered heavy casualties, and were surrounded by the NVA for days. Finally, we were relieved by the U.S. Marines and returned back to Saigon. Then we transferred to other different places, such as Thanh Noi, Dang Thanh, Nam Giao, Deo Nong Nuoc, and Long Khang. Our airborne troops were transported to various bases.

After the American troops pulled out of Vietnam in 1973, the Airborne Division didn't perform as well as many had expected. We were an Americanized division, which had depended upon the American military system in South Vietnam. After the American withdrawal, we lost this highly centralized command and support system, including communication, transportation, and logistics. We suffered heavy casualties and lost a lot of equipment, but there were not much new recruits, nor new replacements.[8]

Memorial service of the Airborne Division in Oklahoma City in 2003.

The toughest battle for me was the one at Long Khang in 1975. One of the infantry divisions was under attack by the NVA at Long Khang. We were sent by helicopters into the fighting zone at night. For three weeks, we fought a tough defense against the NVA attack. I thought we would never get out of there.

After the battle, we transferred to Son Loc, Phuoc Ty, and Dung Tao. When we were stationed at Dung Tao, Gen. Cham Lan and Pres. Duong Van Minh ordered all the ARVN troops to surrender.[9] We didn't know why, but we obeyed the order and stopped fighting.

After that, our unit just fell apart and everyone seemed on your own. I didn't know where to go. Many of my friends got on the trucks heading South, back to home. My hometown had already been taken by the Viet Cong and I heard about the Viet Cong's policy of punishing those who had served in the ARVN like me. I was afraid of going back home and serving jail time. Like the other men, I burned all of my military papers and photo pictures taken during my service.

I found a U.S. cargo ship and the sailors allowed some of us to board. I had no idea where I was going and what I would do after the war. All I wanted was to leave the country and avoid any punishment, since I didn't think I had done anything wrong as an individual Vietnamese. I had served my country and protected my people. Why do I have to go to jail for that?

After arriving in America, I didn't know where to go and what to do. I traveled with several others to Minnesota and worked on farms. I was kind of like a seasonal handyman and moved from one farm to another. I did anything they asked me to. Then I found a job in a local Coca-Cola bottling company. I have been working there ever since. I missed my parents, brothers, and sisters. I missed my hometown and my country, to which I never returned. The country I loved had disappeared long ago.

Chapter 3

Electronic Reconnaissance vs. Guerrillas

Humble and shy, Lt. Nguyen Nhieu always used a low voice during the interviews and our conversations. Sometimes my recorder failed to pick up his words.[1] That day, however, I couldn't believe my own ears when he told me that he was getting married the next weekend. "Congratulations," I loudly shouted, trying to overcome the background noise in the Chinese restaurant. "Tell me about the bride." I was excited and curious. "Her name is Nguyen Nhi," Lieutenant Nhieu said, still keeping his voice low. He showed me her photo. Big eyes and round face, Nhi is a nice looking and happy woman. Lieutenant Nhieu told me that she was well educated and had written a few books in Vietnamese. He gave me three of her recent publications at the dinner table.[2] "All about the war," his voice got even lower. "You may like them. Not me. She is part of it. She lost her legs in the war, and she is in the wheelchair." I was shocked and became speechless. It was hard for me to imagine such a happy and intelligent woman rolling down the aisle in a wheelchair at her wedding.

Lt. Nguyen Nhieu received his college education and was admitted to a law school in South Vietnam. But the ongoing war interrupted his higher education and made him an intelligence officer in the ARVN Navy. He received his formal reconnaissance training both in South Vietnam and in the United States from the best instructors with the most up-to-date technology.[3] The U.S. Navy provided technical support and trained Vietnamese officers for their intelligence mission.[4] Lieutenant Nhieu's story is notable for its details in naval intelligence collection of the South Vietnamese Navy. As one of the largest navies in the world, the ARVN Navy had more than 1,400 ships and gunboats, with 42,000 soldiers and sailors—seemingly everything needed to fight against the NVA and Viet Cong along the coast and in the rivers. According to Lieutenant Nhieu, however, the ARVN Navy failed to play any significant role in fighting the Communist forces and defending South Vietnam during the war. He believes the navy had problems similar to those of the other ARVN services, including political activity, personal networks, and careerism, which weakened the morale of officers and soldiers alike and distracted them from their military missions.

Lt. Nguyen Nhieu

Chief, Electronic Reconnaissance Team, Giang Doan and Ham Doi Naval Bases, ARVN Navy (South Vietnam)

During my college years, in the spring of 1968, a law school in Saigon accepted my application. My mother was so happy since she thought I didn't have to serve in the military, as my father and two elder brothers were doing at that time. She also planned for me to apply for the further study overseas in the Western countries like the United States. In the fall, however, I found out that the war was everywhere and affected everybody in the college. Neither the students nor the faculty members were allowed to travel abroad. All the professors talked about the war in their classes. Antiwar flyers and rallies flooded the cafeteria and dorms. The students were guessing who the secret Viet Cong members were and who the undercover South Vietnamese government agents were on the campus. Some students disappeared from my classes and never came back. Rumors followed them. These students either left the capital city for the Viet Cong guerrilla force or were assassinated by the secret agents. Everybody worried about the outcome of the war, not about their grade in the class. Certainly, your career and your future depended upon which side you were on, not how well you were educated.

I just couldn't learn any more after I had finished my general education in my first year as a freshman. Toward the end of the fall semester in late 1969, a couple of naval officers visited our classroom for recruitment purposes. After their propaganda and offer briefing, I signed up for the ARVN Navy without much hesitation. My decision almost blew away my mother, who cried and yelled at me, complaining why I didn't talk to her before my enlistment. She didn't understand why I volunteered when everybody else tried to avoid the draft.

I explained to her that I believed it was a very good offer. First of all, the ARVN Navy promised one year of training in a naval academy. All the courses I would take were considered as college credits to fulfill my degree requirement. That would include a six-month study in the South Vietnamese naval academy and six-month training in a naval school in America.[5] My mother felt better after she knew about the training opportunity in America. Second, after training, I would be a naval officer working in the office, not a soldier on the front line. Third, I had to serve in the military before my graduation or before I would start to look for a job. You can't get any government position or any decent job in a law firm without a military service record in South Vietnam. Eventually, my mother agreed with me.

In January 1970, I joined the ARVN Navy. For the next three months, I received some basic training at a naval base in Saigon.[6] There were about two hundred naval trainees in our class. We drilled every day and learned how to use small arms. We visited various ships and gunboats and took part in several naval exercises off the coast. I still remember that one day we got on board an American warship outside the Saigon harbor. The American ship was equipped with new technology and powerful weapons. And, American sailors and officers were very friendly.

After the basic training, they sent me with forty other officer-students from our class to a naval academy in Nha Trang City for advanced training. For the next four months, I studied electronics engineering, radar operations, and electronic detection technology at the naval school. Some of the instructors were American naval officers. Patient and kind, they taught us everything from the books to their combat experience. All of us studied very hard. We were told that only the top ten out of forty officer-students would go to America for further training and study. I worked very hard during these months. My strong English background and solid core curriculum at the college had really helped me all the way to the top of the class. By the end of this advanced training, I knew that I was going to America for further study, and that I would become a petty officer first class.

In August 1970, I came to America with eight of my classmates from the Nha Trang Navy Academy. We went to the U.S. Naval War College at Newport, Rhode Island. We were divided into two groups, four of us studying naval intelligence.[7] I studied electronic interception and detection of enemy signals, radio messages, and telegraphs. Even though they cut our training from six to three months, I learned a lot at the U.S. Naval War College. We traveled a lot during this period, including trips to New

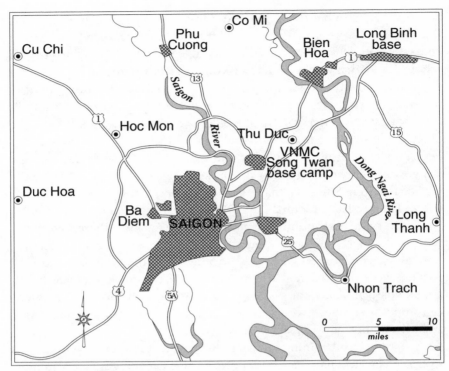

Saigon and Surrounding River Bases, 1964–1975

York, Washington, Philadelphia, Chicago, Norfolk, and Miami. That was an eye-opening experience, and I began to dream of coming to America after the war.

Upon my return, I was promoted to lieutenant by the ARVN Navy in November 1970. The ARVN Navy had two main branches: the offshore sea fleet and the inland river fleet.[8] I was assigned to the river operations at the Giang Doan River base. I served two years in the river unit, and two years with the sea fleet at the Ham Doi Naval Base.

From 1971 to 1973, my assignment was electronic information collection along the rivers for the ARVN Naval Intelligence Center. I led an intelligence team of about forty naval officers and sailors. We were traveling on a small reconnaissance boat equipped with new electronic devices. We were sailing along the rivers with six or eight officers, about three or four days for each trip. We collected electronic information by intercepting radio signals of the NVA and Viet Cong. These Communist radio opera-tors and communication officers must have been very well trained. It was very difficult for us to break their codes and to figure out what they were talking about. After each trip, we analyzed the information and reported the Communist troops' movements and deployments to the navy intelli-gence center.

As the collection team chief, I knew my mission and tried to avoid any engagement with the Viet Cong and NVA in order to protect my team members and electronic equipment. On several occasions, however, we had to fight our way out of a dangerous situation.

In February 1972, for example, we were sailing along the Go Quao River near Rach Gia. On the third day, we discovered information of a large-scale movement of the NVA troops. When the Communist troops moved, we followed them for two days. On the fourth day, however, we lost their radio signals because they had marched too far away from the river. In order to find out their destination, I decided to land our team and fol-low the NVA movements. Before we could relocate these troops, we were ambushed by the local Viet Cong from a village. One of the officers was killed, and two were wounded. I had a minor injury. It was so sad to see your men get killed or wounded because they followed your orders. I still feel sorry about those officers today. But at that moment you are sure that these men are loyal to you and to our government.

I knew that the Communists considered the U.S. and ARVN intelli-gence the most dangerous and that our intelligence would be fatal to their victory. Thus, they tried everything they could to neutralize our opera-tions and destroy our units. As a team chief, I was told from time to time by my superiors that our security wasn't perfect and there could be inside VC agents, that you needed self-protection and trusted nobody, and that you were always prepared for the worst. My officers were transferred fre-quently, and we changed our team base several times.

In the spring of 1973, after the American troops withdrew, I was trans-ferred to the sea fleet and led an intelligence collection team on an escort ship. This was a big gunship, but I had a smaller group, about ten offi-cers, working under my command most of the time. I had a similar assign-ment: collecting electronic information and intercepting radio signals of the movements the Viet Cong [PLAF] and NVA forces.

I was unhappy about this transfer, not because of the new assignment, but because of a missed promotion opportunity. I was supposed to be promoted to lieutenant commander during this transfer. But somebody else got the promotion. That was the problem of the ARVN Navy, in which honest people didn't get promoted or awarded, but those sneaky and dishonest people would get all they wanted. I served as a lieutenant for four years with the Navy. I never got a promotion.

Nevertheless, we had better electronic equipment and a longer range radar system built in the escort ship, which had been operated by the U.S. Navy and then was transferred to the ARVN Navy.[9] It had an up-to-date weapon system with many new technical features. When it patrolled and engaged, we sailed as part of its crew out in the seas. We conducted coastal and oceanic information collection and analysis.

We engaged in a couple dozen naval operations. Most of them were bombarding the NVA coastal positions and supporting our ground operations. Several of them were rescue missions to transport our ground troops out of the Communist attacks. I still remember one confrontation with the Chinese Communist Navy near the South China Sea.

During one patrol in the summer of 1973, we identified several Chinese vessels leaving the international waters around the South China Sea and approaching our waters. Our fleet, including two cruisers and one supply ship, sailed toward the Chinese in order to stop a possible violation of our sovereignty. The Chinese fleet, including two cruisers and two destroyers, didn't stop and continued to sail toward us. Around noon, both fleets met each other near the water boundary [twelve miles off the coast]. And then both stopped face to face in close range. Our cruiser crew rushed to their battle positions and prepared for combat. We were ready to destroy our code books, manuals, and other documents. The standoff took about one hour. Then the Chinese warships backed down and pulled out. But I was surprised that, after they sailed away, the Chinese ships turned around and fired on us. We returned fire. Although the exchange of gunfire was intense, it didn't cause much damage since we were far enough from each other. I didn't know what kind of game the Chinese Navy was trying to play. Our commanders reported our victory against an invading Chinese fleet. My guess was that the Chinese probably did the same thing.

This was another problem of the ARVN Navy. The commanders and officers tended to report victories and make up some good news, and not report the real problems or the truth. We lacked the nationalistic spirit in our officers, most of whom didn't dedicate their lives to the cause. Our navy and South Vietnamese armed forces needed a strong fighting spirit

Lt. Nguyen Nhieu in the United States in 1998.

so that we could have stayed on our course. The spirit would create miracles. Unfortunately, our enemy forces had a fighting spirit, were dedicated to their cause, and won the war. Certainly, they had an evil cause, which didn't lead to the salvation of the Vietnamese people, but led to Communist control.

After the war, I was jailed by the Communist government from 1975 to 1979. After I was released, I returned to My Tho, my hometown. I was treated as a criminal by the neighbors for many years.

Nevertheless, my mother was so happy to see me back home. After my father died, I was her only surviving family since she lost two of three sons in the war. I looked for all kinds of jobs and worked hard for her.

In 1992, my dream was coming true: I came to America through humanitarian organizations' programs. I regained my human dignity. I am proud of my service in the ARVN Navy, and American people here respect that. They appreciated our sacrifice and loss during our fight against the Communists. Living in Fort Worth, Texas, I am working hard to try to settle down, and then I can bring my mother to America. She has suffered enough, and I am her only family.

Chapter 4

Communist Regulars
from the North

Although I met many parents from overseas on American college campuses, I have seen few grandparents from Asian countries. As a grandfather, Sgt. Tran Thanh traveled all the way from Hanoi to Florida to attend his granddaughter's graduation commencement at the university. "My son and daughter-in-law work in the government, so they can't take off from their office," Sergeant Thanh told me. I knew that many Vietnamese officials could only come to America for official business, not for a family visit. Complacent and affable, Sergeant Thanh was very glad to see me and talk about his family story and service in the North Vietnamese Army.[1] He did not mind going into detail on the Communist Party organization, political propaganda, mass mobilization, NVA guerrilla tactics, and battles against American soldiers. "I told American friends my story," he said. "They should know more about Vietnam."

The Vietnamese Communist force was founded on December 22, 1944, during World War II, with a total of five thousand men. In November 1946, North Vietnam, then the Democratic Republic of Vietnam (DRV), passed its first constitution and established its Defense Ministry with Gen. Vo Nguyen Giap as its first defense minister and commander-in-chief of the North Vietnamese forces. In 1950, they were reorganized and renamed as the People's Army of Vietnam (PAVN, or NVA, commonly known as the Viet Minhs during the French Indochina War), with 50,000 troops. By the end of the French Indochina War in 1954, the Viet Minhs totaled 120,000 regulars. In May 1955, the NVA established its navy, followed by its air force in September 1956. After 1958, it formed its armored, antichemical, radar, engineering, and other special forces. The NVA had 380,000 troops in 1964, and 1 million men by 1972.[2]

Tran Thanh was drafted into the NVA like all the adult males between eighteen and forty-five in the North. He received formal infantry training and learned how to use Russian- and Chinese-made weapons.[3] *From the early 1960s, North Vietnam sent its NVA regulars to the South to train and support Southern Communist troops, the People's Liberation Armed Forces (PLAF), to fight the ARVN and the U.S. forces in guerrilla operations. From 1964, Hanoi infiltrated an annual average of 100,000 troops, including some of the best units, through the Ho Chi Minh Trail to South Vietnam. The NVA actually provided the main force of the Communist insurgency in the South.*

In the spring of 1965, Sergeant Thanh's company was sent to South Vietnam. From April to November, he fought in several battles around the Central Highlands and the surrounding mountainous areas. By the 1968 Tet Offensive, the NVA/PLAF in the South reached a total strength of 400,000 troops. In the late 1960s and early 1970s, the NVA/PLAF expanded its operations into Cambodia and Laos. From January 1961 to January 1973, the NVA/PLAF suffered 851,000 military deaths.[4] *It is interesting to see Sergeant Thanh's views on his South Vietnamese Communist allies, ARVN opponents, and the Americans then and now. His story about life in the NVA is valuable because there is little information on the North Vietnamese Communist forces in English.*

Sgt. Tran Thanh

Third Company, 174th Regiment, 316th Division, NVA (North Vietnamese Army)

I love Connie, my granddaughter. Her parents sent her to study in America four years ago. Now I traveled all the way from Hanoi to Florida, attending Connie's graduation commencement in Tampa, and helping her move to New Orleans, Louisiana. This is my first trip to America. Among other things, I like southern weather, seafood, and local Vietnamese restaurants along the gulf coast. Not many complaints, but, as a smoker, it is hard for me to find a "smoking area" by guessing the signs in English and Spanish.

Connie loves Florida, too. Active and dynamic, she participated in many international student activities on campus and didn't miss a local Asian community celebration. But she couldn't attend any Vietnamese

Society (*Cong Dong Viet Nam*) gatherings in the Tampa Bay area, because she is from North Vietnam, or Communist Vietnam, now officially the Socialist Republic of Vietnam. I couldn't believe it when Connie told me what happened to her. There are still two Vietnams in today's America. The war was over almost thirty years [by 2004]. Vietnam and America normalized their relationship about ten years ago. It's history. There is no reason of disliking us, especially our kids. We can become friends. I always start my conversation with an American Vietnam War veteran by saying, "Friends are made after a fight." Most people here liked it after Connie's translation. We truly know each other after we fought the war. And both peoples have learned that we won't fight again. I just did what the Vietnamese people had to do at that time, including the minorities in North Vietnam.

In 1939, I was born to a Black Thai family in a small mountainous village near Lai Chau, North Vietnam. Among Vietnam's minorities, the Black Thai people are different from the White and Red Thais. With a total of a half million, the Black Thais are so called for our darker skin color and black garb of the women. We dwell mainly in the upland valleys of northwestern Vietnam and northeastern Laos. Our family affiliation determines our status and occupation. While a few families in my village formed political and religious elite, others furnished farmers, artisans, and soldiers.

According to the Black Thai tradition, every man is a soldier. He lives a life close to the land and to the warfare. Bravery, self-discipline, physical toughness, stoicism, and martial arts are fundamental to his lifestyle. Discipline, loyalty, and frugality are the ethical values of the mountain warriors and have been an active force in the Black Thai community. For a Black Thai man, his integrity and loyalty are based on the protection he can provide to his family and village. It's a collective effort, or a team defense. In the past, Black Thai villages always faced external threats and foreign invasions such as Chinese, French, and Japanese conquests and occupations. Since long, each village organized its men into a "self-defense team" to protect its people and land. The self-defense team trained the men, organized village defense, and also sent volunteers or conscripts to the national armed forces.

My family has a tradition of service. My father joined the nationalist resistance force against the Japanese invaders during World War II. Two of my brothers served in the Viet Minh against the French invading forces and fought at Dien Bien Phu in 1954.[5] The Vietnamese Communist Party provided a strong military and political leadership that helped the Black

Thai and all the Vietnamese peoples in the North achieve their victory and national independence. My father and my brothers became heroes of our village since they served the country and the people against foreign invasions. Servicemen are respected. Those who were killed in action have their names placed in the village temple next to the ancestors. They are worshipped by younger generations. My childhood dream was to be a soldier when I grew up.

In 1950, I went to a nearby elementary school about three miles from my village. I remember having a one-hour drill every morning, including marching, shooting, bayoneting, and martial arts training. It seemed to us at the time that joining the army and fighting a war would be a lot of fun. I learned for the first time about the Geneva Settlement of 1954 in my elementary school. We were told that the settlement ended French colonization in Vietnam (1876–1954). But a corrupted, dictatorial, and brutal government, the Republic of Vietnam (RVN), controlled the South and was murdering and torturing its people. It made sense to us that the North should liberate the South and achieve national reunification by force.

After elementary school, I returned to my village in 1954 and became a farmer working in rice paddies and coffee plantations. As with all the males between sixteen and fifty-nine, I joined the "Self-defense Force" in 1955. The Self-defense Force was a local militia organization. Based on the rice-rooted, traditional "village self-defense team," it was well established in the rural areas across North Vietnam. The Self-defense Force in my village was under the command of a self-defense committee chaired by the village chief. He was under the command of the county self-defense committee. The county committee was commanded by the provincial self-defense committee. In my village, each family had two or three militia members. Three families formed a group, three groups became a team, and three teams served as a section. All the section leaders sat on the village self-defense committee. I remember that we drilled regularly with light weapons, and that we provided local security and emergency or rescue services. Women and children under sixteen were encouraged to participate in some of our training and activities. The most dangerous job, as I remembered, was hunting mountain tigers in the winter when they came down from the mountains and attacked villagers and their livestock.

After two years of farming and militia training, I was conscripted by the NVA in 1958 as a reservist, like all the adult males between eighteen and forty-five in the village. I served two months every year in a Black Thai battalion stationed at Lai Chau, a small city in northwestern Vietnam. The reserve was local, ethnic, and based on a rotation system. Our company mainly consisted of Black Thai soldiers who came from my village and several surrounding villages. I knew most of the men in the company. We came to the same company under the same commanding officers and preformed active duties, including border patrol, city security, political study, and intensive training. That was the moment of the year for me since there were so many new things to learn during each active duty service.

I learned more combat skills and new weapons, including automatic rifles, machine guns, antitank and antiaircraft rockets, and group-attack tactics. Every month, half the company rotated while the other half stayed for their second month. In my political education class, the company political instructor told the reserves that the American imperialists had invaded South Vietnam with a large number of their troops. North Vietnam now had two enemies in the South: the corrupt RVN government and aggressive U.S. forces. We should be better prepared for a new war against the Americans. After the "Tonkin Gulf Incident" in August 1964, I knew that the United States had escalated its ground war in South Vietnam, and had shifted its war efforts to North Vietnam by increasing its air strikes and heavy bombing. Ho Chi Minh, chairman of the Vietnamese Communist Party, adopted a new strategy: to defend the North by fighting the war in the South. At that time, we believed that we could win the war as long as we followed Chairman Ho. History has proven he was right.

In the fall of 1964, the NVA sent more infantry troops to the South. In the North, the NVA established five antiaircraft artillery divisions and one radar division for air defense. In 1965, it formed two surface-to-air missile regiments.[6] The DRV government launched a massive mobilization to meet the manpower need for its new operations. The NVA divisions began to activate their reserves. Each NVA infantry division formed regionally. For example, most of the soldiers and officers of the 308th Division were from Hanoi, the capital city of North Vietnam. The 308th was also called the "Capital Division," as one of the first six divisions established in the First Indochina War. Our 316th Division was an ethnic minority division in which many soldiers and officers were Tho, Miao, and Thai minorities from the northwestern mountainous region.

In December 1964, the 316th Division command called up all of its reserves for active duty. At the division assembly point, I was assigned to the Third Company, 174th Regiment. I was excited when I reported to the company. I didn't care what was going to happen next. I was not afraid. Two of my best friends, Tuan and Waong, were in my company. We knew that we would take care of each other. In a "three-three formation," the 316th Division, about fifteen thousand men, had three regiments, each having three battalions, with each battalion having three companies. The soldiers of the Third Company were mostly the Black Thais from the Lai Chau area. During the intensive training for the Southern guerrilla operation, the Black Thai soldiers impressed the officers and men by our martial arts, shooting, and hand-to-hand combat skills. We earned our nickname, the "mountain tigers," in the company.

In March 1965, the Third Company departed for the South.[7] We traveled southward by truck along the Black River from Son La, a northwestern city, to Linh Cam, a small town in the central region close to the 18th parallel. Then we rode westward on small trucks entering the Annam Cordillera, the Great Mountain Range. I had heard a lot about this forested mountain range. As a mountaineer, I really enjoyed traveling up to the great mountain by day and listening to mountain tigers roaring at night.

One morning, Lieutenant Ngu told us that we were going to pass the border and enter Laos. He also asked everybody to hand over our personal belongings, which might identify our Northern status.[8] I surrendered my ID papers, a couple of books, and my wallet. But I hesitated about giving up my girlfriend's picture since all collected items would be burned. If her photo got burned, it would mean bad luck to her, and it could mean I would never see her again. I decided to keep her photo. Back on the mountain road, our trucks got slower and slower. At noon, we crossed the border, where a pine tree separates the two countries with a big bi-lingual sign on it, "Viet Nam–Laos."

After entering Laos, we began our journey on the Ho Chi Minh Trail. The narrow and rocky road was in poor condition through the western side of the Truong Son Range in Laos. We had to get off the truck many times and walk through the sections under expansion or repair. Because of enemy reconnaissance and air raids, we mostly traveled at night and rested by day along the trail. The traffic at night was very heavy and slow. Northern troops, artillery pieces, ammunition, equipment, and supplies were lined up for miles, traveling more than five hundred miles, and passing through Laos from north to south.

In April 1965, the Third Company entered South Vietnam from Laos. I remember that after we moved into the South, we received a couple of new officers as well as a new order from the Central Office for South Vietnam, the NVA frontline command in the South. The "new" officers, only new to us, were experienced NVA officers in the South for years. They told us that we were here to assist the South Vietnamese Communist troops, and that we needed to work together with the People's Liberation Armed Forces (PLAF) and the South Vietnamese Communist Party, or the National Liberation Front (NLF). What do you call them, the Viet Cong?

Then our company was assigned to consolidate and strengthen the liberated villages in the mountainous area not too far from the South Vietnam–Laos border, or the tri-state region. As a mountain unit, the Third Company was good at hillside defense work, village underground tunnels, antitank positions, and antiaircraft outpost construction. We worked very hard during the spring of 1965. We built the village defense work day and night. We also tried to share our defense tactics with the NLF/PLAF villagers. But I don't think they trusted us. There may be a couple of reasons for that.

The first reason was a political one between the NVA in the North and PLAF in the South. We had a civil war between the North and South. Then, we had a war against America. The Southern Vietnamese wanted us to help them resist America, but didn't want us to take over the South. They saw the NVA and PLAF as separate entities. We considered them as the one Communist force.

The second reason may be an ethnic one. They are the Vietnamese people, the majority. Some of them were kind of stuck up and didn't want to ask for help from the minorities like the Black Thais from the North. They saw us as the "barbarians." The Vietnamese people, farming the central highlands, coastal lowlands, and the deltas of the Red and Mekong rivers, make up 85 percent of the Southern population.

Through the spring of 1965, the Third Company worked on defense work one village at time. After turning each into a fortress, we moved on to another village. From time to time, we engaged with the ARVN troops in small scale. In many cases, we launched an attack on the ARVN-occupied village in order to expand our territory. A typical battle began with a charge on the ARVN defense point by a squad from the Third. The ARVN defenders called in their reinforcement, or actually their rescue troops, from the nearby town. The rescue troops usually provided firepower strong enough to stop our attack and cover the defenders' withdrawal. During their retreat, we just waited for the ARVN defenders to get on their vehicles and run away from the village.

Sometimes, however, the ARVN came back and tried to retake the village. One day in 1966, the ARVN attacked one of our well-built defense works in a village. The Third Company got the information ahead of time and put together all of its men to defend the village's underground tunnels. Our captain tried to send a message to the enemy troops that we would not easily give up our territory. After a two-day fight, the Third and local Viet Cong guerrilla troops successfully defended the village by a joined force. Although we won the battle, I lost one of my best friends in it. Waong was badly wounded when the ARVN soldiers destroyed part of the underground tunnel and threw several grenades into the section where he was. When I saw him after the battle, he was covered by blood. He couldn't move at all. We were family friends, and like brothers. I couldn't help my tears while holding one of his hands. "Don't," he shook his head, "We are the mountain tigers." These were his last words. We buried him and other comrades who were killed in the battle in the village cemetery. Lieutenant Ngu told us that we had destroyed one enemy armored vehicle, killed nineteen, and wounded thirty-six ARVN soldiers.

In 1968, when our company moved back into Laos, I was promoted to sergeant. In Laos, we engaged with the American troops for the first time, although most of the battles were in small scale. In 1971, I served as a Black Thai combat training master, or a drill sergeant. We stayed in Laos until 1973. Our company entered South Vietnam again in 1974 and participated in several major offensive campaigns to liberate our country.[9] After we won the war in 1975, I retired from the army with honor.

I did what everybody had to do during the war. We did what we felt was right for our country and for our family. We did it so they [our kids and grandkids] don't have to go through it. The war should be remembered as it was. It's over, and it's history. The war can't go on forever. People and things are no longer valued on the basis of whether they are "ours" or "yours." Connie is right. Let's get over it and move on. Well, many Southern Vietnamese have left their homeland. They have a home there. They like to express their grievance and justify their residency in a foreign country like America. We should understand why they are here. They love America, but they don't have to hate Vietnam. I love my country, and I don't have problems with America. Connie loves both countries. I know why she wants to find a job here and stay in America after her graduation. My son and I don't have any problem with her decision.

Chapter 5

People's War against Americans

Nicely framed family photos covered the small living/dinning room wall. A full-size bed made the room even smaller. Inside an old two-room house in the middle of a Southern village, no air conditioning and no computer, I couldn't help but wonder whether Capt. Ta Duc Hao was happy living like this as a war hero.[1] Excited and a little nervous, Captain Hao showed us the enlarged photos on the wall. "This is my father, a two-star general," he said as he proudly pointed to an old man in a NVA uniform with many medals on his left chest. Pointing to others, "They are my children." Captain Hao told me their stories one by one in the same complacent way. All three of his kids went through their colleges on government scholarships. Two of them worked in Ho Chi Minh City as engineers, and one at Da Nang as a lawyer. Satisfied and smiling, Captain Hao sat down with me. He was happy indeed. That's probably what he had fought for: carrying on the legacy and pride from the last generation and bringing new opportunities to the next.[2]

As a young North Vietnamese, Ta Duc Hao was drafted into the NVA in 1965 and sent to South Vietnam that summer via the Ho Chi Minh Trail. From 1964 to 1968, North Vietnam supported the Viet Cong by sending more NVA regular troops to fight a guerrilla, or "people's," war against the American and ARVN forces in South Vietnam.[3] In 1964, the NVA sent infantry regiments to the South. In early 1965, the 325th Division entered South Vietnam. In May and June, the 305th Division had entered the South via the Ho Chi Minh Trail.[4] By the end of 1965, the NVA had ten infantry regiments in South Vietnam. After 1966, the Northern regular troops joined Viet Cong guerrilla troops and became the main strength of the Communist forces in the South. When the Tet Offensive campaign took place in early 1968, the number of NVA regulars in South Vietnam had reached 400,000 men.[5] Both the

NVA and the PLAF suffered heavy casualties. Captain Hao's story describes the engagements with the ARVN and U.S. troops in the Central Highlands in general, and emphasizes the Battle of Ia Drang. The details provide some insight into the NVA military strategy, combat tactics, and operational problems during the mid-1960s. It may explain why the NVA and PLAF suffered heavy casualties during these battles.

Capt. Ta Duc Hao

First Company, Thirty-first Battalion, NVA (North Vietnam)

I joined the People's Army of Vietnam [PAVN, or NVA] in early 1965 because I needed to. First of all, the American air raids [Operation Rolling Thunder] against North Vietnam were so intensive that we couldn't go to school anymore. I felt very sad when I saw that our neighborhood was burning, and that many people died during the bombings. I agreed with our government that we should keep the war and Americans in the South. All the teenagers joined the army at that time. Second, my father served in the army for most of his life and ranked as a two-star general.[6] All of my older brothers had joined the services. I must follow the family tradition. Third, in the North, service was something necessary for your career development, like a college degree. No military service, no good job for you in the future. You need to earn it by fighting the enemy and showing your loyalty to the Communist Party and Uncle Ho. After an infantry training for a couple of months near Hanoi, I reported to the First Company, Thirty-first Battalion, of an infantry regiment. In the company, I learned more about small arms, demolition, and basic defense engineering. During that time, I also heard the men in my company talking about going down to South Vietnam and fighting a war against America. I was excited about participating in the ground war that had been going on in the South for years.

In the summer of 1965, the First Company received the orders that we would move to South Vietnam. Our battalion command sent some instructors to our company talking about the war situation and enemy troops in the South. We learned a lot about the American forces and their weapon systems. We also knew at the time that we might stay in the South for a long period of time. Before the end of the dry season, our company traveled from north to south by train. Then we entered Laos and continued our road trip through the Ho Chi Minh Trail. Sometimes we rode in the trucks, and sometimes we walked by foot. We traveled over five hundred miles crossing Laos, and entered Cambodia. From there, we crossed the border and moved into South Vietnam.

After we arrived in the South, we were under a joint NVA-PLAF command.[7] At first, we engaged mostly with the ARVN troops. When the rainy season began in June, our company received a new order from the joint headquarters: to destroy the enemy's "strategic hamlet villages" in the tri-state region. In the spring of 1965, the "puppet" RVN government and its army continued their so-called pacification program design to bring security and local self-government to rural South Vietnamese people. During the dry season, they occupied many villages, purged the pro-Communist farmers, armed the villagers, and helped them to fortify their villages. The pacification protected the ARVN bases and lines of communication, and sought out the Viet Cong and the NVA in the surrounding areas. In the rain season, the ARVN troops pulled back to their bases and left the pro-government farmers on their own in their "strategic hamlet villages."

We had a chance to retake these villages during the rain season. It was the first time we moved into enemy territory, but there wasn't much action. The armed farmers in their strategic villages rarely confronted the North Vietnamese regulars. When they saw us coming, they hid their weapons and acted as ordinary villagers. We usually gathered the villagers and tried to single out the government agents and hostile village leaders. Then we executed the bad guys and destroyed their defense works. As long as we didn't burn their houses and take away their food, the villagers didn't fight back.

That summer, our company participated in several ambush and small-scale defensive operations. In 1965, the NVA-PLAF command believed that the U.S. and ARVN troops in the South outnumbered NVA troops, and that the enemy had superior firepower and advanced air, naval, and armored forces. Thus, our troops avoided a frontal or formal battle with the U.S. troops, but engaged in traditional guerrilla warfare tactics, such as ambush, hit-and-run, night attacks, cutting transportation and communication lines, and attacking enemy weak points. We harassed the U.S. and ARVN troops, made the war as costly for the Americans as possible, and protected the civilian population as best we could.

In mid-July, the First Company was ordered to defend the village of An Theo. It was a strategic point in the area. After losing it to the NVA and PLAF in June, the ARVN now tried to take it back. The battalion command

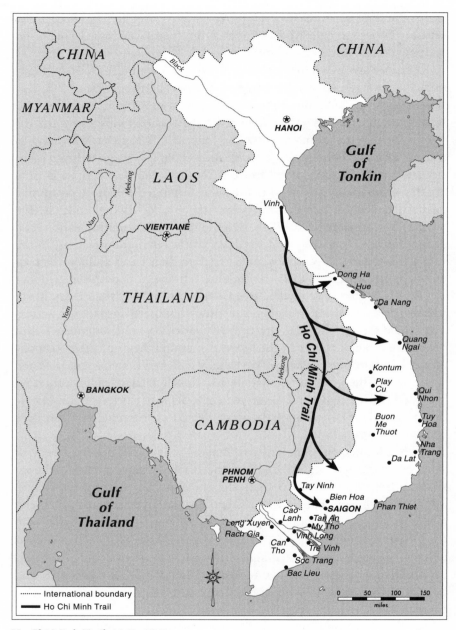

Ho Chi Minh Trail, 1963–1975

ordered our company to move into An Theo overnight. Then we spent a couple of days strengthening the defense works with the help of local Viet Cong and villagers.

On July 18, the ARVN troops arrived. They attacked An Theo a couple of times in small groups, but our company defeated them. Then they stopped their attack, but did not withdraw. They were waiting for their reinforcement. Next day, more ARVN troops arrived with heavy artillery pieces and armored vehicles. On July 20, the ARVN launched a larger scale offensive against An Theo. They had at least three companies with seven armored vehicles. Their artillery pieces bombed the village with more than two hundred 105 mm shells and charged our defense positions several times. Their intensive artillery shelling destroyed most of our defense works. We had to move into underground tunnels to continue our defense. Having failed to take over the village, the ARVN troops stopped their attacks by the evening. They pulled out their troops and didn't come back the next day. We successfully defended An Theo. However, our company and local Viet Cong suffered heavy casualties during the three-day battle. We received our new recruits regularly from the North.

In the fall of 1965, the NVA developed a new strategy, the so-called formality strategy, or a formal warfare strategy. The new strategy included plans and tactics of frontal engagements, medium-scale offensive campaigns, attacks on the cities, and elimination of an entire enemy unit, like a company or even a battalion. Meanwhile, there were different opinions in the command. We heard about the strategic debates at the high command. Anyway, the new strategy lasted for almost three years until its peak, the Tet Offensive campaign of February 1968. Both NVA and PLAF suffered the heaviest casualties since the beginning of the war.[8] Then the high command believed that the offensive strategy was too costly to continue. Thereafter, the NVA returned to its traditional guerrilla warfare.

Since the implementation of the new strategy, our company began to join other companies and engaged in large-scale operations at battalion level. One of the big battles we fought was the Central Highlands Offensive campaign. You called it the Battle of Ia Drang in America.[9] At the end of October 1965, the PLAF and NVA launched a joint offensive campaign against Plei Me, an ARVN stronghold in the Central Highlands.[10] By October 29, the PLAF had completely encircled the ARVN garrison. In early November, the NVA and PLAF launched our attack on the ARVN troops at Plei Me.

In order to eliminate all the ARVN garrison, the NVA set up road-blocks between Plei Me and Pleiku and between Plei Me and An Khe in order to stop possible ARVN and U.S. reinforcement or rescue efforts.[11] Our Thirty-first Battalion was deployed at Hill 558 along Route 21 between Plei Me and Pleiku. One day in early November, our company moved into our positions at the bottom of the hill. We dug some foxholes along our defensive positions between Route 21 and Hill 558. And then we waited. Around noon, we were told that the ARVN reinforcements were coming from Pleiku on Route 21, including an infantry battalion and an armored battalion. We should ambush the ARVN troops at Hill 558 to stop the rein-forcements and ensure a victory of the Plei Me attack. I was a little bit nervous since we had not yet engaged in such a large-scale battle in the past six months. I checked my ammo and medic-aid package again and again.

Before long, a couple of the ARVN helicopters flew over our positions. They didn't detect the concealed NVA troops around Hill 558. About 1400 hours, a long column of the enemy armored vehicles and trucks came along the road. We opened fire when they reached the hill. The enemy troops were in panic under the unexpected attack. They fled to where they came from and left many bodies behind along the road. We were so excited about our successful ambush. Captain Ngu, our company commander, ordered us to refill ammo and send wounded back. He shouted, "Hurry, they will be back." He was right. About one hour later, the enemy troops attacked our positions with the help of the American helicopters. The American armed helicopters from Pleiku attacked our positions with a fierce bombing and shelling. We had to pull out of our roadside positions, and moved up to the hill for better coverage.

About 1600 hours, two more ARVN battalions arrived as new rein-forcements. Then they charged the hill. Even though our battalion fought bravely, we were outnumbered and without any air and artillery support. When it was getting dark, our battalion commanders ordered a with-drawal from Hill 558. We heard next day that the American troops from An Khe also broke the NVA roadblock. On November 14, because of the failures of blockage, the PLAF stopped its offensive on Plei Me. On November 14, more American troops arrived in the Ia Drang Valley and began their counterattacks against the PLAF and NVA. Our command decided to concentrate the PLAF-NVA troops to deal with the American reinforcement.

From November 14 to 19, our company joined the other PLAF-NVA

Capt. Ta Duc Hao (right) and the author in Longxuyen in 2006.

units and attacked American troops at the Ia Drang Valley. During the five-day battle, our company suffered heavy casualties, including thirty-one dead and forty-one wounded. We were replaced by our reserve troops. Our battalion also pulled out of the attack due to its heavy casualties. On November 19, the command decided to withdraw all the units from the Ia Drang Valley. Then we moved west, toward the South Vietnam–Cambodia border. That was a major withdrawal from the Central Highlands. On November 19, our company received new orders to escort a NVA field hospital moving west to the liberated area [the PLAF-controlled areas]. In the afternoon, the American helicopters discovered the field hospital and our battalion headquarters, which retreated with us. The helicopters' firepower inflicted large casualties on our troops. I was shot with multiple wounds on my right shoulder and my neck. I was lucky to receive immediate medical assistance, since our company was escorting the doctors and nurses of the field hospital.

The field hospital couldn't stay anywhere within the borders of South Vietnam. It kept moving west, crossing the border, and eventually withdrew into Cambodia. I and other wounded moved with the field hospital and left South Vietnam in that winter.

In 1966, I recovered from my wounds. I left Cambodia and returned to my unit in 1967 in South Vietnam. I was lucky to be transferred back before the American forces intensified their air raids and bombing in 1969 and eventually invaded Cambodia in the spring of 1970.

Our battalion fought in seven provinces of South Vietnam. I was promoted to sergeant, lieutenant, and then captain. Although I was wounded again in 1973, I remained in active duty until the war was over in 1975. We returned back to the North in the same year. I retired from the army in 1976 during the demobilization and I got married in Hanoi later that year. I talked to my wife and came down to the South in 1978. I knew the South better than the North since I had spent about ten years of my young adult life here. Also I could get a better job here after we won the war and took over everything during its reconstruction in the late 1970s. I worked in the village office in 1979–1985, and then in the town government from 1986 to 2002. I retired from the government position in 2005. I receive government retirement, military pensions, and disability compensation every month. I'm very happy living in this village with my wife. We may have to move to one of the cities since our children need our help. One of them is expecting their first baby.

Chapter 6

No Final Victory, No Family Life

They are still friends. Ngoc and Tran worked in the same office in 1975–1976 at Ty Xay Dung, the largest construction corporation in An Giang Province. Ngoc's father was the CEO, a retired NVA lieutenant general; and Tran was from a small business family and soon fled the country as one of the "boat people." I was surprised to see their reunion after thirty years: emotional hug with tears, instant recall of some old-day gossip, and garrulous brags of their kids and families. Even though they went separate ways, there was no animosity, no regret, and no hard feelings. They seemed happy with the ending. Lt. Gen. Huynh Thu Truong was happy, too, having seen it all: the end of the French Indochina War in 1954, the end of the American War in 1973, and the end of the Vietnam War in 1975.[1]

As a senior artillery expert, Major General Truong's war experience both in the North and in the South reflects the technological aspects of the NVA and PLAF by showing how the Viet Cong adopted new technology and trained its officers. During the early years of the 1960s, Hanoi sent many of the NVA officers with Southern roots back to the South to participate in the NLF and PLAF's struggle against the ROV government. Some of these officers had been recalled to north of the 17th parallel according to the Geneva Indochina Agreement signed in July 1954.[2] Some had fled to the North during Diem's suppressions against the Communists in 1958–1961. While in North Vietnam, they received further training in guerrilla warfare, mass mobilization, political propaganda, and military technology. After they were sent back to the South, these officers played an important role in upgrading the PLAF's weapons and equipment and improving their combat effectiveness.

The NVA high command began to pay more attention to military technology in the late 1950s in order to win large-scale, decisive battles against

the ARVN forces, establishing artillery and engineering divisions and open-
ing artillery and engineering schools to train their officers and commanders.
When the first antiaircraft artillery brigade began its air defense of the capital
city, Ho Chi Minh wrote to the commander that "Without antiaircraft artil-
lery, Hanoi is like a house without a roof."[3] In the summer of 1965, the NVA
established its antiaircraft missile regiments in the North. Meanwhile, the
PLAF continued to improve its weaponry by introducing up-to-date military
technology. In the late 1960s, the NVA transformed from a peasant guerrilla
army into a modern professional army.[4]

Lt. Gen. Huynh Thu Truong

Rector, Artillery Training Center, PLAF (Viet Cong, South Vietnam)

I was born into a well-off family in 1923 in South Vietnam. After high
school, I enrolled in a French Catholic College at Saigon [present Ho Chi
Minh City] in 1944. I studied engineering, mathematics, mechanics, physics, and chemistry. The Pacific war was over in August 1945, and the Viet
Minh established the Democratic Republic of Vietnam [DRV] in Hanoi
with Ho Chi Minh as president in early September. The Viet Minh had
been active in the South.

The First Indochina War broke out in 1946 when the Viet Minh troops
clashed with the French forces in the North. Even though we were French
college students, we didn't like the French colonial government's return
after World War II, with their old-fashioned, out-of-date colonial policy. We
liked national independence and wanted to take Vietnam back from France.
I joined the student protests against French domination of our country.

The Viet Minh members were actively involved in these student movements in Saigon and rapidly developed their party branches all over the
college campuses. I was approached by one of the party branch members in
our college, and I became a Southern Vietnamese Communist Party member in 1946.[5]

After my graduation in 1948, I got married and had an engineering
job to cover my secret mission as an undercover Communist engineering researcher. I had accomplished several important artillery tests and
research projects for the People's Army of Vietnam [PAVN, also known as
Viet Minh] in the North in my company lab in Saigon. The results of my
research were sent all the way from the South to the North.

In 1952, the Viet Minh headquarters in the North sent a request through the South Vietnamese Party Committee in Saigon and asked me to join a newly opened artillery training school in the North. The party committee asked for my own opinion on this. At that time, I believed that I could make more contributions to Vietnam's Communist revolution by joining the army in the North than working as an undercover engineer in the South. Certainly, there was a war going on in the North between the Viet Minh and France. It meant that my decision would soon lead me to danger, hardship, and even death on the front line against the French forces. But I thought that the party needed me, and that there was also a good opportunity for my career. I left my job, a comfortable family life, and a pregnant wife behind. I walked for two weeks with a small group of people all the way to the North until we got to the Chinese-Vietnamese border.

Back then, the Viet Minh force was a guerrilla farmers' army. Short of financial sources and military technology, they didn't have their own artillery instructors and training facilities in the early years of the French Indochina War. The Chinese Communist forces, the People's Liberation Army [PLA], provided artillery pieces, equipment, and training for the North Vietnamese troops. Among the 250 advisers of the CMAG [Chinese Military Advisory Group] were eleven artillery officers, who arrived in North Vietnam on August 11, 1950. In May 1951, the Chinese helped the Viet Minh establish the 351st Division, the first Vietnamese artillery and engineering division.[6] In the same year, the PLA also trained the Vietnamese officers inside China by opening an officer academy, an artillery training center, and engineering schools. While the Viet Minh high command was grateful about the Chinese effort to train the Vietnamese artillery officers, it also worried about the military dependence and Chinese influence. Since the Viet Minh had grown from two divisions up to seven regular divisions by 1952 and was winning the war against the French forces, it should have its own artillery training programs.

After arriving in the North, I served as an artillery training officer at the Viet Minh's No. 9 Quan Khu Phao Binh [Artillery] Training Center.[7] Most of the artillery equipment came from China, including 60 mm, 80 mm, and 82 mm artillery guns. Their best artillery technology was the Chinese-manufactured six-rocket launchers and 75 mm recoilless guns against tanks and defense works.

During the early years at the artillery training center, we translated

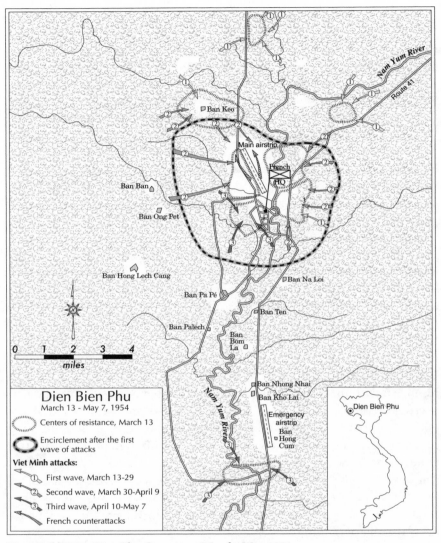

Viet Minh's Dien Bien Phu Campaign, March–May 1954

many technology notes and manuals from Chinese to Vietnamese. I also translated many French technical instructions into Vietnamese and helped our officers to operate captured French artillery pieces.

After my promotion to a major in the Viet Minh, I took part in writ-

ing our own training curriculum, officer assessments, promotion require-
ments, and equipment maintenance regulations. At the training center, I
taught classes, organized routine drills, and assessed joint exercises. We
also developed our artillery planning, operation instructions, mobile tactics, defense deployment, and offensive bombardment. Our program
became more sophisticated, and our classes got bigger. In 1953, we had an
average of 150 officers on the campus all year long. The artillery training
and tactics played an important role in the major battles, such as the Red
River campaign in 1953.

During these years in the North, I missed my wife and my little two-
year-old daughter, whom I had never seen. But I knew her name was Ngoc,
which I'd picked for her before I'd gone to the North. I had to fight for our
victory before I could have my family reunion. We had to fight harder and
win the war by defeating the French.

From December 1953 to April 1954, the Viet Minh forces encircled
the 15,000 French troops at Dien Bien Phu. Our artillery troops played a
very important role in the final battle. The 351st Artillery Division, rocket
battalion, and 75 mm recoilless gun battalion effectively engaged in the
offensives. Many of our artillery officers received their training from our
center. In March, their successful shelling against enemy airfields, supply
depots, and communication lines had isolated the French forces and also
diminished their escape chance. By April, the French troops held only three
points. On May 6, the Viet Minh high command launched its final all-out
attack. In a couple of days, the French surrendered. After eight years' fighting, we finally defeated French colonial forces in Vietnam.

After our victory in the First Indochina War, in the summer of 1954, I
traveled back to Saigon and looked for my family. Thanks to the Southern
Communist Party members who had taken good care of my family, my
wife and my daughter were doing just fine. I moved them all the way from
Saigon to the North. In 1957, I was transferred from the artillery training
center to the NVA Artillery Academy in Hanoi. My family followed me to
the capital city. We had a little boy a year later, when I was promoted to the
rank of lieutenant colonel in 1958.

In the early 1960s, the war between the NLF and the Diem government
of the so-called Republic of Vietnam [RVN] became intensified. Diem and
his forces killed thousands and thousands of the Southern Communist
members and jailed hundreds of thousands of the Communist sympathizers. Chairman Ho always reminded us that "Comparing with the great

hardships that the Southern people and army have to endure, your difficulties remain modest. You have to follow their example, fighting more valiantly and achieving greater victory."[8] Our party and army decided to support the Communist movement in the South by providing military aid and training to the South Vietnamese guerrilla troops.

After nine years' service in the North, in 1961 I was sent back to the South and joined the PLAF [People's Liberation Armed Forces] of the NLF to train their artillery troops. The Diem government referred to the NLF as "Viet Cong," meaning "Vietnamese Commies."

I left my post in the NVA Artillery Academy in Hanoi, and left my family again in December 1961. After we crossed the North Vietnamese-Laos border, we began to walk on foot. Then we entered Cambodia and walked a long way down south. They told me that it took longer going this way, but it was much safer. Then we entered South Vietnam by crossing the Cambodian-South Vietnamese border. After a twenty-three-day journey, we finally arrived at a Viet Cong military base in An Giang Province in January 1962.

The Viet Cong base was at the top of the Ca Mountain, which has many big trees and overlooks the Ca Mau River. Isolated in the forest and less populated, this mountainous area was far away from Diem's controlled areas. The villagers around the base were supportive to the NLF and the PLAF military struggle against the Diem government and the U.S. armed forces in South Vietnam.

We opened a PLAF artillery training school and began to offer classes to the PLAF officers. I was ranked colonel in the PLAF, an automatic promotion of one level up for most officers who returned from the NVA in the North to the PLAF in the South. The PLAF command sent its officers to our school for training in small groups. Usually we had an average of thirty to forty officers in our school. But we got better and more advanced artillery technology.

During the mid-1960s, we began to receive Soviet artillery pieces and equipment, including Russian-made 120 mm and 155 mm guns. Even though they were not available in the South until 1971, we began to learn how to operate and maintain these new weapons. Of course, we also studied American artillery technology since the PLAF had captured a large number of American artillery equipment and supplies. I was promoted to the rank of major general in 1964.[9]

During these years, I missed my wife and my children a lot. It had been

Lt. Gen. Huynh Thu Truong in Saigon in 1975.

more than fourteen years. We could send a letter and received mails without mentioning anybody's real name. It took about one to two months for each mail traveling from the South to the North, or the other way around. I believed that we had lost some of our mail. Nevertheless, I had my tears in my eyes every time when I received their mail. At first, I saw a small piece of my daughter's or my son's drawing; then a few words in their handwriting; and soon a short essay. They could not send any photo picture. The only photos I had were taken fourteen years ago when they were very little. I always wondered if they could remember me and accept me as their father who was never there during most of their lives. I really wanted to end this war by defeating the enemies so I could have my family back and have my own life back.

In the late 1960s, the war situation was getting better and better for the PLAF. Our artillery troops began to show their firepower when the PLAF started its offensive campaigns against the enemy strongholds and military bases. The main artillery operations in the South occurred in 1968, 1972, 1973, and 1974–1975, the later part of the war.

Because of the nature of the guerrilla warfare and lack of road control and transport vehicles, the Viet Cong did not employ large artillery pieces

Lt. Gen. Huynh Thu Truong (PLAF, ret.) in My Thanh in 2006.

until much later. Among their favorite guns were small artillery pieces, like 60 mm mortars and single rocket launchers. We trained them how to repair these weapons and how to manufacture the shells. Our training helped the PLAF troops win the battles against the ARVN and U.S. forces. I was promoted to lieutenant general in 1974. Eventually, we won the war in 1975.

By 1975, I haven't seen my family for fourteen years. My wife still lived in Hanoi, and she'd survived the American air raids and bombings. My daughter, then twenty-three years old, studied in a medical school in China on the North Vietnamese government scholarship. My son, seventeen now, was sent away from Hanoi to one of the government grade schools in the rear areas along the Vietnamese-Chinese border. The North Vietnamese government tried to ensure the safety of the children of all the high-ranking DRV officials and NVA generals, who were fighting the war on the front lines. We, as generals and parents, really appreciated that.

In 1975, I retired from the army. I found a position as the Chief Executive Officer (CEO) at Ty Xay Dung (a construction corporation), one of the major companies in An Giang Province. My wife moved from Hanoi to An Giang to join me. Our daughter continued her study in a medical school in Hanoi. In 1982, I retired from the company. My daughter as a physician also moved to An Giang to practice her medicine in order to take care of us. My son, married with three children, became a chief engineer in a petroleum-chemical company, and lives in Ho Chi Minh City with his own family. I enjoy our family life and my retirement.

Part Two

Hanoi's Comrades

Chapter 7

Russian Missile Officers in Vietnam

I was panicked and didn't know what to do in Kyiv, the capital city of Ukraine, after we were told that "Major T." could not be interviewed at that time. Anthony Song, my contact person and Russian translator, was not.[1] After several telephone calls, Anthony told me that Major T. had agreed to come to see us the next morning. "It's not me," the major explained when we met at our hotel. "My superior got to take a look at the list of your questions. He didn't want me to get into any trouble." Loyal and active in the local veteran chapter, Major T. also asked me to let him remain anonymous and have no picture in the book.[2]

The Soviet Union officially denied any direct involvement in the Vietnam War. Since its collapse in 1991, Russia and other former Soviet republics like Ukraine and Kazakhstan have maintained the same position. The Russian government has concealed the participation of the former Soviet Union's military in the war.[3] Soviet official records on the Vietnam War are closed to the public and scholars. Most Russian veterans do not want to talk about their experiences in Vietnam, and I now know why. In 2007, Moscow published a book on the Soviet involvement in the Vietnam War. With official permission, for the first time, twenty-nine veterans provided their personal stories of the Soviet war experience in Vietnam from 1965 to 1973.[4]

After the Moscow-Hanoi agreement in February 1965, the Soviet Union began sending its SAM missile troops, air-defense radar units, launch site technicians, training instructors, pilots, aircraft maintenance personnel, and logistics officers to North Vietnam. The total number of Soviet troops in Vietnam, however, is still inconclusive due to a lack of accurate sources.

*Russian archives provide few details about their military operations in Viet-
nam since the defense documents remain closed to the public and scholars.[5]
Some Russian historians still use Western sources for their research on this
topic.[6] The Chinese sources base their figures on the number of Russian officers and soldiers who traveled from the Soviet Union to Vietnam by railway
through China. Their statistics show that about 3,500 Soviet military personnel entered Vietnam in the spring of 1965. The total increased to 4,100 in
1967.[7] This number does not include the Russians who traveled to Vietnam
by air. U.S. intelligence believed that 1,500 to 2,500 Soviet military personnel
were in Vietnam in September 1965, including 150 pilots and 300 technicians
engaged in communication and other support activities.[8]*

Major T.

Training Instructor, SAM Missile Training Center, North Vietnam, Russian Armed Forces (Soviet Union)

I was born in Ukraine, the former Soviet Union, in 1944. My father was an
engineer at an aircraft manufacture company in our hometown. After my
middle school in 1959, instead of going to high school, I enrolled in a local
aviation mechanic school, something like vo-tech or a professional school
in your country. With a strong interest in machinery and aviation technology, I did a good job on my grades during the three-year studies. I was also
recruited by the party branch in the school and became a Communist Party
member in the last year of my school. Having graduated from mechanic
school in 1962, I found out that the military service offered a better opportunity than other jobs available in aviation industry at that time.

I joined the Soviet Army in 1962. I guess because of my training in
aviation technology and political credentials as a party member, I was
assigned to the strategic missile forces, the elite troops of all the services
in the Soviet armed forces. Our unit stationed around Moscow suburbs.
As new recruits, we began our intensive training on the new technology.
Due to my outstanding training records, by the end of 1962 I was selected
to be sent to the Soviet Antiaircraft Artillery [AAA] Technology Academy for further study. This academy trained the officers for commanding
surface-to-air missile troops and operating the air-defense system. I spent
two years at the AAA Academy. I took many classes, such as physics, chemical engineering, computer science, calculus, statistics, and military history.

I remember that our instructors quite often used the cases of the French Indochina War to explain military strategy vs. technology in a war between a Communist state and the Western powers. That was the first time for me to learn a lot about Vietnam, its Communist movement, and its leader, Ho Chi Minh. On the campus, I saw some international officer students studying at the academy. They came from the Communist countries like Poland, Cuba, and North Vietnam. They had their own separate classes and much shorter training programs.

Our classes were on a fast path, and our daily drills and weekly field training were also pretty tough. Several of my classmates did not make it and dropped out of the academy. Many of the cadets had a military family background, and some had a general or even a marshal father. We all made good friends and helped each other in and out the classroom. I remained at the top of the class and also served as the party branch secretary for our class.

Before my graduation, the war in Vietnam became intensified in 1964. The superintendent called for "volunteers" to serve in Vietnam. All of the cadets, including our graduating class, Class of 1964, signed up for our service in the Vietnam War. As new officers of the Soviet strategic force, we really wanted to go to war and apply our knowledge and skills to a real-war situation. At the prom, however, we heard some rumors that North Vietnam had declined the Soviet offer to send in Soviet military volunteers and assist the Vietnamese war efforts against the Americans.[9]

After my graduation, I returned to my unit and worked at the battalion headquarters as a staff member in the fall of 1964. A year later, our battalion commander told us that the battalion would select several officers as missile instructors to train the NVA missile troops in North Vietnam. As a well-trained new staff member, I was selected in the summer of 1965 for the missile technology teaching assignment in Vietnam. I was told that the teaching mission would last about one year, and that I would return to my unit after the overseas assignment. I became a missile training instructor with the rank of captain. At that moment, I had learned that the Soviet surface-to-air missiles [popularly known as "SAMs"] had been shipped to North Vietnam to fight against the U.S. Rolling Thunder air campaign. The Soviet SAM sites became operational in North Vietnam in April 1965. The Soviet missile troops began their engagements on July 25, shooting down three U.S. warplanes that day. Now we needed to train the Vietnamese missile troops which could join the Soviet SAM operation and shoot down

more American airplanes. In the summer of 1965, the Vietnamese established their first antiaircraft missile regiment in the North.

In early 1966, I joined the special Vietnam unit of the Soviet missile
troops, so called military detachment #31920, under the command of Maj.
Gen. Alexander Stuchilov. The unit headquarters was in Moscow, and it
provided a two-week preparation for the missile officers and soldiers before
they were leaving for Vietnam. We learned more about the Vietnam War
and America's Rolling Thunder air bombing campaign. But we were not
allowed to tell anyone about our assignment in Vietnam, not even our parents and family members. We were not allowed to wear our uniform with
ranks and names over there. We were not allowed to carry our handguns
or any weapons like a military knife with us.

Then, in May 1966, I got on a train and began my long journey to
North Vietnam. Our train included two passenger cars and twenty-seven
cargo cars fully loaded with Russian antiaircraft missiles, missile launchers, and communication and commanding equipment. Part of our job was
to keep our eyes on these missiles and make sure that they would get all
the way to Vietnam safely. I traveled with sixty other officers from Detachment #31920. I was so glad to find out that several of the officers on the
train were my academy classmates from the Class of 1964. Even though it
was a long trip, we had so much fun, just like having a college class reunion
party for two weeks. First, it took one week for our train traveling to the
Russian-Chinese border. Then we had to change the locomotive and all the
cargo and passenger cars at the border since China uses its own rail-track
system different from the size of Russian tracks. As we waited for the Chinese to unload and reload the missiles, we visited local shops and bought
more hard liquor and junk food, since the meals on the train were terrible
in Russia. We didn't know that the Chinese would provide very good meals
and drink for us all the way across their country. After another week traveling in China, finally, we arrived at the Chinese-Vietnamese border.

At the Chinese-Vietnamese border, we did routine inspections of the
missiles and equipment for the last time and signed paperwork both with
Chinese and Vietnamese officers. The Vietnamese unloaded the missiles,
and sent them to different locations in North Vietnam. The sixty Russian
officers were also divided into several groups and traveled to different
places for different jobs. I knew that some of my classmates would go to the
combat zones for their operational assignments. I got a little bit nervous as
I knew that we were in the war.

Russian SAM-2 missile in North Vietnam.

I was assigned with a couple of other officers to a training center in a mountain north of Hanoi. Established in the spring of 1965, the center had sophisticated Russian-made training facilities, including indoor (actually in-cave) missile launcher model, operation demo equipment, underground classrooms, and comfortable living quarters. Our training program focused on the operation and routine maintenance of the CA-75M [or C-75] high-altitude guided SAM-2 model and later the improved SAM-3 system. More than forty Russian instructors and officers had been teaching and working at this center for more than a year. They had about three hundred Vietnamese students, including commanding officers, headquarters staff, missile operators, radar operators, technicians, and logistics officers. These NVA officers studied missile technology and operation in different programs between one and six months. Most of them did not speak Russian. The Russian instructors totally depended on the Vietnamese translators. Some of the Russian instructors were happy to see us coming. They thought that we would replace them and some of them could go home. Unfortunately, the center just added several new positions in order to offer more missile technology courses to the Vietnamese officer students. Most of the Russian instructors served in the center for two or three years. I did too.

I did not know exactly how many Soviet missile officers worked in Vietnam. My guess was at least four thousand Russian missile personnel in North Vietnam when I served there. I knew that over one thousand Soviet missile technology instructors were training the Vietnamese missile force in the late 1960s. I also heard that several Russian missile battalions from two strategic divisions took part in the air-defense combat operations, about two thousand troops. And more than one thousand Russians as technical, administrative, and logistic units to support our missile operations and training in North Vietnam in the late 1960s. Gen. Alexander Stuchilov was also the chief commander of the Soviet antiaircraft defense forces in Vietnam in 1967–1969.

During my teaching at the missile training center, the senior Russian instructors told me a lot about how to train the Vietnamese officers. The Russian instructors followed General Stuchilov's principle in training. General Stuchilov always said "do as I am doing." His principle guided our training and worked pretty well. We emphasized basic knowledge, practical skills, and hands-on learning. The Vietnamese officers could pick up the Russian missile operating pretty fast by following our moves and memorizing the procedure with a little education or without any missile technology background. Following our operation manuals, we demonstrated missile operation step by step, and showed the Vietnamese officers how.

After basic training, we offered different classes based upon North Vietnam's needs in their air defense against the "Rolling Thunder." The first class taught the Vietnamese officers how to use Russian missiles to shoot down American aircraft at the medium height of 2–3 kilometers [1.2–1.9 miles]. The second class was to show them how to target the enemy bomber at a high altitude, about 5–7 kilometers [3.1–4.3 miles], like B-52s. The B-52 heavy bombers had been a major problem for the Vietnamese air defense at that time. And then, in the third class, we taught them several new methods to shoot down American warplanes at very low altitude, about 300–500 meters. All of the Vietnamese officer-students were impressed by our missile technology. They worked hard and learned fast. Our evaluations and assessments showed that they had mastered the Russian missile technology and were capable of operating the Russian radar/missile system as the major part of the air defense in North Vietnam.

We also worked with the Vietnamese instructors at the center. Some of them had received their technology and language training in the Soviet Union.[10] Familiar with the Soviet military system and speaking some Russian, they served as interpreters or teaching assistants for our training classes. They also translated a large number of our training textbooks, operation instructions, and maintenance manuals from Russian to Vietnamese. I made many friends with those Vietnamese officers. I even learned some Vietnamese for my shopping in the street markets or ordering food in the local restaurants.

As a training instructor, I did not see air defense combat since our training center was way up in the North. However, we read NVA briefings and their combat reports every day to adjust our training methods. We heard stories all the time about our Russian officers and soldiers who engaged in the air-defense combat against the American warplanes on the front lines. We knew we were in the middle of the war. We were happy to see our Vietnamese comrades become skillful in missile air-defense and shoot down more and more American airplanes. For example, the U.S. Air Force employed their new F-111 fighter-bombers in their Rolling Thunder air campaign in early 1968. On March 17, six F-111s arrived at a U.S. Air Force base in Thailand. A week later, the F-111s began their bombing missions. The Vietnamese learned how to deal with the U.S. high-tech aircraft immediately. On March 28 and 30, the NVA missile troops shot down two F-111s in Ha Tinh Province.[11]

Later I learned that, by the end of the war, the Vietnamese had established a strong air-defense missile force, including twelve missile regiments and four radar regiments. Each regiment had four missile battalions and one technical battalion, totaling one thousand troops. In addition, the NVA had a total of six air-defense divisions. Each division had four AAA regiments, one SAM missile regiment, and one radar regiment. There were four air-defense schools, including a missile technology academy and an air-defense officer academy. By 1986, Vietnam had sixteen SAM-6 missile regiments and six radar regiments. In addition, it had seven air-defense divisions, totaling fifty thousand troops.

In 1968, I completed my teaching assignment in North Vietnam and returned to the Soviet Union. We had a very bad homecoming. Since the Soviet government denied any involvement in Vietnam, our war in Vietnam was an "unknown" war. Nobody knew anything about our service. After we came back, we were not allowed to talk about our experience and contribution to the Vietnam War. The former USSR didn't acknowledge our participation in the Vietnam War. There was no medal, awards, or recognition. Later, I got promoted to a major before my retirement from the military.

Our service in the Vietnam War has never been recognized by either the Soviet government or the military. Thus, our sacrifices are not appreciated by the society and Russian people. Many low-ranking officers like me did not receive any pension and privilege for our service in Vietnam, while the veterans from all other foreign wars enjoyed their good pensions and many privileges for their services. I know a sad story about one of the Vietnam veterans. His name is Mr. Boris Verkhoturov. He spent more than two years in Vietnam as a radar operator. One day, his radar was bombed and he was burned seriously. After hospitalization for a long period of time, he retired from the missile force and became a part-time schoolteacher. After his retirement, Mr. Verkhoturov did not get any financial compensation or healthcare from the government for his wounds and burns. The salary from his part-time teaching was not enough for him to pay his medical bills. That is why so many Russian veterans do not want to talk about the Vietnam War. The war we are not supposed to remember.

Chapter 8

The Dragon's Tale
Chinese Troops in the Jungle

It became a reunion party when the eleven veterans and their families arrived at Capt. Zhao Shunfen's home in Harbin, the provincial capital of Heilongjiang, Northeast China. Captain Zhao wanted me to meet his comrades who survived the Vietnam War, and whose friendship seems to last forever.[1] After the potluck dinner, they began to sing together Chinese army songs from the 1960s. They recalled, so many of them, the lyrics word by word. They had songs before their meals and meetings, before each combat, during the drills, seeing comrades off to the hospital or cemetery, and songs to show their loyalty and love to their country, party, and Chairman Mao Zedong. Captain Zhao told me that they were so sad when China had a border war against Vietnam in 1979. They were happy to see that the two countries normalized their relationship in the 1990s and developed new friendship in the early 2000s. Some of the veterans were planning a trip to revisit Vietnam. They wanted to show their families where they had fought China's Vietnam War.

As a Communist state bordering with North Vietnam, the People's Republic of China (PRC) actively supported Ho Chi Minh's war against France in the French Indochina War of 1946–1954. Thereafter, China continued to provide weaponry, equipment, and military training to North Vietnam.[2] China's massive amount of supplies and strong support helped Ho to intensify the guerrilla campaign in South Vietnam in the early 1960s. In July 1965, China began to send its troops to North Vietnam. These Chinese forces enabled Hanoi to send more NVA troops to the South to fight the Americans. The majority of the Chinese troops in Vietnam belonged to the antiaircraft artillery (AAA) force. From June 1965 to March 1969, the PLA sent sixteen

AAA divisions into North Vietnam to engage in air defense against America's Operation Rolling Thunder.[3]

  As part of the AAA force, Capt. Zhao Shunfen's unit entered North Vietnam in September 1966. He returned to China in 1967, after he was wounded in combat. His personal account illuminates for the first time the important role that the Chinese military played in the Vietnam War. His story reveals how the Chinese party organization, basic training, education, and command and control operated in the PLA during these years. It also shows the Chinese perception of the war situation, combat environment, firepower, technology, and homecoming. Interestingly, as both a political and a social institution, the PLA continued to play an important role in domestic and foreign affairs by providing political stability, social order, and technology research and development during the Great Cultural Revolution of 1966–1976, when China was in turmoil. Most young men dreamed of joining the military for their education, social mobility, professional career, political security, or just for their own survival during the Cultural Revolution.*

Capt. Zhao Shunfen

Fourth Company, Third Regiment, Thirty-first AAA Division, People's Liberation Army (China)

In 1945, I was born in a small village in Northeast China, the first of seven children in the family. My childhood dream was to be a city high school teacher when I grew up. Wearing eyeglasses, riding a bicycle to work, and eating in a faculty lounge were all a country boy could dream of. I studied hard in middle school and prepared well for my high school entry examination. I, however, couldn't go to high school after I passed the exam in 1961. At that time, the so-called three-year "natural disaster" began.[4] The farmers had a very difficult time, and some of them died of starvation.

  I remember that my mother cooked crushed corncobs with apricot leaves. We ate everything, but we were still starving. In the summer of 1961, I decided to stay at home, helping my dad in the cornfield by day and helping my mom to take care of my six younger brothers and sisters at night. Using my old books and newspapers under a kerosene lamp, I taught my brothers and sisters math and history at home since they didn't even have a chance to go to middle school.

  In the fall of 1964, the country's economy turned around. My village had the first good harvest in five years. We finally had a break. My father thought about sending my brothers and sisters back to school. My mother began to visit a woman matchmaker in the village and tried to arrange my marriage. I was nineteen, and my dream of becoming a school teacher seemed fading away. Back then, I was too old to go to high school, and there was no job market in the cities. As a farmer's son, I was supposed to be a farmer and stay where I was.

My chance came in November 1964. One day, a recruiting team from the People's Liberation Army [PLA] paid its annual visit to our village.[5] All of the eligible male villagers, between eighteen and twenty-five, were summoned to the village chief's house. There were about forty young men at the meeting. I was really interested in the army's offer. "Our army is a big school," the recruiting officer said. "You will learn a trade through your service." More attractive to me was their retirement plan. "You have choices for retirement after your service," the officer promised. "You can either retire back to your village here, or choose to work someplace else, like a job in the city." I wanted to join the army to get out of the village, but I was not sure of my parents' opinion.

Surprisingly, my parents supported my decision when I told them that evening. My mom, frustrated in her inability in finding me a bride due to the economic condition of the family and village, thought army service may give me a better chance to find my own girlfriend. My dad felt sorry for keeping me out of school for so long. Hard manual labor and progressive malnutrition made me short, skinny, and I had developed asthma. The army would feed me better and address my health problems. I didn't expect this. My parents were relieved that their son joined the army. My younger brothers and sisters were envious about my travel by bus and train, having my photo taken, and sending it back home. They never dared to think about such things. Overnight, two other men and I became the heroes of our families and the village. On the day I left home, however, I saw the tears in my mother's eyes. I knew she was happy. I will never forget that cold winter day in December.

After the new-recruit orientation in the spring of 1965, I was assigned to the Fourth Company, First Battalion, Third Regiment, First Antiaircraft Artillery Division, Shenyang Military Region.[6] The division had fought in the Korean War. But our guns and equipment were old. We had the same weapons used in the Korean War. We had 100 mm, 76 mm, and 57 mm antiaircraft artillery pieces, and 37 mm antiaircraft machine guns. The

Russian-made 100 mm big gun could send its shells up to 30,000 feet altitude. I remember the different guns were mixed to arm each battalion. The combination could provide a fire zone from 8,000 to 30,000 feet. The Fourth Company had 120 men, operating eight artillery pieces and several machine guns. As a new recruit, I didn't get a big-gun post. I became a machine gunner to protect the artillery positions, but I had no complaints. I enjoyed drilling in the morning, riding on the truck, talking to the men across the countryside, and eating in the army mess hall.

My favorite part of the daily routine was the one hour of "political study," or "motivational education." I called it "reading and writing class." I had so much fun picking up the books again after having left school four years previously. The company political instructor taught world history and Chinese literature in order to help the soldiers understand the Communist theory and the thoughts of Mao Zedong, chairman of the Chinese Communist Party [CCP]. Like the Soviet military system, the Chinese army has a dual system with a chain of command and a chain of political control. Each company had a political instructor, who was usually the secretary of the party branch in the company. The company political instructor took part of the decision-making responsibility with the company commander. Each battalion also had a political instructor, who was part of the battalion command. Each regiment, division, and army had a political commissar, who was the secretary of the party committee and shared the responsibility with the commanding officers. Each regiment, division, and army also had a political department to implement political tasks and education. The political instructor/commissar system has been a major instrument of party control and political penetration in the PLA.[7]

Under that instruction, I learned more Chinese characters and grammar so I could write essays to express my own understanding of the Chinese revolution, exchange my ideas with others, and build my loyalty to the party. My first essay, six pages long, was an application for Chinese Communist Party membership. I really wanted to join the party at that time. I had no doubt about it. Nobody twisted my arm. I still believe that it was a right decision, and that it was probably one of the most important decisions in my entire life. About six months later, my application was accepted by the CCP branch in our company. I became a CCP member just before our new mission in the Vietnam War.

We learned about Vietnam and the war through our political study in the spring of 1965. "China and Vietnam are neighboring countries," the company political instructor told the men. "We have been good neighbors for the past one thousand years. Today, China is a Communist state, and North Vietnam also has a Communist government. We are Communist brothers in addition to our traditional friendship." He told us that imperialist America was invading Vietnam. It separated the country into North and South Vietnam. America was the common enemy of both China and Vietnam. The Vietnamese people's future was dependent on international Communist aid and support. Then he raised a question: "What should we do when the bad guy breaks into our good neighbor's home?" "We should help," the men answered. "That's right," continued the instructor. "If we don't stop the Americans in Vietnam, they will invade Cambodia next, then Laos, Thailand, and eventually China."[8] The instructor told the men that assisting Vietnam was defending China. The instructor's interpretation of the Communist "Domino Theory" made sense to the men, who remembered America's invasion of Korea and its occupation of Taiwan.

In July 1965, when I became a Communist Party member and corporal, Chinese troops entered North Vietnam.[9] China sent surface-to-air missile, antiaircraft artillery, railroad, engineering, mine-sweeping, and logistics units into North Vietnam to help Hanoi defend the Democratic Republic of Vietnam [DRV]. The Chinese forces in North Vietnam operated antiaircraft guns, built and repaired roads, bridges, railroads, and assembled factories. We enabled Ho Chi Minh to send more NVA troops south to fight Americans.

In October, the First Antiaircraft Division received an order from the PLA high command in Beijing to be prepared for engagement in the Vietnam War on a rotational schedule. We learned later that the high command used Vietnam as a training ground and rotated the Chinese troops there. China could rotate all of its antiaircraft artillery troops within five years, according to Beijing's schedule. Each division was to operate in North Vietnam for six months, but no longer than eight months.[10] In late 1965, our company instruction began to introduce the American air force, including its fighters and bombers. Through our training, we learned some Vietnamese words, like "*Chao ong*" (How are you?) and "*Cam on*" (Thank you), to communicate with local Vietnamese people. I was amazed that the pronunciations of many Vietnamese words are the same in Chinese. We also learned some English words, like "Don't move!" and "Surrender or die," which we might need if ever confronted by American pilots.

In the summer of 1966, the division began a cross-country movement, from Northeast to Southwest China, more than 2,500 miles. The division assembled in early September at Ningming City, Guangxi Province, about thirty miles from the Chinese-Vietnamese border. At Ningming, we had a four-week foreign war orientation. One thing all the Chinese soldiers and officers had to do was to take off our Chinese uniforms: no Chinese badges, no Red Star cap insignia, no PLA rankings, and no Chinese names. We put on Vietnamese light green uniforms and gray caps without ranks. The men laughed at each other. We looked just like the Vietnamese soldiers if we didn't talk. Our division, the First, was renamed the Thirty-first AAA Division in the new order of battle for the PLA forces in North Vietnam. The division headquarters sent some Vietnamese translators to serve at regiment, battalion, and company levels. A searchlight battalion was assigned to the division for night operations, and some medics and technicians were also added to each regiment.

In the morning of September 28, 1966, my regiment left China and entered Vietnam. The traffic was very heavy and slow, about twenty or twenty-five miles per hour. Supply trucks, artillery pieces, construction equipment, and PLA troops were rolling southward, forming a long column on the road. We crossed the border at the Youyiguan [Friendship Pass], which connects the main transportation line between the two countries. No military vehicles stopped at the pass. The traffic became even slower after they crossed the border.

That was my first time in a foreign country. Just like the others, I was so excited. I found that North Vietnam was just like Southwest China. Many palm trees and banana trees were along the road; some rubber plantations were in the middle of the bamboo forest. The Vietnamese houses, rice paddies, and stubble fields looked like those in China. And their trucks, motorcycles, and tractors were all made in China. But their bicycles were French style, looking better than the Chinese brands. The Vietnamese men, women, and children were very friendly to us. They stopped what they were doing and waved to us when our artillery column passed by.

Entering North Vietnam, the Third Regiment kept moving south on Route 1 highway. We passed Lang Son (a city about twelve miles from the border) in the afternoon and exited at the "forty-three mile" point on Route 1, then turned onto a muddy, country road. After a six-hour bumpy ride into the mountains, we finally stopped before midnight in a quiet, deep forest, about seventy miles from the border. In the dark, I was surprised to see a nicely built field camp waiting for us in the middle of the forest. It included bamboo shelters, showers, and pinewood beds. In fact, our regiment replaced another from the Beijing Regional Command, which had built everything needed for operations before rotating back to China.

The Shenyang First Division, renamed the "Thirty-first Column" in North Vietnam, provided air defense over Lang Son Province, including its cities, railroads, and highways. Lang Son, a northern border province in the mountainous area, has only two medium-size cities. Since they are so close to the Vietnamese-Chinese border (about twelve and fourteen miles), the American airplanes didn't raid these cities. Americans didn't want to risk a conflict with the Chinese air force by flying into Chinese air space. Thus, the Thirty-first Column focused its main efforts on Lang Son's transportation network. Two regiments positioned themselves along Route 1, a sixty-mile section from north to south through the province. The Third Regiment was assigned to protect a local road and a bridge between Route 1 and Thai Nguyen, along the Lang Son-Hao Binh provincial border.[11] The rest of the troops and division headquarters were stationed three miles off Route 1, eight miles south of Lang Son City. The division's supply depot and field hospital were located in the same area. Our battalion was assigned to protect that bridge on the local road. We worked all night and didn't sleep the first night. I had to position my machine gun up the hill on the south side of the bridge. It was rainy, foggy, and muddy, with many insects and thick bushes. My twin-barreled machine gun seemed much heavier than it had been. After I'd done my job, I helped others push the big guns up the hill, as a CCP member should do. They barely made it before dawn.

American airplanes paid their visit the next morning. The First Battalion received the call from the regiment headquarters about 0920 hours that six F-105 fighter-bombers were coming in their direction. At 0935 hour, the battalion's first outpost, about thirty miles south, called in and reported that four F-105s, at middle speed and an altitude of 18,000 feet, were flying from southeast to northwest. Five minutes later, the second outpost, about ten miles south of the bridge, called, "Four 105s are coming!" The same messages were passed on from the battalion headquarters to the company commanders.

"Ready," the captain yelled in the loudspeakers on the hill. The approaching jets' engines sounded like a rolling thunder. The captain ordered, "100s, 76s, fire!" The big guns opened their fire before I could see the American fighters. Although we learned a lot about the American fighters and bomb-

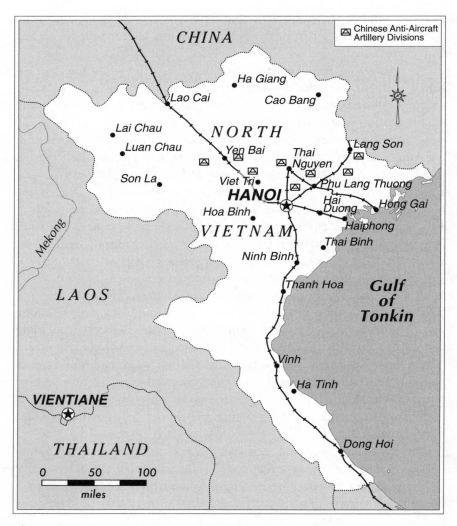

Chinese AAA Divisions in Vietnam, 1965–1968

ers, I didn't realize they were so noisy and fast. The hill shook, the sky was smoking, and the air smelled of burning gunpowder.

I barely heard the captain's order, "37s, fire!" That was for me. I looked hard into the sky. Two of the fighters split and seemed intent on striking our positions. I aimed at one of them and pulled the trigger. My machine gun roared and sent bullets flying toward the fighters. They didn't dive, just flew over the hill. I turned my gun 180 degrees and kept firing until the planes disappeared from my sight. "Cease fire," the captain ordered. I, sweating and out of breath, realized that the whole battle took only minutes. "Oah, oah, oah!" We jumped out of our positions and cheered when we knew the American fighters had gone. Even though the American airplanes just passed through the area, it was important for us to taste a real combat. We now felt confident. We knew how combat was, and we knew that we could make it. At lunch that day, we toasted each other with tea for our first battle.

Our real headache was changing our positions after each engagement to avoid American retaliation. We had to move our guns and ammunition into new positions before the next morning. After our first engagement, the company pulled the guns out of the positions on the south side of the bridge, moved them down the hill, across the bridge, and into the forest north of the bridge.

The next morning, American fighters and bombers came back. There were six of them. We were lucky. They struck our old positions on the south side of the bridge. The fighters fired rockets from a distance, tearing down trees, burning bushes, and starting a wall of fire no one could escape. Then the bombers dropped heavy bombs on the positions, smashing the rocks and wiping out pretty much everything on the hill. The American firepower was so fierce that I became nervous just watching it from my new position. I was not scared. I was young, and not scared of death. But what had overcome me was the overwhelming firepower, which somehow had neutralized my mind at the moment. My gun seemed useless; I felt insignificant. I began to hate the American airplanes, their firepower, and the furious air strikes that had minimized my world and my existence. From the north side of the bridge, the Fourth Company opened fire on the fighters and bombers. Surprised, the American airplanes tried to pull out and escape from the well-organized Chinese fire.

I hated the heat and jungle in North Vietnam as much as I did the air strikes. All of our men were from North China. The weather in Vietnam was too hot for us. In October, Vietnam's dry season began. We often operated in temperatures between 100–110 degrees. We were sweating all day long. The next spring, the endless monsoon rains arrived, ensuring we stayed constantly wet. Some of us became sick. When I accompanied one of our men to the division field hospital, I was surprised to see the hospital full of sick soldiers.

In November, the bridge collapsed during an air raid. The engineering troops (also from China) worked day and night to repair the bridge. For almost two weeks, there were no air raids and no engagements. Somehow we didn't enjoy the relaxation long before the men got bored. Boredom had never been considered a problem until then. In December, the air raids became intensified again. I was wounded on December 19, when a large group of the American warplanes attacked the bridge. Their first dive was so low that I could see the numbers painted on their planes. They came so fast that my gun didn't get them at all. They fired upon our positions with a rain of bullets.

I could hear my comrades' screams and cries behind me. I felt bad since my 37 mm had failed to protect them. Jumping out of the trench, I set up my machine gun at a higher position before the airplanes' second dive. "Come back down here! It's dangerous there!" someone cautioned me. I ignored the warning and stood high without any cover, trying to aim at the coming airplanes. I guess I was mad, or crazy, or something just like that.

The fighters made the second pass one after another. I could hear the bullets from the aircrafts passing by me and felt the hot air from the jet engines' exhaust. Standing up, I kept firing and firing, until the captain ordered a cease-fire. A shock of pain struck me as soon as I released the trigger. I sat down and couldn't get up again. The terrible pain came from my legs. I knew I got shot. Biting my tongue and trying not to scream, I looked down, checking my legs. A couple of bullets went through my left leg, which was covered by blood. I tried to stop bleeding before the medics found me. "Lay down!" the medics said, "Don't move!" I just felt so exhausted and fell into sleep after the medics gave me a shot. I wasn't the only one wounded. I learned in the Chinese field hospital that my company suffered twelve dead and thirty-seven wounded in the battle, including one of my best friends. That was a pretty heavy casualty rate for an AAA company.

After my condition became stable, the field hospital decided to transfer me from Vietnam to China for further treatment. On January 5, 1967, I left Vietnam for China. When the truck passed the Vietnamese-Chinese border, I said *"Chao ba toi ve"* ("good-bye" in Vietnamese) to the country and people I had been fighting for during the past four months. I said *"Zaijian"* ("good-bye" in Chinese) to my friends who came to Vietnam with me, but would never return home.

The Chinese soldiers had sacrificed their lives for a foreign country.

Capt. Zhao Shunfen (PLA, ret.)
in Beijing, China, in 2005.

They were buried in Vietnam, and their real names were not allowed to be put on the tombstone. I just wonder how they can be remembered. Can their parents eventually go to Vietnam and visit their sons' graves? We never know. I didn't know why the tears were in my eyes when I passed the border. On the way, I saw more Chinese troops, supplies, and equipment were being readied to be sent into Vietnam.

I returned to my company in March 1967 when our division rotated back to China. I received an award for my actions in the battle, and became a sergeant in that spring. At that time, China was in the middle of the Great Cultural Revolution [1966–1976], a nationwide turmoil, which paralyzed the civilian governments, started many local conflicts, and caused millions of deaths. Mao Zedong decided to employ the PLA to restore order and prevent possible civil war in the country. Moving to center stage, the military took over civilian governments at provincial, district, city, and town levels, sending officers to schools, factories, companies, and farms. Looking for a large number of officers to run the cities in Northeast China, the Shenyang Regional Command asked each army, division, and regiment to contribute its share and select officers as representatives. Like most of the officers, I didn't want to leave my current duties. But the regimental command developed a list, including my name. As promised, I and most of the officers who were going to work with civilians received an immediate promotion. I was promoted to captain.

As a captain, I became a military representative who took part in the local administration. I chose to work in a high school at Harbin, capital city of Heilongjiang Province, 150 miles from my hometown. My dream finally came true at the point when I didn't want it. And my parents liked my new job and were so happy to see me back. In the summer of 1968, I became one of the three PLA representatives working at the Eighteenth High School in the city of Harbin. In 1971, the military representation was terminated and, like most of the PLA representatives, I decided to stay at this civilian position. I retired from the army in 1972. A year later, I became the principal of the Harbin Eighteenth High School. In 1974, at age twenty-nine, I married a history teacher at the Eighteenth High School. Busy with two small kids, I managed to finish high school in 1978. It took me ten years studying in evening and weekend classes to get my college degree in history. Since I retired from my administrative job in 2002, I have been teaching world history classes at the Eighteenth High School. I enjoy teaching, and the Vietnam War is one of my favorite topics.

Chapter 9

Chinese Response to the U.S. Rolling Thunder Campaign

Maj. Gen. Qin Chaoying was right about Maj. Guo Haiyun when he intro-duced me to him in Beijing.[1] *Straight and jocular, Major Guo was a typical PLA officer with a good memory of his war-fighting in the past and an ada-mant pride about his experience in Vietnam. He served as battalion chief of staff in the First Regiment of the PLA Sixty-fourth AAA Division, which entered Vietnam in April 1967. He, his staff, and their air-defense troops fought tough battles during the U.S. Rolling Thunder campaign against North Vietnam. They also worked hard to fill the "technology gap" between the Chi-nese air defenses and the Russian antiair missile system. According to the major, the Chinese could not match the superior Soviet missile technology for North Vietnam's air defense. In 1967, the PLA high command ordered its AAA troops to intensify their training in order to shoot down more Ameri-can airplanes than the Soviets. Major Guo recalled that the Chinese troops had two rivals in Vietnam: "the American imperialists in the sky and . . . the Soviet revisionists on the ground."*[2]

To strengthen their air defenses in North Vietnam and compete against the Soviet Red Army, the PLA sent more AAA divisions. According to Le Duan, general secretary of the Vietnam Lao Dong (Workers' Party, VWP, in 1976 renamed Vietnam Communist Party), by April 1967, the Chinese forces in North Vietnam totaled 130,000 men.[3] *This rapid involvement with a large number of forces remained undetected by American intelligence.*[4] *The PLA high command hoped that their numerical superiority might enable the Chinese troops to overcome their inferiority in equipment and technology. It seemed rational to the Chinese leaders, who believed that a weak army could defeat a strong army by employing tactics such as surprise attacks and an active defense. Maj. Guo Haiyun and his staff had to devise an effective air defense against the U.S. Rolling Thunder.[5] Later on, Chinese leaders realized that their experience with guerrilla war tactics and the "people's war" doctrine did not help the Vietnamese much in their war against American forces. Mao Zedong had to concede situational differences to the DRV leaders in Beijing in 1968, stating, "You are meeting new situations at present, so a lot of your ways of dealing with them are and ought to be different from ours in the past. We learned how to fight step by step and frequently suffered defeat in the beginning; it was not as smooth as for you."[6]*

Based upon their Korean War experience, the Chinese high command started to rotate their AAA divisions in December 1965. In their rotation, each division operated for six to eight months in Vietnam. Most Vietnamese officers did not like the Chinese rotation system.[7] The Vietnamese believed that it took a couple of months for a Chinese AAA unit to adapt to the weather, terrain, and combat conditions. When the unit became combat effective and able to shoot down American airplanes in the fourth or fifth month, it had to prepare for its departure. Then the new unit would repeat the same cycle again.[8]

Maj. Guo Haiyun

Chief of Staff, Second Battalion, First Regiment, Sixty-fourth AAA Division, People's Liberation Army (China)

I joined the PLA at the age of sixteen in 1948, the last year of the Chinese Civil War [1946–1949], when the PLA needed more new recruits to win the final battles against the Nationalist Army. After the civil war, I was sent to a PLA artillery school in Shenyang to study artillery technology in 1949. After the Korean War broke out in the summer of 1950 and China sent its troops to Korea in the fall, our school was changed to the Shenyang Antiaircraft Artillery Academy in 1950 in order to establish an air defense both in North Korea and in China against the American air power. I studied aviation technology, radar systems, antiaircraft defense, and Russian in 1950–1955.

All of the PLA's antiaircraft weapons and equipment were made in the Soviet Union back then. China had imported Russian-made 85 mm and 37 mm antiaircraft artillery guns since November 1949. More models of 100 mm, 76 mm, 57 mm, and 37 mm guns were purchased during the Korean War.[9] After 1955, the PLA imitated the Russian 37 mm gun and made it double-barreled in 1965. In the same year, the Chinese produced copies of Russian 57 mm and 100 mm antiaircraft guns. They were all equipped with Russian-made antiaircraft fire-control radar.

After my graduation in 1955, I was assigned to the Twenty-fourth Army, which stationed in Shenyang Region. In its antiaircraft battalion, I served as a platoon leader, company commander, battalion staff, and battalion deputy commander from 1956 to 1965. In the summer of 1965, when the PLA began to send its AAA troops to Vietnam, the high command collected all of its antiaircraft units from the army, navy, and air forces and reorganized them into eleven AAA divisions, which were under the command of the air force. Having left the Twenty-fourth Army, our battalion was regrouped into the Second Battalion, First Regiment, Sixty-fourth AAA Division. I was promoted to the chief staff of the battalion in 1965. To meet the rapidly increasing demand from Vietnam, the air force established nine more AAA divisions between 1966 and 1969.[10] Most of the divisions, however, were armed with the 1950s Russian-style 100 mm, 85 mm, 76 mm, 57 mm, and 37 mm antiaircraft guns.

To make these newly established divisions combat ready, the General Staff headquarters of the PLA provided three-month training for the staff officers at battalion, regiment, and division levels. We spent two months in Southwest China, learning new communication technology, radar systems, cooperative operations, and Vietnamese. Then, in early November 1966, our group crossed the border and entered Vietnam for further real-war situation training. We stayed at the Third Regiment headquarters of the Sixty-fifth AAA Division, learning more about America's Rolling Thunder air campaign, Vietnam's landscape, command and control, plans and operations, and cooperation with the NVA command centers. Our training group returned to China in late December 1966.

In retrospect, the Chinese air defense was inadequate in 1965–1967.[11] Obviously, there was a huge technological gap between the American and Chinese forces, much larger than in the Korean War. Gen. Yao Fuhe, our division commander, who served in the Korean War, pointed out that "when the Americans developed the post–World War II jet fighters in 1950, we used Russian-made World War II radar and AAA pieces. We had a five-year technology gap in Korea. Now, when the Americans had the most advantaged aircraft in the world by the mid-1960s, we still used the same air-defense weapons. There was a twenty-year technology gap in Vietnam." I had heard the Chinese officers of the Sixty-fifth Division complain about their out-of-date artillery pieces and inferior radar systems. The Chinese-made 57 mm and 100 mm antiaircraft guns, the major AAA pieces for the Chinese divisions in 1965–1967, did not have high performance in the air defense of North Vietnam.

In April 1967, our Sixty-fourth AAA Division began to enter Vietnam. As the rotation policy planned, we replaced the Sixty-fifth Division and took over the air defense of the railways from Lao Cai to Yen Bai, about 140 kilometers from north to south. This was one of the two main railroads for China, Russia, and other Communist countries to ship in their economic and military aid to Vietnam. Our division headquarters considered Yen Bai to be the major defense point, deploying three regiments with 138 artillery pieces and 99 antiaircraft machine guns. Our battalion was part of the air defense of a railway bridge outside the Yen Bai city.

On July 4, we had our first engagement. On that afternoon, four American F-105 bombers came to attack the bridge, escorted by four F-4C fighters. Waiting until they reached about 4,500 meters from our position, we opened fire. Shocked, all of the warplanes pulled up and fled away. All of our commanding offices and soldiers were happy about our first engagement without any casualties.

Our next engagement was a large-scale AAA battle against American Shrike missiles on July 20. In 1966–1967, the U.S. F-105F and F-105G airplanes began to employ AGM-45 Shrike antiradiation missiles against the Chinese and Russian antiaircraft radars. A Shrike, usually launched from twelve to sixteen miles away, followed the radio waves from a search radar or gun-directing radar, and then destroyed the target within fifty seconds. Shrike missiles inflicted more casualties to the Chinese divisions, and some of the units were almost blind due to the loss of their radars. After entering Vietnam, for example, the Sixty-fifth Division lost seven search radars and nine gun-laying radars within three weeks in early 1967.[12] Even though the PLA high command planned on many new research and development projects to improve radar technology, the political turmoil of the Great Proletarian Cultural Revolution had made implementation of these R&D projects very difficult, if not impossible, in 1967–1970. The new models of search radar and AAA guns did not emerge until 1971.[13]

Figuring we'd have to adapt to Shrike missiles and increasing U.S. bombing, our battalion and regiment headquarters relied on our own resources,

Chinese AAA troops in Yen Bai in 1966.

or the people's war approach and the low-tech tactics. Most of our commanding officers at battalion and above levels were the Korean War veterans, who had experience in fighting against American warplanes.

In the morning of July 20, nearly one hundred American warplanes approached the Yen Bai area. When the enemy airplanes reached thirty to forty miles from our positions, our search radars detected the targets and sent in the data to the gun-laying radars. Then the search radars used on-and-off switch and low volt wave to deal with the Shrike. The search radar was turned off before the F-105s reached their Shrike missile fire range [fifteen miles]. In the meantime, our gun-laying radar spotted the targets and passed the information to my battalion command center. My staff members calculated the data and sent out the artillery fix. Then the gun-laying radar shut down their long wave, while the operators shook radar antenna left and right, up and down, to make it hard for Shrike missiles to follow their radar wave. Waiting until the airplanes entered the air-defense fire area, the operators turned the long wave back on to direct the fire on the airplanes. Even though the American airplanes fired thirty-one Shrike missiles at all of our radars, including our battalion radars, there was no major damage by the Shrikes.

Then we issued fire orders to all 100 mm, 85 mm, and 37 mm guns. From the north side of the bridge, the Fourth Company opened fire on the fighters and bombers. The American airplanes tried to pull out and escape from the well-organized Chinese fire.

"We got it! We got it!" yelled the Fourth commander so loudly that I could hear him from the radio over the heavy bombing and intense artillery shelling. I looked up. One of the bombers was flying away with black smoke trailing, the plane swinging like a drunkard. "Second Squad," I called in no time. "Look for a crashed plane and American pilots."

A dozen soldiers picked up their rifles and rushed into the jungle. We were instructed by the division and regiment commands to check on crashed planes and to capture any surviving pilots in order to evaluate the air defense and improve our performance. The Second Squad had to rush to the crash site first and guard the "operating area," so the Vietnamese or the Soviets could not enter, according to the agreements. If the Soviets got there first, the Chinese could not interfere in their "operations." We had to compete against the Soviets, as we always said that we fought against the American imperialists in the sky and against the Soviet revisionists on the ground.

In fact, we needed to know American aviation technology. After the Sino-Soviet split in 1960, we lost the only source for the air force modernization. Our participation in the Vietnam War opened up a new window of opportunity to learn from the U.S. Air Force, the most advanced in the world. Our high command instructed our troops to search for pilot logbooks, codes, records, and training manuals; also instrument panels, communication devices, radar equipment, and electronic systems, weapon controls, missiles, launchers, and cameras.

During my field training in 1966, I saw several groups of Chinese defense engineers, technology experts, and weapon designers from Beijing traveling to the crash sites for their research and to the POW camps to interrogate American pilots.

Nevertheless, the Chinese-Vietnamese as well as Russian-Vietnamese agreements requested that all captured pilots be turned over to the NVA within two hours, and all the weapons and equipment be turned over to the NVA within twenty-four hours. The Vietnamese command, however, knew that the Chinese and Russians were researching and pirating the American high-tech equipment and hardware, and shipping them back to their countries. The Vietnamese were neither allowed to stop the Chinese nor Soviet military vehicles, nor to search Chinese or Russian military personnel.[14] Two days later, our search squad returned without finding the crash site. We did not change our combat report that the Fourth Company had shot down one American airplane on July 20.[15]

The NVA command was not satisfied with our low-tech war-fighting, or guerrilla, tactics. They requested our commands to submit to the NVA command within twenty-four hours after each engagement.[16] After each battle, we had routine paperwork, counting ammunition, assessing [or rather, guessing] the results, and reporting to the officers. The NVA needed the number, if any, of American planes shot down, American pilots captured, Chinese casualties, bridge and road damage, civilian casualties, ammunition used, technical problems, communication failures, or any other problems.

In the early winter, our division command did not satisfy its combat objectives since we didn't shoot down as many American airplanes as other divisions. The command launched an "active defense," moving out of our defense perimeter and looking for an engagement, instead of waiting for one.

Our regiment command planned to ambush the American airplanes at their rendezvous points after their raids and on their way back to base. With the planes off guard, with no bombs, low on fuel, and at slow speed, the Chinese guns might have a better chance. One company from my battalion participated in the first ambush battle with other two companies. The ambush point was very crucial. The first location was chosen about thirty miles south of the defense area, near Bac Ninh, sixty miles north of Hanoi, North Vietnam's capital city.

I led my company to our position, which was in the middle of the impenetrable jungle. We had to cut through the trees and bushes in order to move the big guns into the positions. Movement through fifteen-foot-high elephant grass and knee-deep mud not only slowed our position construction, but produced considerable fatigue as well. To better conceal our movement and deployment, no cooking, hot water, or hot food was allowed. We ate powdered rice crackers and canned meat for weeks. And, most frustrating, the American airplanes didn't meet there.

We had a small force with small guns and without medium-range search radar. We had to change our positions three miles eastward during the second week. Early in the third week, on December 16, eight American airplanes came, flying south, at slow speed, low altitude, and in a noncombat formation. Our commander waited until all the planes flew into our ambush zone, and ordered to fire. My company aimed at the targets and fired several rounds. One plane was hit by the intense explosions of our first-round shells. Before the American pilots figured out they were ambushed, another was hit and on fire. The rest of the airplanes pulled up to a high altitude, but did not leave. They made a big U-turn, regrouped, and attacked our positions. They made two passes, firing upon our positions. And, then, all of a sudden, they'd gone. Our company was lucky having only five wounded, but the other two companies suffered heavy casualties. It was reported that we shot down one warplane and damaged two. Our ambush was a big success, and I believed that Mao's guerrilla tactics still worked in today's high-tech warfare.

In January 1968, our division, the Sixty-fourth Division, rotated back to China after nine months in Vietnam. It was reported that the division shot down 109 American airplanes and damaged 85, while 40 soldiers and officers were killed and 246 wounded.[17] After our return, our regiment moved to Tangshan, Hebei Province, in 1969. In 1970–1975, our antiaircraft weaponry and equipment were improved drastically due to our problems in the Vietnam War. For instance, the PLA designed and manufactured its own 85 mm all-weather, automatic antiaircraft artillery gun in 1972. It produced its own command and communication equipment in the same year. Its AAA forces had a total of 10,000 antiaircraft artillery guns by 1972. The PLA also began to produce an improved model of 37 mm double-barreled guns in 1974. By the mid-1970s, we had new radar systems, such as Models 572 and 589 low altitude search radar, Model 586 fire-guiding radar, and Model 405 offshore search radar. I took part in these technology improvements. I was promoted to major, serving as a battalion commander, regimental chief of staff, and regimental commander.

However, since the late 1960s, the missile technology began to play a more important role in China's air defense. By 1972, the PLA Air Force had four surface-to-air missile divisions, including fifty-five SAM missile battalions. While producing more missiles and upgrading missile technology, from 1976 to 1980, the air force started to downsize its conventional AAA forces by disbanding six antiaircraft artillery divisions. I retired from the active PLA duty in 1981. While enjoying my retirement, among my favorite things is to tell my combat experience in the Vietnam War.

Chapter 10

Russian Spies in Hanoi

I got the name and contact information of "Mr. B." from a former KGB agent at an international conference on Intelligence in the Vietnam War.[1] Then we communicated via telephone and e-mail before our meetings and interviews a year later. Serious and phlegmatic, Mr. B. always chose his words carefully and tried to provide short answers to my questions.[2] Having worked with Chinese sources and recruited the Chinese Vietnamese informants in Hanoi, he spoke fluent Chinese and knew the Chinese intelligence community very well. Mr. B. told me in the interviews that the former Soviet Union had helped the Chinese to establish an intelligence system during Stalin's regime in the early 1950s. Thus, the Chinese intelligence service was a mirror image of the KGB. That is why not only their methods, tactics, and organizations, but also their mind-sets were similar. Even the titles, numbers, and positions in both secret services and security ministries were identical. It made their rivalry a "war of twins," as the former KGB agent called it, after the Russo-Chinese split in the 1960s. From 1965 to 1970, North Vietnam was an arena for Russia's spying on China.

The Soviet Union increased its intelligence activities drastically in Vietnam after Moscow shifted from its policy of "staying away" in 1960–1964 to a new policy of "lending a hand" to North Vietnam in 1965. Mr. B.'s story of his life as a KGB agent in Hanoi gives some details of the Russian intelligence training, organization, missions, and recruitment in North Vietnam in 1966–1968.[3] It is interesting to see how the Communist intelligence services spied on each other. In the following story, he also indicates the internal problems of the KGB, such as the lack of institutional security and job protection, distrust and peer conflicts, lack of retirement and social welfare, bureaucratic ignorance and carelessness of appointment, and politics in intelligence. All of these undermined the KGB from within and reduced the effectiveness and integrity of the Russian intelligence system. Mr. B. wishes to remain anonymous in the publication of his personal story. He has joined the "Glasnost Foundation," an international anti-KGB organization headed by Sergei Grigoryantz, a human rights activist.

Mr. B.

Russian Agent, KGB (Soviet Security and Intelligence Service), Russian Embassy in Hanoi, North Vietnam

During my college years, I was recruited by the National Security Committee, popularly known as the KGB (*Komitet Gosudarstvennoi Bezopasnosti*). After my college graduation in 1964, the KGB sent me to the counterintelligence school in Minsk [the current capital city of the Republic of Belarus]. I received formal intelligence training for two years. During my school years at Minsk, I met some Vietnamese intelligence officers who were trained by the KGB intelligence and counterintelligence. I also met some of the experienced KGB officers in their forties. They came to the school for a short training of new tactics and technology. Some of them made new Vietnamese friends in the school. Then, in 1965, the Vietnam War there became the KGB's first priority.

After my school years at Minsk, I was assigned to the KGB's Sixth Department at the KGB headquarters.[4] The Sixth Department conducted the interception and inspection of correspondence. My job was to examine the interceptions and reports on the correspondence both in Vietnam and China. I enjoyed working in the office while I continued my studies of Vietnamese language, history, and politics in Moscow.

In 1966, I received my first overseas assignment, as I expected, to Vietnam. At that moment, the KGB needed to build quickly its own intelligence sources in Vietnam because of the rapid increase of the Soviet involvement in the Vietnam War after February 1965.[5] Before 1965, the KGB station in Hanoi consisted of only five undercover agents, since the Soviet embassy had not yet established a military mission. Yepher Ivanovo was one of the early KGB agents working in the embassy, with a covering position as a third secretary. Fluent in Vietnamese, he reported the war situation to Moscow and provided the assessment of U.S. air bombing of North Vietnam. The KGB also collected information on the U.S. military technology, equipment and weaponry quality, troop morale, and war preparation.

Later, the high command of the Soviet armed forces established the military mission in the Soviet embassy at Hanoi. The head officer of the KGB served as a military missionary at the embassy in Hanoi. His deputy served as vice consul general. Another officer was a consul (middle level diplomat), Agent Georgiy Pechernikov. At that time he was the only agent who could speak some Vietnamese. His lingual capacity kept him very busy. He had to attend all the diplomatic events, read all the information and reports in Vietnamese, and meet all of our Vietnamese agents at least once a week. That exhausted him and caused him some health problems. Soon after his return to the Soviet Union, he retired from the KGB because of his poor health. He died in 1996. Two other undercover agents served as a cipher clerk and a driver at the embassy.

In 1966, the KGB doubled the number of its agents from five to ten at the embassy; and by 1970 the number increased to fifteen. When I arrived, I found out that many of the agents could speak some Vietnamese or at least could read Vietnamese. They worked intensively and effectively. For example, their accurate reports and timely assessment helped to improve the Russian missile technology in combat. After the Soviet Union provided Hanoi with SAM-75M missiles, the air defense in North Vietnam reduced the effectiveness of the U.S. Rolling Thunder air campaign in 1966–1967. The U.S. air forces, however, soon developed new technologies and tactics to deal with the Russian missiles in 1968. The Vietnamese missile troops could then only shoot down one American airplane with an average of firing ten to fourteen SAM-75M missiles. The KGB agents in Hanoi focused their efforts on collecting the air-defense information and making accurate assessments. Based on the information, the Russian missile experts improved the combat effectiveness of the SAM missiles by developing new SAM-125 missiles, which enabled the Vietnamese to shoot down one American plane by firing an average of three to four SAM missiles in 1971–1972.

Having been well trained, the KGB agents adapted to the working environment, weather, and people quickly. All Russian agents in Vietnam liked its traditional cuisine. We cunningly used it for making our Vietnamese agents relaxed during the meeting or recruitment. Some of the Vietnamese spies had received some of their training in the Soviet Union. Their familiarity with the KGB system made our work much easier. But I knew that they never trusted us. When we were in Hanoi, the North Vietnamese counterintelligence shadowed us. Well, it seemed natural, even though we were all Communist agents and fighting the same war against the Americans.

Even the KGB didn't trust its own people. All of the Russian agents in the embassy kept an eye on each other and reported any suspicion of any possible collaboration with foreign intelligence. The KGB headquarters had internal control to protect itself as an institution at home and abroad. It aimed to discover traitors and potential defectors. The distrust and peer spying, of course, hurt many honest agents and officers. Unfortunately, it had been part of KGB culture or tradition. It was a professional disease inside the KGB. Sometimes it just drove you crazy. In the meantime, however, the KGB didn't try everything to protect its own agents. For example, one Russian agent lost her cover in Hanoi. After calling her back, Moscow headquarters appointed a new female agent as a replacement to the same position and in the same office of her unmasked predecessor. That made it clear for everybody that the newcomer was a KGB spy, too. The cover became transparent. This bureaucratic ignorance and carelessness had victimized many KGB agents.

The Soviet military intelligence in Hanoi was in worse shape. It remained inadequate when I got there in 1966. Although the GRU [*Glavnoye Razvedyvatel'noye Upravleniye,* or the Foreign Military Intelligence Directorate of the Red Army General Staff of the Soviet Union], just like the Defense Intelligence Agency in the U.S. Defense Department, set up a station in the embassy, they didn't have a single Vietnamese speaker. I knew that their job was to obtain American military technology and weapon samples from the Vietnamese. They also provided the training for the NVA special force, which conducted sabotage, assassinations, and other secret missions. I heard that the Russian military intelligence agents also interrogated American POWs, especially the American pilots who were shot down during the Operation Rolling Thunder air bombing campaign against North Vietnam. Since the KGB and GRU had their separate systems, we didn't have much communication or exchange except seeing each other at the embassy's weekly business meetings.

My cover at the embassy was a press consul in the News and Media Section. I worked with journalists, reporters, and the News and Press Bureau in the DRV's State Council. My assignment was to collect political and military information on China and Beijing-Hanoi relations. At that time, the

KGB worked hard against China, an immediate threat to Soviet security and international relations. To fulfill my assignments, I attended many of the press conferences, talked to the news corps in the city, recruited Vietnamese and Chinese reporters as informants, translated useful information from Vietnamese to Russian, and wrote reports. I spent a lot of time writing reports. I was supposed to write ten pages of my spy reports every day. Then, these reports were coded into telegrams and sent to Moscow. Each of us was so busy and stressed that we really didn't know what other agents were doing. We were not sharing any information with each other. It was prohibited on the ground of security.

At that time, China was in the middle of its "Cultural Revolution." Although Beijing remained closed to the West, it had many channels to inform Hanoi of its "great achievements" in the mass radical movements. From my sources in Hanoi, I received news every day on Chinese leaders' speeches, power struggles in Beijing, collapses of the local governments, military involvements, armed conflicts, and casualties. I selected the important information and translated them from Vietnamese to Russian. It was very time consuming, and I worked until midnight almost every day.

I didn't have much time to recruit the Chinese informants or agents. Anyway, the Chinese or Vietnamese-Chinese civilians were unreliable human sources. If you talked to a Chinese citizen or a Chinese reporter in public, he or she would turn around and walk away after they found out you were a Russian. Some agreed to work and accept our offer and money, but they would give you virtually worthless information. According to my experience, they were so tricky. After they received our money, these Chinese agents always double-crossed by eagerly confessing to the Chinese counterintelligence in North Vietnam.

Another factor that had made the KGB spying on China the most difficult operation was the similarity of the two Communist intelligence systems. It has been a replica of the KGB, which had created the Chinese intelligence in the early 1950s and trained the Chinese officers and agents until the early 1960s.[6] In other words, both intelligence agencies grew from the same root. Up to the early 1960s, the leading posts in China's intelligence were held by Soviet KGB intelligence officers from Lubyanka. After the Soviet-Chinese split, the Soviets returned home. Nevertheless, most of the top Chinese officers and agents from the 1960s to 1980s had received some training in the Soviet Union during their early career in the 1950s.

The life at the embassy was comfortable, even though the Vietnamese government didn't treat us very well. They tried to play a political game of balance or neutrality between the Soviet Union and China. They wanted to show the Chinese that the Vietnamese government was not one of Moscow's puppets. Sometimes their unfriendliness just went too far. For example, the Soviet embassy was always the last one among the diplomatic community in Hanoi to get their invitations to a reception or a party. To improve the relations, our embassy tried so hard to please the North Vietnamese government. The relationship between Hanoi and Moscow got better after Ho Chi Minh's death in 1969.

To avoid any unpleasant incident, the Soviet embassy had so many rules. We couldn't do a lot of things we needed. They didn't give any special consideration to the agents. I met Col. Nikita Karatsupa at the Soviet embassy in North Vietnam. As senior KGB officer, his mission was to train Vietnamese colleagues [agents] in Hanoi.[7] Although he was well-known in the KGB as a hero, Colonel Karatsupa didn't have a good apartment in the embassy because he was aging and retiring, without much future in the Soviet politics. He complained to Maj. Gen. George Preobrazhensky, deputy chief of the KGB in charge of the rear regions and neighboring countries. General Preobrazhensky talked to the Soviet embassy about the colonel's poor health condition. The embassy reluctantly moved Karatsupa into a bigger apartment. He retired from the KGB after his Hanoi assignment.

I left Hanoi in 1968 for another assignment in Japan. I believe that our hard work and valuable information made a significant contribution to Moscow's decision-making toward Vietnam, which had resulted in the defeat of the Americans and the victory of the Vietnam people and government. I heard that the Soviet-North Vietnamese relationship was drastically improved in 1969–1971. Thereafter, Hanoi divorced Beijing and established a complete and strong cooperation with Moscow. I never had a chance to revisit Hanoi, where I served our country during the Vietnam War.

Part Three

Saigon's Allies

Long Days and Endless Nights

An Artillery Story

Funny and optimistic, Sgt. David McCray always made our interviews very enjoyable meetings. No wonder he was popular in his Non-Commissioned Officer Candidate School class that went to Vietnam, or that he organized their first reunion in Washington, D.C., many years after the war. Sergeant McCray was drafted when he was a student at the University of Oklahoma and was sent to Vietnam in 1970.[1] Going to war for most meant tearful good-byes at home, followed by days or even weeks of homesickness and loneli-ness while in training, and shocking experiences in their early engagements in South Vietnam. Indeed, many of them were unprepared for what they would experience in combat against Communist forces in an unfamiliar land. Uneasy and nervous after his induction date, David did not fully understand what was going on in Vietnam.

The environment provided the first obstacle for a newly arrived soldier. Memories abounded about the oppressive heat, with the average monthly temperature of 90 degrees often soaring into triple digits. In the winter months, Vietnam's dry season, troops often operated in temperatures between 100 and 110 degrees. During the summer and fall the endless monsoon rains arrived, ensuring the soldiers stayed constantly wet. Exposure to the jungles proved as harsh and deadly as the Viet Cong. Infested with snakes, mosqui-toes, ants, and leeches, soldiers dealt with discomfort, pain, and even death from the environment. Common afflictions included bacterial and fun-gal infections (referred to as jungle rot), malaria, and hepatitis. Pride and a sense of belonging are key components of effective army units.[2] Sergeant McCray's story shows how a newcomer could survive 'Nam during his first three months and become an effective soldier in Battery E, Forty-first Artillery, the "Whispering Death."

Sgt. David E. McCray

Battery E, Forty-first Artillery, Fourth Division, U.S. Army

I served in the U.S. Army from February 1970 through December 1971. I was drafted and put under orders in December 1969. Since I was in school, I was allowed to finish the current semester, which ended in the middle of January 1970. The county in Oklahoma I lived in, McClain County, for some reason put me under orders that prevented me from going into the lottery the following month. I was the only fifth-year senior that was treated this way. When I was drafted, I was a student at the University of Oklahoma carrying fifteen hours and working at a service station in Norman, Oklahoma. I would work twelve hours a day for thirteen straight days with one day off because it was necessary to pay for my education. I was in some ways relieved to be drafted.

I took basic training in Fort Polk, Louisiana. I was in [Charlie Company, Fourth Platoon, Second Squad] for eight weeks. I took both my Advanced Individual Training [AIT] and Non-Commissioned Officer Candidate School [NCOCS] training at Fort Bliss, Texas. They were both in the first AIT brigade, and in the AIT, I was in C battery for eight weeks. In the NCOCS I was part of the training battalion for twenty-three weeks.

I was trained to be a squad leader, 16F40 MOS (Military Occupational Specialty).[3] My duty was to operate air-defense artillery equipment for dusters and quad fifties.[4] The squad leader, usually a sergeant E-5, and section chief, usually either a sergeant E-5 or staff sergeant E-6, were remotely attached to other firebases or landing zones to pull perimeter defense at night and run convoys during the day to supply the bases with ammunition or other supplies. The squad leader was in charge of one unit and the section chief was in charge of two units. The section usually had two sergeants, E-5, and the section chief, E-6, would serve as liaison to the attached unit's commanding officer. In my case it was usually the 173rd Airborne.

I went straight from NCOCS to Vietnam and traveled to many places in the country. I reported to the Oakland Army Base outside San Francisco, California, on December 31, 1970, just prior to noon. I spent three days there and was transferred to Travis Air Force Base for deployment to

Sgt. David E. McCray (first from right) and Battery E in 1971.

Vietnam. We left Travis and flew to Anchorage, Alaska, and had a short layover for refueling. From there we flew to Tokyo, Japan, with another short layover for refueling. We left Tokyo and flew directly into Bien Hoa Air Base just outside Saigon, South Vietnam.

After spending the night at the Bien Hoa Air Base, I was transferred to Nha Trang for assignment with the First Field Forces. Next I was sent to Tuy Hoa for deployment in the Sixtieth Artillery in Charlie Battery, dusters, Fourth Division.[5] From Tuy Hoa I went to Two Bits Firebase for four or five weeks, next to Landing Zone [LZ] English for five to six weeks and finally to LZ Uplift for about three months at the end of May 1971.[6] Charlie Battery went into "stand down" and I was transferred back to Tuy Hoa for reassignment to E-Forty-first artillery in Pleiku in the Central Highlands.

I spent four to six weeks at Artillery Hill in Pleiku and four to five weeks at Firebase Tin Can on the tri-border area of Laos, Cambodia, and South Vietnam along the Ho Chi Minh Trail. Next I was transferred back to Artillery Hill in Pleiku for four to six weeks, and in late August or early September I was transferred to Cha Rang Valley. This would prove to be my last base in Vietnam. I stayed there from September to December pulling perimeter defense at night and running convoys during the day. During this time we ran many convoys from Quin Nhon ammunition depot to remote firebases along QL-19.[7] However, this was the best duty I had in Vietnam.

The biggest memory about my service was when we were driving into Cam Rahn Bay. We hit several traffic lights with the normal red, yellow, and green lights. It finally hit me that I had not seen any other colored lights since I had been in Vietnam. It was a special signal to me because I knew that I was going home after all. For my entire period in Vietnam I tried to take one day at a time, although I had kept what we called a "short timers" calendar. Several times I had close calls at moments when I did not expect it. Because of this, I had tried to keep myself from getting too excited about coming home. I was afraid of making a big mistake. I was not due to leave Vietnam until January 5 and had expected to spend Christmas and New Year's Day in Vietnam. Now I knew for sure I would be home before Christmas.

I elected to leave the battery headquarters in Tuy Hoa a few days earlier and trusted a clerk in battery headquarters to complete the medals for everyone. When I left, the medals were in process, but it was never completed. To my knowledge, no one in my section, including myself, received his or her ARCOM [the army commendation medal given to almost all soldiers serving in a combat zone]. This bothers me to this day because I spent my entire tour in the field. The clerk I entrusted to complete the paperwork had put himself in for a Bronze Star and ARCOM. To my astonishment, since I have been back I have discovered this was the norm for most of the clerks in Vietnam. They had the company officers sign hundreds of papers on a daily basis and it was easy for them to push through. Even when it was passed to battalion headquarters their buddies would get them signed in the same manner.

Another searing memory was when my mother, my dad's two brothers, my brother, and my sister dropped me off at the Oakland Army Base to report for my Vietnam tour. It was all I could do to keep from breaking down in front of them. They were not taking it very well and I was trying to be positive and in control. If one of my buddies had not come up to us when we exited the car, I am not sure I would have been able to maintain control. A guy named Tom Mahoney made things a lot easier for me when we ended up being stationed in the same section in Vietnam for a short period, which made the transition a lot easier. The first night in Vietnam, at the Bien Hoa Air Base, there was a sapper attack and we were warehoused in a barracks without any weapons during the attack. That would be the first of many scares.

Something funny that happened to me was while we were on bivouac at Fort Bliss [in Texas]. We were staying in bunkers similar what we had in Vietnam. These bunkers were large enough for five of us to sleep in and keep our guard status for the night. During one night, when one of the squad members came in to wake his replacement for his shift on guard duty, a loud rattle was heard in the bunker. All of a sudden five guys were frozen. Not knowing where to go or what to do, they all started shouting for help. Several of us came running to see what was happening. Upon discovering there was a rattlesnake in the bunker with them, we went to get flashlights to find out where the snake was. It turns out the snake had crawled under one of the guys' sleeping bags near his feet and the guard disturbed the snake when he walked in. They managed to get the snake out and those five guys did not want to stay in the bunker for the rest of the bivouac period. However, they had no choice because the weather had turned cold because the three-week period was during late September and early October.

I had many, many scary experiences during my service. One that sticks in my mind happened so quickly that I didn't have enough time to get scared until it was over. It happened on my last night in Charlie Battery before we went into "stand down" the last of May. We had been getting rocketed and mortared from such an angle that our dusters did not have a field of fire. The commanding officer of the 173rd Airborne told us at about five o'clock that evening that they were going to deploy one of our dusters to high ground at LZ Uplift. LZ Uplift straddles QL-1 highway. East of the highway was a hill where the communication center was located. We moved after dark to prevent anyone outside the base to know where we were going to be located, or so we thought. We had a bulldozer push up a parapet for the duster. We laid a landline to the nearest bunker and I made radio contact with Fire Direction Center [FDC], where all authorizations are issued for fire missions, for our firing coordinates. These were normal procedures, to have two-way contact to the FDC if needed.

During my establishment of radio contact, the last thing I remember was seeing a blue flash. A rocket had hit near the base of the parapet the bulldozer had already finished. After the blast I found myself twenty to thirty feet behind the duster with the breath knocked out of me. Luckily the soft dirt, parapet, and duster protected me and I was only disoriented.

I got up and ran smack into the bulldozer, bruising my hip and leg. Once I managed to regain my senses, I ran back to the duster. We were not given permission to return fire that night. We received no firing coordinates for over another hour. It was a very unusual night, and it seemed as though the Viet Cong knew we would be moving before we did. It was not unusual for things like this to happen. The "all clear" had to be given by the local ARVN before we were given coordinates.

Another scary incident was a convoy escort to LZ Moon. We were to arrive at a firebase south of LZ Uplift by 0900 hours and escort an ammunition convoy to LZ Moon, which had been under attack for several nights. We arrived on time at the firebase, but to our amazement the convoy was not ready to go. This was highly unusual, although we were not concerned about the delay. As the day wore on, we began to get concerned because of the time it took to get to LZ Moon. It was not a great distance, but the road was a dirt road and went through the jungle with elephant grass growing very close to sides of the road. It was very slow travel. About 1600 hours the convoy was ready, and I was very nervous by then. I knew that in order to get to LZ Moon before dark we would need some luck. Of course, we were not lucky. Less than a mile off the QL-1, the engineers discovered the road was mined. Procedures for a mined dirt road called for the engineers to sweep the roads. I think the engineers only found a couple mines, but it really slowed us down and made the engineers very cautious. When dark fell we were only halfway to our destination and we could see LZ Moon getting hit. The captain that was in charge had us pull into a circle in the elephant grass and make camp for the night. The four dusters were the only firepower we had, with a few infantry types. That was the longest night of my life and probably the scariest. We were never attacked and extremely lucky. Due to our vulnerability, a couple of experienced squads could have taken it to us in that elephant grass. The next day a helicopter arrived and picked up the captain and we were sent back to our LZ. To this day, I do not know what happened at LZ Moon.

A third scary episode I will discuss included an incident that happened at Firebase Tin Can on the tri-border area of South Vietnam, Cambodia, and Laos. The firebase was only two to three miles from the Ho Chi Minh Trail and was the size of a football field. On this base were two eight-inch guns, two 175 mm guns, two 155 mm guns, two dusters, and two quad fifties. My guess was that there were only about fifty personnel on this base. The quads protected the north and west side of the base, on the east side was a MACV compound with an ARVN base, and the west and south side of the base were covered by the dusters. The west side faced the Ho Chi Minh Trail.

I usually took the first watch on guard duty at night until 0100 hours and left the other four for two separate shifts from 0100 hours until daylight. Ever since my Vietnam days I have become a very light sleeper and any strange noise will wake me. I am sure this night contributed to this trait. Sometime during the early morning hours I awoke feeling as if pins and needles were sticking me. I immediately rose and began counting the guys. I was startled to discover that no one was on guard duty. I woke everyone and we ran to our assigned positions. I was in my boxer shorts, flack jacket, and helmet with my M-16. As I began walking along the razor wire, a figure jumped up from the wire and began running back through the claymore mines. The next morning we discovered that many of our mines had been disconnected without our knowing it. We all learned a very good lesson and I changed our procedures. The guard on duty was not allowed to come into the bunker until properly relieved of his guard duty. In addition, if the individual did not come out on first call, I was to be notified immediately. To this day, I do not know what or why I woke up. I guess God was watching over us.

My favorite memory in the service was after we graduated from NCOCS in October 1970. We then had to serve six weeks of on-the-job-training in the AIT units. Some of us trained the trainees at motor pool, classroom, physical training, marched them to classes, rifle range, etc. I was chosen as the physical training drill instructor, among other duties. I really liked this duty. I was in tremendous shape and could outrun all but a couple of the trainees. I really worked them hard, and when my time was up they all were in really good shape. I was running about five-minute miles in combat boots, fatigues, and tee shirt at that time. We did physical training every morning and every evening. During the day I marched them to their classes. It was a cup of tea to me. I was glad I did not get the motor pool duty because it was too boring for me. In addition, for the first time since I had been in the army, my fellow graduates and I had our evenings free. When we were off duty we were free to go to town, play tennis, or go to the NCO's club. It made the army more like a job for the first time.

The worst thing that happened to me was finding out my AIT buddy Darrell L. Ponder was killed in Vietnam. I do not know the details except that he was killed during a sapper attack on the base. I heard one of his peers panicked and ran over him in a quad fifty truck. I still do not know for sure if this is true.

The biggest lesson I learned from my military service is that life is not guaranteed. Live one day at a time. You can save for the future, but try to enjoy each day. We in America have been blessed. Those who have not served in the military under a time of duress or served in an impoverished country have no idea how blessed we are. I think either the Job Corps, military, or similar service should be required for everyone after either high school or college. We owe this to our country. Maybe then our citizens would understand more about how veterans have made life better in the United States.

There were a couple of people that I met in the military that influenced or impressed me extremely. Their names were 1st Lt. Stephen Muse and 1st Lt. Dominick Crea. They were both West Point cadets that were assigned to our unit for a while in Pleiku. Both were obviously very bright and could do things without listening to the NCO's opinion. However, both were proactive listeners and would take into account our opinions as well as our ideas to approaching different problems. I really had a good relationship with both individuals. Lieutenant Crea served as the company commander at the end of my tour.

My entire tour of duty in Vietnam lasted from January 6, 1971, until arrival at Fort Lewis, Washington, on December 12, 1971, for ETS [Estimated Time of Separation] on December 13, 1971. I remained in the Inactive Reserve until February 10, 1976.[8]

My homecoming is still hard for me to talk about. I need to go back to my departure first. My mother, sister, and brother had driven me to California to visit my dad's mother and his siblings' families. I had a good time and all of my relatives paid attention to me and made me feel special. We left southern California for the Bay Area to report to the Oakland Army Base. My dad's two brothers drove up there and we visited my mother's relatives.

The night before reporting for my Vietnam assignment, at that relative's home, I overheard a reference to me as a baby killer by one of those relatives, who refused to leave their room to talk to me. If this wasn't bad enough, when I was transported by bus from the Oakland Army Base to Travis Air Force Base we were met with protesters at the gate with a barrage of tomatoes. This had quite a negative impression on me.

Upon my estimated time of separation from the army [or ETS, used in conjunction from separation from active military service] from active duty

Sgt. David E. McCray in 2004.

in Seattle, I was spat upon in both the Seattle airport and the Denver airport. I did not have that experience in the Dallas Love Field Airport or the Oklahoma City Airport, but the damage had already been done. I found myself embarrassed and ashamed of my uniform. The first thing I did was to borrow a pair of jeans from my brother and a shirt before I made the trip to Pawnee, Oklahoma, to see my mother. To this day these memories haunt me, especially the cruel comment by the relative. The joy of seeing my immediate family was overshadowed by what had happened before my deployment and return from my service responsibilities. In addition, I had brought back gifts to my family and tried to give a handmade hat to my two-year-old nephew. My brother told me it was unacceptable for a child to wear a hat from a war. Last year, I finally gave that hat to my nephew.

After I got out of the military I returned to college, while working full time. I graduated with a bachelor's degree in biology and a minor in mathematics and physical education in 1974, and an accounting degree in 1978. I was promoted into the accounting department for the company I had been working for and began my career in accounting. In 1998, I started searching the Internet to find the forty members of my NCOCS class that went to Vietnam. I located thirty-six of them and organized a reunion in Washington, D.C., which tied to the Dusters, Quads, and Searchlights Veteran Organization. Eleven members of the class and some of their wives attended. It was quite an emotional reunion.

Chapter 12

And Then They're Gone . . . Just Like That

Maj. Curt Munson has few regrets about having volunteered for the marines and Vietnam. As a young man, he was willing to face challenges and take risks. It is still true these days when he sits in his big office as the investment representative for one of the largest national financial corporations.[1] Major Munson was one of the U.S. Marines sent to Vietnam after 1968 as the war became unpopular at home. In early 1968, the NVA and PLAF forces launched a general offensive campaign against the American and ARVN forces during the Lunar New Year (Tet). After the Tet Offensive, Gen. William C. Westmoreland asked for 206,000 additional troops for South Vietnam. Pres. Lyndon Johnson turned him down and shortly thereafter announced his decision not to run for reelection. Nevertheless, 25,000 American troops were sent to South Vietnam as replacements.[2]

Major Munson joined the marines in the spring of 1969 when he was eighteen. The American soldiers who fought in Vietnam had the youngest average age of any American war. They were younger than those who had served in World War II (1941–1945) and the Korean War (1950–1953). In February 1970, Curt was sent to Vietnam. He came back home a year later. It has been forty years since Munson returned from Vietnam, but even after that long, he's clear and decisive about his most important memories. After his tour in Vietnam, he went on to spend twenty years on active duty in the marines, plus four years on reserve status. He retired in 1993 as a major, after serving in such exotic locations as Somalia, Israel, Syria, and Egypt. Munson served as a UN Truce Supervision Officer, commanded the marine detachment on the aircraft carrier John F. Kennedy, *served in Desert Storm, and taught at the U.S. Army Field Artillery Center and the Marine Corps Command and Staff College.*

Maj. Curt Munson

H&S Company, Third Battalion, First Marine Division, U.S. Marine Corps

In 1969, the Vietnam War was raging and I was a freshman at the University of Arkansas. I knew that I wanted to participate in the most significant event of my generation, and didn't want to spend the rest of my life on the outside looking in. Ironically, that is just where Vietnam veterans wound up.

I chose to join the marines in the spring semester of 1969 once I decided to drop out after the term. Because I was eighteen, healthy, and out of college, I was pretty resigned to serving somehow. The son of a highly decorated World War II veteran and career soldier, and having always lived on army bases, my decision to join the marines broke with tradition. Joining the Marine Corp was essentially a minor act of rebellion, but was influenced by Leon Uris's book *Battle Cry*, which depicted them as men of honor and greatness. I knew I had committed myself to a tour in Vietnam, although at that point, if someone had asked me, I would not have known much about the issues involved. Most of my exposure to the war came from the John Wayne film *The Green Berets*, with its one dimensional and jingoistic view of the war, and Walter Cronkite. Going to school in Arkansas, I wasn't really aware of the antiwar factions. My thinking about going to war was that it was something I wanted to do, as part of my generation, as part of history, and as a part of growing up. As I say that, it seems amazingly naive to me, but there it is.

In late July 1969, I reported for boot camp at the Marine Corps Recruit Depot, San Diego, California. The objective of boot camp was to prepare basically trained marines, so we drilled, learned first-aid, Marine Corps traditions and history, physical fitness, and the care and shooting of our weapons. After I finished with boot camp in October, I went to Infantry Regiment Training [IRT] and then to Basic Infantry Training School [BITS]. I was a little smarter by then, and was ambivalent, both relieved and concerned to be designated an infantryman. I had to keep reminding myself that infantry was what I wanted, but it gave me pause as well. After

twenty days' leave, I went back for a week of .50 caliber machine gun training and then reported to Staging Battalion for final training and preparation for deployment as a replacement. Acclimating us to the idea that we
were going to go kill people was a big part of the training in boot camp.
Even more than John Wayne, it tended to dehumanize the enemy, to por-
tray them as fodder, just somebody we needed to go and kill. You must
get people's minds right about that, and it is one area in which the Marine
Corps did a pretty good job.

By the time I boarded the Boeing 707 that took me to Vietnam on
February 16, 1970, I felt like I was well trained, but more importantly, we
were fit enough for the challenges of being infantry in a tropical climate.
I thought I was ready, but it wasn't until I'd been in Vietnam for several
months that I realized no training would do as much for me as simply serving in an operational company for awhile. That was where the real learning
took place.

Upon arrival, I reported for duty with the Third Battalion, Fifth
Marines, First Marine Division. The unit was then located in what was
known as I Corps, the northernmost allied military sector in South Vietnam, just south of the Demilitarized Zone (DMZ) separating the South
from North Vietnam.

I was assigned to H&S [Headquarters and Support] Company's mortar platoon, but I actually served with Mike and Kilo companies of Third
Battalion. I was initially assigned to the An Hoa fire support base in the
rugged terrain known as "Arizona Territory,"[3] about thirty-five miles west-
southwest of Da Nang.

In March 1970 I joined my battalion at the marine firebase on Hill 65.[4]
After I joined Mike Company we rotated through several smaller firebases.
Finally, in August 1970, my battalion relocated to Fire Support Base Ross,
in the Khe Sanh Mountains.

I served almost my entire one-year tour in Vietnam as a forward
observer [FO] with Mike and Kilo companies and as a section leader in the
Third Battalion's mortar platoon. As an FO, I was responsible for the fire-
support planning and execution for an entire company of infantrymen, to
include mortars, artillery, and close air support. Sometimes I shared those
duties with an artillery observer, and once with a forward air controller, but
much of the time I was by myself. Imagine a nineteen-year-old being given
that job. It just floors me to think about that now.

My scariest experience in Vietnam occurred while Mike Company was

Maj. Curt Munson at the Khe Sanh Mountains in 1970.

conducting operations from Hill 270 South, in the Khe Sanh Mountains, near An Hoa. It began with what was supposed to be a normal medevac mission off our hilltop by a Marine CH-46 helicopter. It should have been the most routine thing in the world. Unfortunately, the landing zone [LZ] on Hill 270 was smaller than my dining room. Because the LZ was so tiny, the chopper had to hover with its front end off the forward slope in order to load casualties over the rear-end ramp. As the ship maneuvered into position its tail rotor struck the ground.

The torque, along with the sudden stop of the tail rotor, brought the whole bird down, shattering the rotor blades and sending pieces flying through the air. In seconds, the helicopter rolled off the hilltop and down the side of the mountain. I had been standing next to the LZ ready to help load Greg Cluff, our artillery observer, down with malaria, onto the helicopter. I could scarcely believe what I was seeing. That chopper was filled with guys from my company. The chopper finally got hung up in our concertina wire, more or less upright, and immediately began to burn. I had been literally as close as I could be. It would have been almost churlish for me not to participate in the rescue. Without thinking, I actually dropped Greg on his ass and ran down the side of the mountain to where the helicopter was and just happened to reach it first. There were quite a few casualties already aboard, and those that could were climbing out of the bird. They were a little banged up, but when you are nineteen years old (as almost everybody was) you can survive all kinds of things.

The copilot had jumped out already. He left his flying partner [the pilot] in the right seat. He looked at me when I ran up and said, "He's dead. Don't worry about him." I was already at the pilot's door, so I reached up and grabbed him. Apparently he'd heard the copilot, because he made enough movement to prove to me that he was alive. I couldn't lift him out of the seat from below, so I ran underneath the helicopter to the copilot's door and climbed on board. The helicopter was in flames at this point. When I got into the cockpit I realized that one of the reasons I couldn't move the pilot was because the instrument panel had broken free and fallen into his lap. I used my leg to lift the panel up and out of the way. After that I lifted this full-grown man up over the armored seat and handed him out to our company gunnery sergeant like the pilot was a little baby. I was scared out of my gourd. I've heard stories all my life about little old ladies carrying their refrigerators out of the house during a fire, but that was my first experience with being that adrenalized.

A couple weeks later I was notified that I'd been recommended for the Navy-Marine Corps Medal. I finally got it when I was back in college. For twenty years I wore a medal that I received for thirty seconds of commitment. I received several other decorations during my career, but that was still my senior award when I retired.

In an infantry company, casualties are the cost of waging war. I became more blasé as my tour progressed, even fatalistic, but I never got used to it. I saw so many guys lose their legs to booby traps that I was convinced my number was coming up. A rifle company is a pretty tight-knit group.

I had friends that were killed or wounded. That is the worst thing that happened to me. Each event was sad, but one of the worst was when Don Tucker got killed. We'd been together since before arriving in Vietnam and by then he was a really good friend of mine. Another pal named Bob Morris got the wound I kept expecting for myself when he lost both of his legs. I still think about them. Donny Tucker was killed in an ambush. Morris tripped a booby trap while on patrol. I was there for Morris's wound, but not Tucker's death.

When I visited the Wall when it came here [the traveling Vietnam Memorial exhibit] I made a rubbing of Donny's name. When I got home that night, I wrote him a letter to kind of bring him up to date on what had happened to me in the years since I'd seen him last, as an act of closure, I suppose. I was in tears when I finished. He was just barely nineteen when he died. Way too young. He is always going to be nineteen. He was in my squad at Staging Battalion, just this shy kid from North Carolina.

Tucker's death is probably the sad thing that stayed with me the longest, longer than others who were wounded, even though sometimes their wounds were terrible; longer than anybody else that was killed. Whenever someone died, the enormity of it was almost bone crushing. You'd see a guy horsing around just before a patrol, laughing and full of life. They would be at a 100 percent of their capabilities. Their parents spent seventeen, eighteen, or nineteen years raising them up straight and tall. Men have to be physically fit to even qualify to join the marines. They were alive and completely potent and capable one minute and dead as a hammer the next. When it happens, you think, "This is like you are being screwed with, the worst nightmare that's possible." It *just* happened! He was standing there a couple of seconds ago. If we can just turn the clock back ten seconds, we can make it not happen. How tough could that be? Sometimes, you'd actually look around like you're going to find some key or clue that will let you turn back the clock. Surely you could undo something that happened that recently. But you can't. You can't bring anything back that's already happened. It was terrible. How awful it is to take somebody who's at the height of his physical prowess, and then he's gone [snapping his fingers] just like that.

Another sad story that has stuck with me occurred when one of our guys shot himself accidentally through his knee (passing his weapon to another marine while climbing up a ravine), and died of shock in a couple of minutes. He died before the helicopter could even get there. We had other guys who suffered the most grievous wounds . . . losing legs or an arm and they'd be alive and wisecracking about sending you a bottle of bourbon from the States when the helicopter got there. This guy took one look at his leg and it killed him. He went into shock—just freaked out. I will never forget that.

Another very vivid memory of my tour was the weaponry available to fight the war. We had the ability to bring an enormous amount of firepower to bear on a target. I remember standing on a hilltop and watching a B-52 strike that was within my range of vision and observing the shock waves blast through the jungle. At the company level, we had no ability to request a B-52 strike. Because of the lead time, it's just as well. As I stood there watching the bombs explode, it occurred to me that if there actually was any enemy in the target area they were just unlucky.

At my level, though, as an FO I could call in close air strikes, artillery missions, and my own mortars. I had a wide variety of weapons at my disposal. For a nineteen-year-old that was a pretty heady experience.

One of my favorite memories from Vietnam was mail. The support I got from my family and Janis (then my girlfriend, now my wife) and from Janis's family was vital to me. For others in my unit, however, the mail sometimes brought bad news.

I lost track of the number of "Dear John" letters guys in my company received. Whether the letters came from wives or girlfriends, too few of the relationships survived a year of being apart. After the initial shock and sadness, guys frequently became pretty sanguine about their own breakups, and the letters themselves tended to make their way around the company. If you weren't emotional about them, some were actually pretty funny. Others gave you pause to think how vicious a girl who'd actually said she loved a guy could be after she'd found somebody new.

When you are young, a year stretches out like an eternity. Before I'd been in country nine months even, it seemed like my whole life had occurred right there [in Vietnam]. I can't even imagine what the guys in World War II went through, leaving the States in 1942 and coming back in 1945 or 1946. Vietnam was a total immersion for me. The work was all-consuming and at times everything else was just a distraction. I recall thinking it would be a miracle if my family and friends remembered me at all. Sometimes I could hardly envision them. I remember thinking, "What if I don't recognize anybody when I get home? What if they don't recognize me?" These were irrational fears and I knew it, but it was one way to recognize how much I had changed during my time away.

I learned a good many human or cultural values, the best and the worst, from my time in Vietnam. First, that selflessness was pretty darned common. In an infantry company I think it crossed a lot of barriers—a lot of cultural and racial lines. When we were "outside the wire" [outside the perimeter fence], whatever our ethnicity or life experiences, our mutual interests meshed perfectly. We all wanted to come back. I remember at times being with guys of totally different backgrounds and thinking how much we had in common. And then once we were back inside the wire, we didn't have a thing in common. An idea frequently enforced by the various peer groups.

Vietnam was the most racially charged experience of my lifetime. It wasn't when we were in the bush. It was when we were on base camps. I worked with guys in the bush, blacks and so forth, that I thought, man, we're really friends. And then they wouldn't speak to me when we were behind the wire because they couldn't handle the social pressure of the ostracism from their running buddies. That made me sad.

When I left Vietnam I was convinced that the South Vietnamese army was ineffective and of poor quality. In retrospect, I have come to realize that my experience was limited to poorly trained militia units that operated on or near our firebases. We couldn't depend on them for even the most basic things, like staying awake on watch or maintaining the integrity of their equipment. I blamed that on their training. In combat, confusion and fear are really easy to mistake for one another (and one usually leads to the other). If they weren't good soldiers, maybe it's because the ones I worked with didn't know what they were doing. I never had any experience with their Rangers, Marines, or other good units.

Still, I think that for a Vietnamese not to be a good soldier is ironic as hell. The militia men I saw were guys who would seem to me to have the greatest level of commitment because they were fighting right next to their homes. Yet they showed it the least. Finally, a lot of people forget that we had other allies in Vietnam, such as Australia and the Republic of Korea (ROK). I never worked with Aussies, but we did operate with the ROK Marines and they were terrific.

I respected the enemy, even though I didn't think that they were great soldiers as a rule. I had two completely different segments in my tour. The first several months, I was in an area where our enemy was predominantly Viet Cong. The VCs were similar to the militia units (sometimes actually the same guys) that I was talking about a minute ago. They weren't very well trained. If a VC unit ambushed us, for example, they would initiate the ambush by firing an AK-47 on full automatic. You'd get a couple rounds up head high, then recoil would cause everything else to go over our heads. If you attacked into one of their ambushes, they would disperse. They wouldn't stay their ground. They didn't fight it out. Although they could be ingenious in the construction of booby traps, they didn't have the soldier skills that were required to fight us one on one.

The last several months of my tour were in the Khe Sanh Mountains, where we had NVA. And that was a completely different experience. They were much tougher soldiers; very competent. They were equipped properly and they had weapons in sufficient numbers and so forth to do a good job. It was scary to meet those guys. I had a lot of respect for them. But I don't want to take anything away from the Viet Cong because they lacked soldier skills. They were doing a job that was incredibly difficult, and under very tough circumstances.

My tour in Vietnam ended with my flight home on February 15, 1971. I flew out of Da Nang Air Base. I passed through Los Angeles Airport very early in the morning, so I didn't see any of the war protesters that marred homecoming for a lot of Vietnam veterans. I was disappointed to have my camera stolen in LA. I hadn't developed any pictures yet, and all the film I took while there was with it. Without photographs I was afraid I would forget—I have not.

On the positive side, while I was sitting in the airport with my buddy Ed Spry, the actor Dale Robertson rode by in one of those little golf carts they use to ferry people around. He had the driver stop, hopped off, and came over to shake our hands. That really meant a lot to me.

I had a better homecoming than many Vietnam veterans. I was met at the airport by my mother, then-girlfriend now wife, Janis, one of my three brothers, and my grandmother. I think my mother was most prepared to see the changes in me. She had seen my father when he got back from World War II. Having my parents available to talk to was extremely important because I did not know what to expect. I had terrible dreams for a year or so, and all the other things that veterans typically experience. At no time did I ever receive any sort of official warning about the resocialization process, and of course, nothing about PTSD [post-traumatic stress disorder]. Talking with my parents and learning that my dad had similar experiences after World War II let me know I wasn't losing my mind, and that my feelings and dreams were a fairly common experience that would recede over

Maj. Curt Munson in 2008.

time. Fundamentally, my family was sound, and my upbringing was sound, so I was pretty sound. I think most combat soldiers experience some level of post-traumatic stress disorder and depression after the scary part is over. Having a family like mine made it easier to bear.

When I returned to college at the University of Arkansas in the fall of 1971, I was never interested in any of the antiwar protests or movements. I was cordial to the Vietnam Veterans Against the War [VVAW] guys I knew, but I never went to any of their meetings. The whole business seemed inappropriate to me somehow. I wore my field jacket on campus with the Marine Corps emblem on it, and I was proud of it, but everybody wore one. I would never have defaced mine with a peace sign or magic marker messages.

I didn't want to talk about my experiences when I came home from Vietnam because I discovered right away that while people would ask you what it was like, they didn't really want to hear the answers. You could see that as soon as you didn't have a two-second quip that explained everything, their eyes would glaze over. I was happy not to talk about it. Even [later on] in the Marine Corps, I never really talked about Vietnam that much because nobody was all that interested. It was irrelevant to the kind of training we were doing, for a more mechanized, European-type scenario. It was easy to avoid the topic.

I think it was inevitable that the war ended the way it did. I think there were a couple of dynamics that came into play there. One of them was the idea of individual replacements, a terrible mistake. It was a way to make the effort sort of a commoditized event. Not the best way to fight a war, but a perfect reflection of Robert McNamara's management—we were all just spare parts.

The other was war exhaustion. At the time, I wanted the war to end. I wanted it to end very much. I can remember how frustrated I was when Henry Kissinger and the North Vietnamese delegates to peace talks in Paris spent so much time worrying about the size or shape of the table, and how frustrated we all were. I just wanted it to be over before my little brother wound up over there. I wanted it to be over for a variety of reasons, but the main reason was because I thought, at the time, we had lost.

My opinion has changed. By now enough time has passed for a better historical and political perspective to have been achieved. Like most Americans, I failed to understand the full implications and what we did as a nation in Vietnam until 1991—the year the Soviet Union collapsed.[5] In the next decade or so, a lot of the academics, reporters, and others who were protesters in the Vietnam War will have retired or passed from the scene. What I'd like to see is for some young rabble-rousing historian with no personal stake in the war to come forward and say, "Communism was a real threat—the Soviets were a real threat! And these guys [the Vietnam vets] did something really valuable."

The other thing I have come to realize in the years since 1989 is how great the impact was on the people of Vietnam. If you watch TV programs where Vietnam veterans go back and meet with NVA veterans or VC, I'm amazed at how many of them are missing limbs. How many of them have been seriously injured. How many lost children and spouses and parents and others that we would not normally have considered to be combatants as a result of the incredibly intensive combat and the weapons we brought to bear. Almost as bad as the dead and maimed is the impact that still exists, from unexploded ordnance, poverty, and other problems linked to the war. Those things are heartbreaking to me. I'm much more empathetic now than I was. I have a more balanced perspective on all of that. I can feel strongly about the wars I've been in without being a war proponent. I wish our country would talk more and fight less. Nearly fourteen years after my retirement from the Marine Corps, I still have strong feelings about my time in the military. It's called service for a reason.[6]

Chapter 13

No John Wayne Movie

Real Bullets, Real Blood

Lt. Gary Doss flew one of the UH-34D helicopters, known as the "Ugly Angels," and landed it at the university parking lot. The retired military helicopter and Lieutenant Doss's presentation were well received by the students from the Vietnam War history class. In his story, Lieutenant Doss describes how a nineteen-year-old Oklahoman joined the U.S. Marine Corps, received his training in California, and engaged in bloody combat in the same year.[1] Over 794,000 U.S. Marines served in Vietnam, more than the total in World War II. The Corps suffered 101,574 casualties, including 14,821 dead.[2] The marines began combat operations in spring 1962. Then its helicopter task force moved to the I Corps Tactical Zone (the five northern provinces of South Vietnam). More marines were sent to northern South Vietnam in 1965, when the First Marine Aircraft Wing began its offensive mission. Lieutenant Doss served in the First Marine Aircraft Wing.

When Lieutenant Doss got to Vietnam in 1966, the war situation had deteriorated. Gen. Wallace M. Green Jr., commander of the U.S. Marine Corps, and Lt. Gen. Victor H. Krulak, commander of Fleet Marine Force Pacific, employed more helicopters in ground combat operations in 1966–1968, leading Vietnam to be described as "the helicopter war." As a door gunner and mechanic in one of the Seahorse helicopters, Lieutenant Doss became part of the "Ugly Angel" squadron. Their Sikorsky choppers ferried marines in and out of battle. His story is typical of the experiences endured by a majority of the young marines.

Lt. Gary Doss

Squadron HMM-362, First Marine Air Wing, Ky Ha, U.S. Marine Corps

As a kid growing up in Oklahoma, the only times I ever really heard about war were in John Wayne movies and the TV news. After I got out of high school, I went to work construction for my dad's company. I didn't really know what I wanted to do, and by 1965, when the draft started to become a big issue, I started getting cards and visitors from the military. After I took a basic qualifications, skills, and interest test, I got more mail from the services and realized I had more qualifications than I thought. One evening, an officer from the Marine Corps visited my house and told me I qualified for what they called an aviation guarantee program. Although this sounded interesting, I still didn't want to join, not right before the holidays. I finally enlisted right after the New Year in 1966.

I went to boot camp in February, and flew to San Diego with seven others from Oklahoma City. The ones I remember are Rusty Kirk, George Smith, James Harris, and Richard Allen. Kirk was killed in Vietnam and awarded the Silver Star. All the horror stories fell short of the reality of camp. The Marine Corps wanted to tear you down, mold you, and create you into the marine poster child. They did a pretty good job by marching, drilling, and restricting you, not even letting you call home. Due to the war situation in Vietnam, boot camp was reduced to eight weeks from the normal twelve weeks, but even though it had been compressed, everyone still wanted to be done with it.

I eventually graduated from boot camp and went into Infantry Regiment Training [IRT], where I was immediately assigned to Uniform Company as a machine operator. The training took up to four weeks for me and several other guys who were assigned to the motor pool or air wingers. The notorious "wing wipers" [air wingers] were not a "part" of the Marine Corps, as some would say, so we got our own special training. We got only the basics of training, learning how to shoot all sorts of weapons and basic camouflage training. I graduated from IRT and was assigned to NATTC [National Aviation Technology Training Center–Memphis] in Millington, Tennessee [just north of Memphis]. There I went through reciprocating engine training, including how to operate different machinery, and repair, pull apart, and troubleshoot the reciprocating engine. I enjoyed that part, but we were still pretty restricted on time and what we could do, like in boot camp.

In Millington, I met Phillip Jackson from North Carolina. We developed a lasting friendship and oddly found ourselves together for most of our time in Vietnam. Shortly after we met, we discovered that we had a lot of things in common. This common ground surfaced quickly and allowed Jackson and me to remain together at the camp. The day of graduation as class 636, we all got a message while marching back in formation during a graduation exercise. The runner had fiery information in hand: all of us were going to Okinawa to await further transport. We were allowed a short leave before our flying halfway across the world. We first arrived at Treasure Island, and I thought that would be the last I'd see of Jackson.

But we both were shipped to Honolulu, then to Guam, and still together to Okinawa in December 1966. We stayed in the transit barracks there, and every day we would get into formation, fall out, and listen to loud speakers for information about who was going where. A good number of us were called to go "FFT-RVN," which sounded like some recreational vehicle to me. I realized quickly that "RVN" stood for "Republic of Vietnam" [South Vietnam], which meant you were going somewhere pretty serious. In a few days, Jackson was called to "FFT-RVN," which was hard for me because by this time we were pretty close. My name was called the next day, and I was off to Fatima Marine Corps station to catch a C-130 to Da Nang in South Vietnam.[3]

This continues to be one of my most vivid memories because of the enormous activity when I arrived in Vietnam. A few hours after landing, I oddly met up with Jackson again. In the transit shack, we discovered we'd be following each other again, going to an air base called Chu Lai.[4] "You two guys are going to Ky Ha, that's a helicopter base up the road that gets mortared every night," a guy informed us in the barracks. I didn't want to believe it. Jackson and I found out that Ky Ha would be our home, and I got stationed in Hams 36, part of Marine Air Group [MAG] 36, which was part of the First Marine Air Wing [USMC 1st MAW] in South Vietnam.[5]

I found out at Ky Ha that the guy down at Chu Lai was only half right. It's true that it was a helicopter base, but we didn't get mortared every night. Jackson and I always watched the helicopters fly away and wondered what it was like on the outside, on the other side of the wire. The choppers we had were UH-34D Sikorsky helicopters, or known as the "Ugly Angels."[6] We heard stories from the men about how they were flying all the time, day and night, running back troop insertions, refugees, mail runs, test hops, reconnaissance missions, and all sorts of things. I thought that they really

Lt. Gary Doss and the "Ugly Angel" at Ky Ha in 1967.

knew how to stretch a good table because they got so many things done in a short time period. These guys would come back and work on their birds all night so they'd be ready to fly the next day. Ky Ha wasn't a bad deal. It had hot showers, a little chapel overlooking the valley, and a great beach. It would have been an excellent resort area because of the beautiful breaking water and the sunset on the South China Sea.

I never forget one night, a guy went out to fly and the next day somebody we didn't know came by to pick up his gear and inventory his stuff. He never came back again. At that point, I just accepted that as the way it was. Jackson went to the helicopter squadron before me, and I wondered if someday I wouldn't see him again. In a few days I got my orders.

I was to go on to the front line with the squadron and Jackson. This was something new for me because I hadn't been out of our base too far. My farthest trip had been from shore to the base. I was astonished at the fact that those stories at the base were real. It didn't take long to go from hop to hop to hop in the helicopter in a small time frame along the front line. We would be in a number of different places in just a few hours. One thing we could execute was taking the wounded from battlefield to the hospital in forty-five minutes, an incredibly short time period. This was remarkable compared to the Korean War because the wounded had to be transferred back in a vehicle, whenever and wherever it was going.[7] The speed we could get things done meant many more lives being saved and being able to extract soldiers just at the nick of time.

One of my first missions was with this kid named Poindexter from Georgia on a resupply operation. We would drop off food, water, munitions, or take on somebody needing relief for heatstroke or whatever and replace them with somebody else. The skill of carrying out these missions was very precise. We would fly in at a high rate of speed and flare the old bird up on its axis to cut down air speed. By the time we touched the wheel, we'd be unloading our stuff. Usually if we were just off-loading, we'd just tilt up on the bird's axis and be in and out of the zone in a matter of seconds. Sometimes seconds is all you had. We would, of course, on-load as well, but this was much more difficult because it meant we would spend more time on the ground. The name of the game was to be in and out of the zone as quickly as possible. The less time we were in the zone, the less time in the target area, and the less time we had to take casualties.

One day, we took off looking for a medevac bird. Medevac missions were to transport injured from the field by helicopters to a hospital where they can receive medical or surgical care. I was in the gunner seat during this mission. The wind streamed into the cabin and the rain started just after we took off. The weather fell on us and made it extremely hard to see and maneuver. Suddenly, the huge explosions were going off all around us, jerking the helicopter. I didn't know if we were in an artillery zone or somewhere else we shouldn't be. Those helicopters were built for all weather conditions, but it didn't matter if you couldn't see.[8] Thankfully, as we lowered in the sky the weather settled down a little. I tried to orient myself as we dropped down out of the clouds because there was still a lot of rain coming in, and that's when I saw streaks. They were coming up from the tree line to my left and under the helicopter while we were flying over this little village. It finally occurred to me what was happening, when the crew chief hollered, "Men, we're taking fire!" That resistance was plenty incentive for the chief to open up with an M-60 and start blasting away. I saw a man in the village positioned and shooting his automatic at us along with a little kid running out of a little hooch pointing a huge gun at us. I tried to get my weapon out and over the pivot point to fire, but it wouldn't quite get out that far, so I had to watch him fire at us. Immediately I could hear the bullets hit our bird. We were able to fly a little bit and set down in safety, and it amazed me how one second you were being fired at, and the other moment you were safe. We landed where there was a group of marines in an outpost. We sucked down our ration cigarettes because we were all nervous and keyed up about the experience. Poindexter talked about the men he hit in the village. When I surveyed the damage to the helicopter, I found bullet holes a couple of feet from my position. The pilot fired the bird back up and I checked the gauges to make sure everything was okay. We left that zone and flew from 1,500 to 1,800 feet altitude to get out of range of small arms.

In the daytime, our bird would usually be accompanied by another gunship helicopter and a Huey, or a chase bird with one jet engine and two side by side pilots, an open canopy cargo area with two gunners, two external M-60s on each side, and 2.75-inch rocket pods on each side.

One day, a Huey flew in our close air support while we were down into the zone for the extraction. My pilot called to the ground about the situation. They answered that they were surrounded, and taking fire from all sides. The Huey pilot radioed that he's coming down to make his pass. He flew low to detect the suspected targets, proceeding to unload on the targets to keep them quiet long enough for our bird to get in the zone. It was our turn. My pilot laid our bird over and corkscrewed that thing down out of the sky, shoving me way back into the seat. The power of the reciprocating engine was amazing. He cut off the power to fall in a sort of controlled crash, and as we circled in I could hear, "You're taking fire, you're taking fire!" My pilot said, "Ain't that a bitch," and drops her down out of the sky. We landed right in the middle of a dry rice paddy in a little terraced area. I could see one guy was dragging one of the medics by the helmet. That guy wasn't getting up. I noticed all these dirt clods kicking up from enemy fire, but I jumped out and helped this guy on board. We took off again. My pilot asked the Huey about the air support after we got out of the zone. He said his guns locked up on his first pass and all he could do was make a pass or two to make it look like he was doing something. That was just one of those days. All's well that ends well, and I was blessed.

Another day involved Jackson. We drew some reconnaissance insertions so they could do silent surveillance for a while. We dropped three different sets that day. Jackson was in the other helicopter, and I was in the lead bird with the commanding officer flying pilot. The senior pilot was always the first in the zone. We ended up doing a little basic maneuver and made the drop. You were always keyed up in a free-fire zone, but the insertions remained mostly uneventful. With recons, you didn't want to give away your position and wanted to get in and out without too much delay, and I lived to fight another day.

Lt. Gary Doss (center) and one of the graduate research assistants in 2003.

Another time, a reconnaissance team was doing surveillance for a few days and was spotted by the enemy. Our job was to extract them. The recon team was running around and updating us about where they were, and we'd try to locate their position by some of the terrain and landmarks they described. We eventually arrived at the location, and saw them on a side of a hill taking some intense fire with KIAs everywhere and several wounded. A guy on the ground told the pilot via radio that there were people listening to the radio that wasn't on their team. Our pilot asked the soldier if he "popped" smoke, [to] tell [him] what color it [was]. The soldier returned, "We're poppin' yellow smoke." We pinpointed their location. The lead bird, my bird, flew into the zone and performed a rescue for the most seriously injured first. Our method of rescue came down to hovering over the zone to perform the extraction using a hoist. The guy on the ground needed assistance or a basket, and we didn't have a basket. So the next best thing was that I was lowered down on the hoist. I could smell the gunpowder and see and hear the crackles and radios—the war was going on here.

I had such an inner battle going on inside because I had yet to see my twenty-first birthday and I was lowered into what seemed like a death trap. During a normal hoist extraction, we would reel off the amount of cable needed prior, beforehand, then drop it into a zone to save time. But since I was riding this thing, it had to be lowered slowly, inch by inch. I decided that it would save precious time if I could roll off the hoist and drop a distance to the ground. My heart was in my throat, and I checked the .38 caliber on my hip. I suddenly hit a phase that I didn't know what to do, and I stopped for a second and said, "Lord be with me," and this perfect peace came upon me. I thought later that I should have prayed, "Lord get me out of here," since that prayer went so well. As I was standing in the doorway of the helicopter about to go down, everything went into slow motion. At this moment I realized that we weren't even in the zone. The crew chief said he lost contact with the ground at the last second and the soldier couldn't direct us the last few hundred feet to their position, but we'd be coming around for our final approach.

It turns out that I would have to sit ringside and watch my best friend's bird fly into the zone. I could hear the helicopter Jackson was in and could see the dust kicking off their bird from the fire they were taking. Then I heard words from the pilot that just cut through my soul, "Both my crewmen are hit," but they continued the rescue with the hoist on the ground. The good thing I saw was someone in their bird taking the hoist into the helicopter after I watched it being raised up, so at least one crewman must be left alive. My crew went back and picked up some more crew and a spare Sparrow Hawk team because we underestimated how vicious that zone would be. Close air support was also called. We would go back and forth to complete the mission all day bringing back both alive and KIAs.

Later that day, I walked over to Jackson's bird and was astonished by all the blood staining the belly of the helicopter and the bullet holes everywhere. I was heading back and a shadow crossed my path in the flight line. It may seem impossible to recognize a man by his shadow, but I knew it was Jackson, and it was. I looked up at his smiling face and said, "You're a dead man, aren't you?" He said, "No, buddy, I'm sure not." He told me that they couldn't fire on the zone because of friendlies in the area, and by the time they got in the zone the bullets were hitting them like hail on a tin roof. Jackson said that the bullets were hitting everywhere and he got one in the back. He said, "I knew I was dead and just reached around just to feel how big the hole was, except then I got hit right here in the chest." Jackson escaped death that time and so did I. We would both live to fight on.[9]

Chapter 14

More Than Meets the Eye
Supporting the Intelligence Effort

I have known Lt. Col. Terry Lynn May since 1993 as a colleague and a good friend. The retired army officer had a great sense of humor, wisdom beyond his age, and a sincere passion for sharing and honoring the military experiences of the Vietnam War veterans. I attended his funeral service in 2003 after he lost his battle to leukemia. Among the family, friends, and prominent people in attendance were the city mayor, ROTC officers, and local veterans. I often sit in the middle of the park that was dedicated to his memory in 2005, watching the kids playing around and thinking about how to remember Lieutenant Colonel May in a meaningful way.

Lt. Col. Terry May served as the commander of the Forty-fifth Military Intelligence Company, U.S. Army, from 1969 to 1970 in Vietnam. His specialty, aerial reconnaissance and imagery interpretation, and his experience as an army intelligence officer reflect military intelligence at the company level. He describes his Vietnam tour as bizarre, unpredictable, intense, exhausting, and daunting.[1] At the national level, generally speaking, the U.S. intelligence community believed that its efforts had worked during the Vietnam War.[2] A conference on Intelligence in the Vietnam War, however, provided a mixed picture of U.S. intelligence, including electronic information collection, signals and imagery intelligence, counterintelligence, infiltration operations into the North, psychological operations, the Phoenix program, provincial reconnaissance units, analytical resources, politics of intelligence, and interagency cooperation and conflicts between the CIA, DIA, and other intelligence organizations. While many presentations came up with a positive conclusion, others insisted that the U.S. intelligence's judgments proved prescient much of the time but found little receptivity. At other times during 1965–1968, the intelligence community found favor with policymakers but turned out to be wrong.[3] The CIA also believed that they provided intelligence on Vietnam that was better than that of other official contributors.[4]

Lt. Col. Terry Lynn May

Commander, Forty-fifth Company, 525th Military Intelligence Group, U.S. Army

My Vietnam adventure actually began in the early summer of 1969, when I got my written orders for Vietnam. I had just left Fort Bragg, North Carolina, to attend an army intelligence school in Baltimore, Maryland. I went there to become an aerial reconnaissance planner and photo interpretation officer with a specialty of aerial reconnaissance and imagery interpretation. I was a brand new captain, had been married for not quite three years, and had two infant children: sixteen months and two months.

I had voluntarily become part of the U.S. military establishment and was prepared to go to Vietnam. As a professional soldier, the right or wrong of U.S. involvement was not a hot political or personal issue for me, at least at the time. I was prepared and proud to do what I had been trained for, and I thought I had a good understanding of the enemy. But I never thought that what I would do in Vietnam was something so entirely unexpected and different from what I had been trained for.

The Vietnam conflict had been going strong for almost four years, and I had known since my sophomore year as an ROTC cadet at Central Michigan University that service in Vietnam was almost inevitable, and equally essential, for any officer considering the army as a career.

I flew out of Lambert Field, St. Louis, on December 22, 1969. A few hours later, I was at Travis Air Force Base, north of San Francisco, changing into a short-sleeved khaki uniform. I was in a crowded room with hundreds of other soldiers of all ranks. We tried to mask our real emotions with wisecracks and joking around. I noticed from the ribbons on their uniforms—their military awards and decorations—that many were headed back for another tour. I felt like a rookie suiting up for his first game in the major leagues. After what seemed like an interminable flight, with stops in Hawaii and Guam, I remember how my pulse quickened when we made our final, and very steep, approach to Bien Hoa airfield, some twenty miles east of Saigon. Bien Hoa was a principal port of aerial arrival for U.S. forces.

It was about 0200 hours there, and a real time warp. We left the plane quickly, its engines still running in case a mortar attack demanded quick departure. We walked into a wall of heat and humidity. As we moved toward the terminal, on the right side of a roped pathway, servicemen on their way home walked on the other side of the rope to the plane we just left. You could not possibly find a sharper contrast of emotion. We were virtually silent, but the guys going home sure had a lot to say to and about us, most of which was triple-R rated.

At that time, officers could indicate an assignment preference during in-processing. I remember being quite embarrassed when an amused personnel sergeant chided me for the preference I had indicated, "PACEX." He enjoyed telling me the acronym stood for the Pacific Exchange System, responsible for operating the post exchange, or PXs, in country. Alas, PACEX was not the high-level intelligence-exploitation center I thought that acronym might stand for and where I had hoped to find air conditioning, fluorescent lights, and comfortable officers' quarters.

On Christmas Day, 1969, I found myself assigned to the 525th Military Intelligence Group, headquartered in Saigon. The unit adjutant, or personnel officer, who processed me in was Ephram Zimbalist III, son of Ephram Zimbalist Jr., the famous movie and TV star. Just one of my many bizarre Vietnam experiences. The next day, I received my pinpoint assignment and was transported by jeep to the Forty-fifth Support Company, located at Parker Compound on the banks of the Saigon River. I was one person in the huge support infrastructure seldom heard about. Military analysts call it the "tooth-to-tail" ratio. As part of the supporting "tail," I was one of the fifteen or eighteen people supporting, in some capacity, each combat infantryman doing the fighting. My war, as an Army Military Intelligence Company Commander, would be one of responsibility for a very large group of soldiers, over five hundred men. My duties included their mandatory training, supplies, transportation, military justice, personal counseling and career development needs, and personal security. I also had to keep track of and maintain over two hundred widely scattered vehicles.

During that initial drive through Saigon, I couldn't believe the sights, sounds, smells, and congestion. Blaring horns, heavy diesel exhaust fumes, wall-to-wall people speaking a sing-songy language of which I knew not one word. I wondered if the North Vietnamese Army or the Viet Cong would ever even get a chance to kill me. I was glad to break out of downtown Saigon and roll through the gate of Parker Compound. I spent my entire tour there, serving first, for four months, as executive officer for the company, and then the balance of my tour as commanding officer. I had anticipated neither of those assignments nor anything of their kind.

The small installation measured no more than about thirty by fifty yards. The old, two-story original villa, which housed our orderly room, a couple of other administrative offices, the mess hall, and officer quarters, sat in the middle of the property. Around the perimeter was a ramshackle assortment of old, stucco-walled, tin-roofed buildings and guard towers behind layers of military barbed wire. These outbuildings housed the enlisted personnel, our arms room, supply room, a small club, a one-chair barbershop, and a tiny PX. The latter two each measured about eight by ten feet. On the extreme northeast corner of the greater Saigon area, Parker Compound had originally been a French equestrian academy and stables, probably built in the early 1900s during the heyday of France's century-long colonial administration of then-Indochina.

We were called a "support" company as an operational security measure. The cover name was supposed to conceal our true identity and purpose: a military intelligence organization, the Forty-fifth Military Intelligence Company, part of its parent organization, the 519th Military Intelligence Battalion. That unit was headquartered at Ton Son Nhut Air Force Base, on the north side of Saigon. The cover effort included our wearing infantry, rather than military intelligence, insignia on our uniforms. I quickly learned, however, that this ruse probably only fooled other U.S. units, and certainly not the Vietnamese, either the Southern or Viet Cong variety.

Parker Compound was immediately across the Saigon River from "Indian Country," as it was called: an area unsecured by U.S. forces. After dark, there could be no movement from the compound unless by armed convoy. Organized relief forces were at least thirty minutes away.

Most nights we could see artillery flashes and helicopter gunships working on the near horizon. While we had a barbed wire perimeter and armed MPs in guard towers twenty-four hours a day, we knew we were dead meat if the Viet Cong really wanted to own Parker Compound. Rumor had it that the Vietnamese owner of our little installation was making large, regular payments to the VC to ensure his property was protected. I'm not sure he cared that much about us, though.

The bulk of the soldiers in the Forty-fifth Company were intelligence specialists working in a wide variety of analytical and reporting functions in many different locations throughout the greater Saigon area. The military intelligence effort for the war was headquartered there. Most worked twelve-hour shifts, six or seven days a week. I had every rank assigned to the company, from private to colonel. Only the lower-rank enlisted troops lived at Parker Compound, a couple hundred total. I was also billeted there for most of my tour, along with several lieutenants on my staff.

The men of the Forty-fifth Military Intelligence Company (there were no women assigned) were the young soldiers, both officers and enlisted, who as intelligence specialists and managers were responsible for analyzing enemy ground strength, disposition, location and intentions—"order of battle," as it was called. They were also responsible for such functions as identifying infiltration routes and rates, and analyzing captured documents, materiel, weapons, and prisoner-of-war interrogation reports. They interpreted aerial photography and operated the computer systems housing the in-country intelligence database for the war effort. Their contribution understandably never got much publicity or credit, but it was absolutely critical to the planning and conduct of the war.

As a whole, they were a great bunch of troops: bright, mature, and responsible. Fortunately, and thankfully, they weren't exposed to the rigors and risks of combat field duty. I'm also proud to say they also had very, very few problems with drugs and alcohol. This was the time of the draft, and many of the young enlisted soldiers had college degrees. My company clerk had a master's degree, and everyone working on my administrative staff had some college. Virtually all had been drafted.

I never thought I'd be given so much responsibility, so quickly, with so little time, training, and experience in the U.S. Army. I was usually worried if I could get the job done. My gut was in a knot for most of that year. In many ways, however, I was lucky to have such a challenging job. My hours were very long, however, and I seldom had any free time. The only true privacy I had was when sleeping. I routinely worked seven days a week, at least twelve hours a day; frequently much more. Between the work and the heat, my weight eventually dropped from about 170 to 147.

My tour in Vietnam frequently featured bizarre vignettes and observations that have stayed with me all these years. Running into an army friend and learning that he had the responsibility of using then a new and dramatic bit of technology called a facsimile device, to send to the White House daily copies of aerial reconnaissance photos. We later learned that the president and secretary of defense were personally involved in selecting tactical air strike targets. I soon began to realize that with so many South Vietnamese political and societal infrastructure problems and corruption, and with such high-level U.S. political involvement regarding small-scale tactical decisions, something was terribly wrong and out of whack about this war.

While I have some good memories from my time in the war, many are serious, poignant, and sobering. I became fast friends with a Vietnamese Army engineer officer who was a devout Christian and strong proponent of democracy for his country. Just a few years ago I learned he had spent twelve years in a North Vietnamese jungle "reeducation" camp before being able to flee to the United States with his family. Traveling to my Battalion Headquarters, located adjacent to the U.S. Army Mortuary at Ton Son Nhut AFB, and seeing one large cargo helicopter after another land to unload body bags of U.S. dead. My executive officer's best friend was killed elsewhere in the country, and on the day the army casualty notification team arrived to inform his wife, it was their wedding anniversary. Also, the flowers he had ordered weeks ahead of time through the Saigon PX wound up being delivered while the notification team was doing their grim business. Having to go toe-to-toe with a drunk first sergeant. A legend in his own mind and old enough to be my father, he had become insubordinate and disrespectful, not to mention losing sight of his roles and responsibilities.

I also stood the toughest inspection of my entire army career, at a time when the soldiers in the company were working double shifts providing intelligence support for the invasion of Cambodia. Several busloads of inspectors spent a part of three days with us checking our compliance with about a million different army regulations. This was a time of drug problems for some units in Vietnam. They not only physically checked the troops' foot and wall lockers, but also my desk and lockers; even my laundry bag. This was certainly one time when being an officer and commander meant nothing. They even climbed into our water tower looking for drugs or other contraband. None was found. Needless to say, we felt these tactics and policies were personally and professionally insulting and humiliating.

My low point came after four months in the country, when I had already been there for what seemed like forever, and realized I still had twice as long to go. Wondering, the longer I was there, what eventually would happen to the country after we left, I saw very black clouds on the horizon.

Even for a "Saigon Commando" like myself, there were some scary times and moments, especially knowing that our compound was undefendable and extremely vulnerable, particularly after dark. Standing on the porch of our building and having a spent rifle round from several thousand yards away plink to the floor about ten feet away. Driving my jeep to battalion headquarters and seeing, in my left peripheral vision, a Vietnamese child about ten or twelve years old lob an object at me and run like hell. Fortunately it was a light bulb, which broke on the street in front of me, and not a grenade. Sitting in our little club one night at Parker Compound during a severe storm only to suddenly realize that those weren't lightning strikes up the river about half a mile, but rather incoming rocket fire near a bridge. They sound a lot alike. Army regulations also required me to conduct quarterly reenlistment briefings. Imagine trying to deliver an inspiring, motivating address to a theater full of young soldiers, virtually all of whom were drafted and who never had a single thought about reenlisting.

Eventually it was almost time to go home. The last week seemed like it would never end. I remember being too excited to sleep well. Of course the ultimate emotion was actually making it to my DEROS, or "rotation" date; the day to go home. Normally, the night before was cause for a terrific "good-bye" party. After working so hard and so closely with my fellow soldiers in such an intense setting, the good-byes were also somewhat bittersweet. Despite the excitement of leaving the war behind, it was also tough to say good-bye to the men with whom I had gone through so much. Nevertheless, this was what I had been waiting for, the opportunity to drive out of Parker Compound for the last time.

On that "wake-up" day, as it was called, it seemed like the minutes stood still. The ride to the airport was a blur of memories and anticipation. Then came long, slow lines for U.S. military and South Vietnamese customs inspections. We were all probably pretty paranoid by that point, just knowing that we'd either get shelled, or that somebody had screwed up the paperwork to go home, or that the plane would be delayed. My pulse was racing.

Finally seeing the "freedom bird" sitting there on the tarmac with its inviting open door was a hugely emotional experience. I was really leaving. I would actually be back in the "land of the big PX" within about twenty-four hours. I would actually soon be reunited with my wife and kids.

Frankly, I can't remember much about the flight back, except the utter sense of anticipation, knowing that in just a matter of hours, not months

Lt. Col. Terry Lynn May in 2003.

or weeks, I'd be restored to the long awaited role of husband and father; of finally being present and accounted for, and not represented by letters, pictures, and an occasional phone call.

After an intermediate stop in Hawaii, we finally landed at Travis Air Force Base, north of San Francisco. It was late November, after dark, raining, and a cold 49 degrees. We were all in short-sleeved tropical uniforms and about to freeze. We were then bused to San Francisco International Airport for connecting flights. Arrival there accounted for one of the most bizarre memories I have.

Because of antiwar protesters and picket lines at the airport, we were instructed to dismount the buses, proceed immediately to the men's rooms, and change out of our uniforms into civilian clothes. Then we were to make our way, by ones and twos, to our connecting flights. This was so we wouldn't be hassled or spat upon. What a homecoming. That stood in absolute stark contrast, of course, to the homecomings of our service personnel after the Korean War and World War II.

The next part of my homecoming was equally memorable, and at the extreme opposite end of the emotional spectrum. My wife had flown to San Francisco with the kids and was waiting at a hotel for me. The kids were already sound asleep when I got to the room.[5]

In Vietnam we used to kid about how putting down our duffle bag would be the *second* thing we'd do after finally reuniting with our spouse. I simply say that no romance novelist could do justice to that tenderest of moments when we realized, in each other's arms, that at long last the war was finally over for us.

I learned a lot from my experience in Vietnam. Some of my major lessons learned were that: I had been properly prepared and trained to get the job done; learned to have confidence in myself and was pretty damned good at leading, organizing, and problem solving; learned that I could do lots more than I thought possible; had loved taking care of the troops, and learned so much from the sergeants; was proud of what I had accomplished and my service to country; gained a much greater appreciation for our nation, our way of life and values, and how lucky we are to be citizens of this country; gained a greater appreciation for life itself, for how fragile it is, and how much family really means; and realized that some of the real heroes of that war were the devoted and loving military wives who kept things going at home and provided so much support and comfort from a distance.[6]

Part Four

Doctors and Nurses

Chapter 15

Medevac and Medcap Missions and More

I first read Third Class Seaman Ron Peterson's story in the newspaper. Then Lt. Col. Terry May introduced me to the local Vietnam veteran group that Ron Peterson joined.[1] Peterson had joined the U.S. Navy Reserves when he was only seventeen as a junior in high school, and was sent to Vietnam in 1965 when he was twenty-one. During his one-year tour, Peterson served as a navy corpsman in the First Marine Air Wing at Da Nang. Within the U.S. military establishment, the Marine Corps and navy had a unique relationship when it came to medical support during the Vietnam War. While the army and the air force have their own service-specific medical system at all tactical echelons, the navy provides the medical support for the marines.[2] According to Peterson, in any battlefield, training exercise, or garrison environment, navy corpsmen (medical technicians) were the combat medics and clinical personnel supporting the marines. His experience in Vietnam came during the earlier part of that war and, as such, is quite unique.

Considering his own time in the navy and his having a son who is a ten-year veteran of the Navy SEALs, Ron Peterson has strong views and advice regarding military service. He had the unique perspective of having worked with Vietnamese citizens while in Vietnam, as well as with Vietnamese émigrés during his follow-on civilian medical career in the VA system. After his Vietnam tour, Peterson returned to higher education at Southwest Texas State University and then enrolled in the Physician's Assistant program at Duke University. Following his graduation, Peterson began a distinguished thirty-year career working at a number of prestigious hospitals, primarily in internal medicine and urgent care. Along the way, he helped establish Physician's

Assistant programs at Alderson-Broaddus College in West Virginia (where he earned a B.S. degree) and at Baylor University. He served at VA medical centers in Texas for some thirty years, retiring in 2000. Now in his sixties, Peterson works part-time for a physician at a metropolitan health center.

Third Class Seaman Ron Peterson

Medevac Corpsman, First MAW Base, Da Nang, U.S. Navy

I had joined the navy reserves while still in high school, attending boot camp in San Diego between my junior and senior years. I had some friends in high school, and we talked about it [enlisting], and thought it would really be a neat thing to do. We kind of joined together. It was part of the delayed-entry program. My mother was just about to kill me because we signed up. But I was sure this way I'd be able to go to college and then go on wherever I wanted to. Our goals were to be able to be in the reserves, yet go on to college.

Part of my plan worked. I had been in the navy reserve for almost two years and had just finished my freshman year in pre-med at Southwest Texas State, where I first met Judy (later my wife), when gathering war clouds on the other side of the world changed my life forever. I didn't expect the call for active duty. It was May 1964, a time when most Americans weren't yet thinking about a place called South Vietnam.

I began my training for a qualified corpsman and combat medic, which was quite extensive, about six months long. I did my 'A-School' [advanced individual training] as I went on active duty. It was Hospital Corps School in San Diego. That's about a four-month program. As you finish your "A School," you're assigned where you're going to go next. At that time, because of the Vietnam War, a large number of people were assigned to the Fleet Marine Force. After the "A School," I attended what was called the Field Medical Service School. That's where you got indoctrinated into the marines; kind of a little marine boot camp. It was also field medicine, where you learn how to do field bandages and things like that. It was about two months long at Camp Pendleton.

From Field Medical School, I was attached to Headquarters Squadron 1 of the First Marine Air Wing in Iwakuni, Japan. It was about forty miles from Hiroshima. That was supposed to be my thirteen-month overseas tour. I was there five months and then the whole First Marine

Air Wing moved to Da Nang, South Vietnam. I was in Da Nang for eight months.

From everything I heard about the Viet Cong and NVA troops, they were very capable in the sense of guerrilla tactics. They were exceedingly good. They were difficult to get a handle on, in the sense that you had them and you didn't. They had ways of hiding and going underground and not being able to be found. The other thing, of course, was that it was so difficult to tell the good people from the bad people. Some of the things we heard played out and continued to prove that they were a very wily enemy.

I believed what most Americans believed: that it [Communism] was a bad thing, and that if left unchecked could lead to other countries falling under that same type of regime. There were all these theories about what Communism and these dictatorial types of governments could do. It was a very bad thing and I believed that if we didn't take a stand there, then we may have that on our back doorstep. I have much stronger feelings now than I did at that time. As a young person you believe that your leaders are making the right decisions. I thought what we were doing was an important thing, a positive thing. I did not see it in the light of the war protesters.

I knew when I first went in that there was a great chance that I would end up going there. Early on I was kind of caught up in the fact that it was an important thing, especially the closer I got, when I was in Japan. Everyone left in stages, to go to Da Nang, but I didn't get to go in the first couple of groups. At that point I wanted to go. I was very happy that I was going to be part of something I thought was important, not only for other people, but a big impact on my life. It would be a big factor in the perspectives I have and in how I carried out the remainder of my life.

I was just twenty-one, and being exposed to wartime events in a foreign country certainly was a shock to my system. And yet it was something I really wanted to do. As you get involved with a group like the marines and where I was, you get caught up in that and feel like that's where you ought to be. But to step off the plane in Vietnam and know you're going to be involved in that type of a conflict was certainly a very vivid memory.

There were many times it was scary, when we'd take mortar rounds during the nighttime. The mortaring was pretty often. There were always rounds going off, even during the daytime. It became so common you almost didn't think about it. When there was a real threat we'd be alerted that we'd be having incoming. That would oftentimes be once or twice weekly, and then we'd go for a period of time and not have any. And of

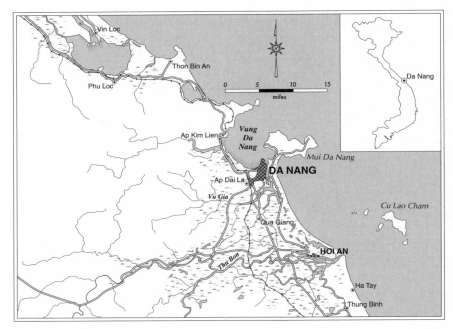

Da Nang, South Vietnam

course you never knew exactly where those were going to hit. During the monsoon season it would be raining very hard, and in addition to that there would be incoming mortar rounds, and getting up in the middle of the night when it was dark and trying to make your way to a bunker.[3] Having it happen at night always made things more interesting. I can certainly remember being frightened on more than one occasion.

Luckily, I and the people I was with never had any injury. But all around us there would be serious medical problems that we'd be involved in treating and transporting out to the larger hospital, the triage hospital, called Charlie Med, or C-Med, where most of the more definitive treatment, surgery and so forth, would be handled.

Another security concern was an adjacent Vietnamese village, nicknamed "Dog Patch." Villagers worked in the marine unit's area during the day, yet mortar rounds frequently came from the village at night. And being there early on [in the war], nothing was very well controlled at that point. We lived where you could look from our tents right into the "Dog Patch." So we were always uneasy in the sense of feeling secure.

I was involved in several areas in the dispensary. Treating patients in sick call, working in the lab and in the pharmacy were all part of my duties. There were many occasions of having to suture marines due to daily work injuries and minor combat wounds. Some of their injuries occurred when the guys partied a little too much and had lacerations from falls or confrontations with fellow soldiers.

One day as I was looking for a medical record at the dispensary check-in desk, I was aware that someone had walked in and was standing at the desk. I continued to look for the record as the individual stood patiently for me to help him. Finally, he said politely, "Is there anyone here who could fix my broken sunglasses?" As I looked up, I realized "Moses" was standing in front of me! It was Charlton Heston that I had so rudely ignored. He continued to be such a polite and appreciative person while we all fell over each other trying to fix his glasses. He then agreed to go outside and have a photo shoot with us. He was on a USO visit to Vietnam. It was indeed a fun and memorable day.[4]

I volunteered many times to fill in for other corpsmen and fly on helicopter medevac [medical-evacuation missions]. We went wherever the action was, marine or army, within fifty to one hundred miles of Da Nang. Our routine duties were not to fly medevac, but I did get to fly medevacs on occasion. Basically, we'd fill in for other corpsmen that were at another unit, called MAG-16, or Marine Air Group 16.[5] I think they were at Marble Mountain, right on the ocean front.[6] It was real close to Da Nang, maybe ten miles. We'd fly and pick up wounded American soldiers and bring them back. On many occasions they would already be deceased, so we'd be bringing back the body bags at that point.

Sometimes we'd go into zones that were clear and other times there would still be hostile fire. I can remember a few times at night, flying in, and seeing the tracer rounds come up, actually taking some hits that were not detrimental to the helicopter. I certainly remember being very frightened at that time. But I made it fine, and never had any serious accidents while I was aboard. Those were very vivid memories. Luckily, I didn't do that full time. I was with the headquarters squadron, and usually worked in the dispensary there. I provided medical care.

We'd fly into any number of places around that whole Da Nang area, wherever there was action going on. It was to wherever there were hostilities going on and our soldiers were receiving injuries. It could be army or marines, and it was in a fairly tight radius, probably fifty to one hundred miles around Da Nang.

The first really significant and indeed fatal injuries I treated were when I flew a medevac mission for the first time. The soldier had what proved to be a fatal wound of the chest and abdomen, and all we could really do was to attempt to stop the bleeding, apply battle dressings, and get IV fluids going. He really was past our ability to do much for him by the time we arrived at the site. Unfortunately, there were many times when this was the scenario. On other occasions, however, we were able to stabilize wounds and get them back for more definitive treatment. The first time I was involved [in treating combat injuries] I was very frightened, not so much about the danger of the mission itself, but more about whether or not I would be up to the task of helping someone who may be critically injured. What I found out was that in the heat of the situation our training took over, and I was able to function better than I had anticipated I would.

I got the opportunity to do what was called a Medcap [medical civic action program] mission. That's where we would go out and treat some of the indigenous people for their illnesses and injuries and insect bites and what have you. Of course they had extensive disease. They were very supportive and happy to have us. We believed we were really being helpful. There was one negative side to that, however. And that is this: there were occasions where we would put dressings on some of those people for various problems and then these very people would be found later, killed, after attacking Americans. They'd still have those dressings on them. It was still very hard at that point to tell who was on your side and who wasn't. That was a continuing problem; somewhat of a universal problem there, not just with us. We had numerous Vietnamese that worked in our dispensary, and on a daily basis we had to trust that they were the good people. Some of them were, some of them were not, as we found out.

Our living conditions were pretty sparse, yet certainly better than the marines who were out in the field, because at least we had either dirt-floor tents or, later on, hard-floor tents to sleep in. When I first arrived in Da Nang we slept in large, dirt-floor tents. I recall there were eight to ten men per tent at that time. Later on, my condition improved, maybe because I passed my E-5 exam. In any event, I was moved to a 'hard-back' tent that had wooden framing and floors. Those tents were like the Taj Mahal by comparison. We had much more room, with our own desk, chair, bed, and private storage area. And only four men per tent. It's amazing what this could do for morale. It also made me feel guilty at times knowing how the ground troops were living out in the field.

One of the funny things I remember was during the monsoon season, when it rains tremendously there. Around our tents we would have trenches built that we could get into in case we sustained mortar attack, which occurred frequently on that compound. We'd have a place to get into very quickly. One time in the middle of the night when it had been raining very, very hard, and we were all very soundly asleep, all of a sudden we heard this big splash and a big scream. The chief [chief petty officer] in our tent, his whole cot and everything, had fallen off into the trench, because the dirt had given away from the water washing it out. He came out looking very distraught.

Usually before we'd go to bed we'd sweep out the tent and clean it up. And then we'd get up in the morning and there would be thousands of little prints all over, in the dirt. There were very large rats that were all over our area, and of course the prints were from the rats. At the medical tent, in the dispensary, we treated many marines who had their toes chewed by rats at night. Many times the marines weren't aware that a rat had been in their bed. The rats were large and looked as big as squirrels. And they had shrews over there, a very aggressive smaller animal. I remember that as a very bad problem there. Actually, one of our sanitation jobs was to collect them and to test them for various diseases, particularly rabies, in case we had to treat the troops. But rabies never was a problem.

Our leisure time was somewhat limited, but like most GIs when we had time, we would write home. Or we'd read old letters and trade books with our friends. Once or twice a week there would be a movie, and that was always a fun time. I have been a runner for years, but I really started running in Vietnam. The Da Nang Air Base was large, and at certain times it was safe to get out and run on the dirt roads around the base. On one occasion, I was running with a friend when mortar rounds started coming in. I'm not positive, but I think I may have run the fastest mile that I have ever run, either before or since. Luckily, we made it back to our area without injury or further incident. I got to take one week of R&R to Okinawa. Some of the guys got to go as far as Australia, but lucky me, I drew Okinawa. It really wasn't bad at all, especially considering our usual living conditions.

I experienced losing good friends in combat and know what that feels like. I had a couple of close friends who were killed, and those are certainly vivid memories; corpsmen that were there, that were actually killed either on their helicopter missions or waiting to go. I actually had one who was killed at night, sleeping on his helicopter. The VC came in during the night and blew up the helicopter and he was killed. Interestingly enough, he was the brother of Tab Hunter, the movie star. He was the chief hospital corpsman and was killed just sleeping on that helicopter. Usually the chiefs didn't even go on those missions. He was just one of those kinds of guys who wanted to be involved. One or two friends were killed after I left Da Nang. That was kind of tough to hear about. It's still a very negative feeling for me.

So, there was not at that time a lot of dissent, either at home or amongst the troops. I had lived around lots of different types of people, including Mexican Americans and blacks, so I worked with them again, and that was not anything new for me. I felt for the most part that we were a unit. We worked together. There were not a lot of people, from my perspective, mad or upset about how they were treated. I understand that later a lot of that changed and that the troops even began to question why they were there. I think a lot of this, why I didn't see that, had to do with the time I was there. People were dedicated to their jobs and seemed to be excited about doing it, about serving, about getting it done and getting home.

My tour in Vietnam ended in April 1966. As opposed to the many Vietnam veterans who had a bad homecoming experience, or none at all worth remembering, I never felt any negativity. I was not even aware of that for so long. Although, after I was back for awhile was when a lot of that [protests] really got worse. I had a very, very supportive family who always kept in touch with me. I had quite a huge number of people there in Austin when I flew in. I remember it to this day. They couldn't have been more loving, more caring, more excited to see me. They certainly treated me as a hero, although I didn't feel I deserved that. They continue to support me to this day.

The whole experience is to feel that you were benefitting a good cause. I believe that was an important thing that we did. I've never experienced any negativity in my life as a Vietnam veteran. That probably had to do with the positive, great support I had. I was certainly treated as a hero when I came home. I was disappointed since many lives were lost. It took a lot of time, a lot of humanity, a lot of death and destruction on both sides. It was really very disappointing and anticlimactic; and ending the way it did was certainly not the way most Americans would have wanted.

After my Vietnam tour, I spent my last few months of active duty aboard a navy destroyer-tender at Charleston, South Carolina. In the fall of

1966, I returned to Southwest Texas State University to complete my education. But not for long.

I happened to see an article in *Look* magazine about the new Physician's Assistant program at Duke University. They were accepting many former military medics and corpsmen. I applied and was accepted into the third class in 1967. I went from central Texas to Duke University. That was a very liberal place. I saw many antiwar demonstrations. That was extremely interesting to me as a Vietnam veteran. After I had been there awhile, it started to make me contemplate more and more why we had been there and why all these people were so upset about it. I began to have new thoughts at that point in time, still feeling that what we did was the right thing. There were people who think we should have gone on and tried to finish that war.

After two continuous years of intense study, I graduated in 1969. I began to work at the VA [Veterans Administration] hospitals. I know from working with Vietnam veterans and taking care of them that a lot of them have had terrible problems as a result of the war. It got to the point where a lot of them could not get on with their lives. I really had trouble with that because I thought, okay, we did the best we could, now we needed to pick up and carry on. But I saw how the war impacted people and how they couldn't get over it. I think it had a lot to do with their family background and structure. I've seen many veterans [in the hospital] who have not done well because of their background.

During the war, you're fired up to go and make a difference. You feel like you can be of great benefit. Of course, after getting there, being afraid at times was certainly a part of it. Saddened by the death of not only friends, but also innocents, the civilians. Being disappointed and angered that some of the people you think are friends are not friends and are killing your friends and your soldiers' friends. And as the time drew near to leave, thinking, "Boy, am I happy to get out of here!" Happy that you're gone, happy that you've participated, saddened by what's going on, and disappointed by the way it ended. But, overall, I would still consider it a positive experience in my life.

Nevertheless, it had a definite impact, dramatically, on my life. To come from a very blessed land, blessed family background, and to be exposed to what is going on in the world that is not good, and to know that although we were not as successful as we wanted to be, that we still had a good impact.

I have very positive feelings about the Vietnamese people I've known and worked with since the war. The ones that I worked with that proved to be true comrades when I was there, I had great respect for. Because of the things I saw, I was not very trusting for a long period of time because you could never be certain who was and was not the enemy. I think the Vietnamese people were very, very smart as a general population. I think they are very dedicated to whatever their goal is, to attain that goal. They're willing to stick it out, no matter what, whether it was to get out [of Vietnam], or if it's the enemy or if it's not the enemy; whatever that goal is, they will stick with it. They're very tenacious. They're a very strongly family oriented people. I really have a lot of respect for them as a general rule.

I still think we had a very positive, significant impact on an area of the world that needed help. And then, to come back and to feel even more blessed because of the freedom that we have in our country, and all of the wonderful things that we have in our country as opposed to many, many places in the world that still, to this day, don't know our freedom. Those are probably the most important things I learned from that [my tour in Vietnam].

Chapter 16

Drowning Tears with Laughter

Students were enchanted by 2nd Lt. Judy Crausbay Hamilton's enthusiastic attitude and unique war experience when she talked to my history classes about Vietnam.[1] Women were not drafted into the military in the 1960s, but Judy signed up and served as both an air force and an army nurse during the Vietnam War.[2] She worked in the air medical evacuation squadron in the U.S. Air National Guard from 1965 to 1967. Then she asked the air force to put her in-country as a flight nurse. After they told her that only male nurses were sent "in-country," she left the air force for the army. She went to Vietnam from 1967 to 1968, serving as an army nurse at the Ninety-first Evacuation Hospital, III Corp, and other field medical facilities.[3]

After the Vietnam War, many veterans combated their emotions with anger, others turned to alcohol or drugs, and many withdrew from society. Second Lt. Hamilton learned to channel her horrifying experiences into memories, some of which bring laughter. Serving as an army nurse, she saved the lives of American, South Vietnamese, and North Vietnamese soldiers. She cared for soldiers during times of great danger. There is no doubt that she endured stressful times. However, she has learned to cope with the stressors of war in a most unique way.[4]

The following chapter covers Judy's story of courage and patriotism in 1965–1969. Her vast experiences offer a unique perspective to the war. One of the wounded soldiers wrote to her many years after the war: "Last night I must have woke up a dozen times, each time enjoying the excitement of having established contact with you again, and remembering just how much you were a very bright light during a very dark tour of duty. Before my twentieth birthday I had been wounded in action three times, the worst time being the multiple GSW's that brought me to the Ninety-first Evac in November of

1968." He expressed his gratitude for her caring in a time of dire need. "For over twenty-five years I have simply wanted to say 'Thank You' for your care, concern, and kind words spoken daily during that six week period. You were truly an angel existing in a living hell. . . . Certainly you came in contact with hundreds of wounded soldiers, and there was nothing particularly unique or outstanding that would cause you to remember me. But for me you were not only the first American woman I had seen in seven months, but a great source of inspiration in an otherwise totally depressing environment."⁵

2nd Lt. Judy Crausbay Hamilton

Flight Nurse, Air National Guard, U.S. Air Force, and Ninety-First Evac and Can Tho Hospitals, South Vietnam, U.S. Army

I joined the military after completing nursing school at Baptist Memorial Hospital in 1965. I served in the U.S. Air National Guard from 1965 to 1967 and served with the U.S. Army from 1967 to 1969. Women were not drafted into the military. Some women went to nursing school through the army, and they were indentured to them for three years. I went into the military to travel. My brother was in the navy on the USS *Enterprise,* and he also served in Vietnam. I have always been a nurse. I worked as a pediatric staff nurse at Children's Memorial Hospital.

After I joined the Air National Guard in 1965, I attended flight nurse school for about eight weeks at the School of Aerospace Medicine, Brooks Air Force Base, San Antonio, Texas. I attended army boot camp at Fort Sam Houston, Texas. As flight nurses, we went to flight nurse school and came into the air force as officers. So we did not go through air force basic training.

Air force nursing was totally different from civilian nursing. We performed everything inside an aircraft. All of our nursing was done during flight. The great difference between air force flight nursing and civilian nursing was that you did not have someone to answer your questions. Most of the time flight nurses did not have anyone to help with medical procedures that might be needed in flight. Occasionally we would fly with one flight surgeon on board. A flight surgeon would fly with us only if we had an extremely critical patient. So we flew many times without flight surgeons. That was a big difference between civilian and flight nursing. During this time, the military nursing was completely different because we were dealing totally with casualties from Vietnam.

2nd Lt. Judy Crausbay Hamilton and her aero-medical evac team in 1966.

Then I received air evacuation training with an active duty air force aero-med unit located at Yakota, Japan. Next, we flew into Clark Air Force Base [Sapangbato, the Philippines]. During this time, the military flew patients back from Vietnam to Clark Air Force Base. We loaded the injured soldiers, marines, and seamen into C-141 transport aircraft at Clark and then flew them to Japan. From Japan we flew these men back to the United States.

One of my most vivid memories took place during a routine mission, while I was assigned to the 137th Air Medical Evacuation Squadron, which was on their way to Vietnam. During this mission, my air force rank was second lieutenant. There was a rapid decompression on a C-141 aircraft that landed before we arrived at Wake Island. The rapid decompression occurred at 35,000 feet with approximately one hundred GI soldiers going to Vietnam. We took those soldiers and placed them on our C-141. One of these soldiers was severely injured with a case of cerebral bends.[6]

We flew the injured soldier back to Hickam Air Force Base and placed him in a navy decompression chamber. Afterwards, I flew with these soldiers to Vietnam. I took care of that patient in the back of the aircraft, with the assistance of my two corpsmen [medical technicians]. We had a really scary flight because the patient almost died on me several times in flight. I had no medications for an emergency situation. There were very few things available that I needed to work on this patient. However, we did get him back to the decompression chamber. An article in *The Oklahoma Journal* recaptured this extraordinary event:

> The patient needed oxygen, but the troop system could not be used; the technicians used a low-pressure bottle, which had to be filled every 15 minutes from the forward part of the cabin. The crew flew abnormally low and, at Lt. Crausbay's suggestion, over pressurized the cabin to a simulated altitude 1,000 feet below sea level. At one point, the patient's pulse rated to 200—far above normal. Drugs, which would have countered the condition, weren't available. Remembering a technique from training, the Air Guard Nurse applied arterial pressure which reduced the pulse to normal.[7]

Fortunately, I had two medical technicians with me from our guard unit with experience in air evacuation. They were really tremendous and did a great job. The story also ran in a 1967 issue of *The National Guardsman*, and included a humorous compliment. "The guardsmen had been on 31 sleepless hours of duty. But it was Lt. Crausbay's first visit to Hawaii and she wanted to make the most of it. She washed her hair and went out on a date."[8] Major General Weber wrote me a letter, "Congratulations on a job well done and we are most appreciative of the fine publicity you brought to Air-Evacuation."[9]

Whenever we did our air evac missions over to Southeast Asia, the GI patients were so receptive and grateful. You could not do enough for them. The soldiers were so mortally wounded and damaged. I remember one soldier whose torso was in the middle of the litter. I asked him: "Don't you need to move up in the litter?" The litter was flat and not tilted up. I tried to move him and found that he did not have any legs. He fit perfectly in the center of the litter. I felt so terrible. One soldier had a tracheotomy [a breathing tube in his neck]. He would not go to sleep for fear that it would plug up and he would die in his sleep. I told him that "If you just close your eyes and go to sleep, I will sit here by you and watch you for a couple of hours. . . . I will just sit right here by you."

I said to myself: "When I get back to the States, I want to get around those patients more. I want to go where they are first injured. I don't want to just take care of them forty-eight hours later, or a week or so after their injury."

So I asked the air force if they would put me in-country Vietnam as a flight nurse. An officer said: "No, we are only sending male flight nurses in-country Vietnam." Then, the guys in the Air Guard told me that "You know Judy, if you were in the army, I bet you that they would send you to Vietnam in a New York minute."

So I contacted the army and asked them if they would actually send me in-country Vietnam. The army officers told me; "Yes, we will guarantee you an assignment to Vietnam." Therefore, I left the comforts and camaraderie of the air force for the army in 1967.

I did this after I realized that many of the Guards did not serve in-country Vietnam. This is really what instigated my transfer to the Army Nurse Corps. I would have stayed with the air force had they assigned me in-country Vietnam.

I served in the U.S. Army from 1967 to 1969. While in the army, I served four months at Fort Ord, Monterey, California, on an orthopedic ward. The hospital ward received casualties returning from Vietnam. There was an AIT and basic training program [boot camp] located at Fort Ord. Therefore, we received AIT and basic training casualties as well.

One of the things that I found so special before getting stationed in Vietnam was working with the casualties returning from Vietnam. These soldiers were fresh from Japan and pretty fresh from Vietnam. They were obviously wounded to the extent that they were not going back to the service, so they sent them back to the U.S. and tried to place them in a military hospital close to their homes. Many of them at Fort Ord were from Redondo Beach, Los Angeles, and other close locations. The soldiers would usually arrive at Travis Air Force Base and then would be transported to Fort Ord Army Hospital. They came in massive influxes. When a patient arrived, his family was notified where the ward would be. If the patient was well enough, the family could take him out on leave. Nevertheless, they needed to stay there at the hospital for reconstructive or follow-up surgery. The patients were allowed to go out on passes with their family.

I remember this one patient who came to the ward. He was an old man, twenty-five years old! I say this with tongue in cheek, because everybody was between eighteen and nineteen. He was an older guy without any legs. He had lost both legs in Vietnam. We did not have a lot of amputees at this ward. The patient arrived about noon and his wife was coming to the ward from Los Angeles that evening.

Before her visit, I asked him, "Does she know what happened to you?" "Yes, she knows." We were waiting eagerly for her to come. I mean "we," the whole ward, about fifty GIs and a half dozen nurses, was waiting on her arrival. No one knew if she would reject him or accept him. When she arrived on the ward, she looked at her husband. The only thing she said was "Get your things together. I've got a motel room for us."

You know, this lady was our queen! We could not have done enough for her! That is all he needed to hear. That one incident really gave me another picture of Vietnam that I will never forget. I had not seen the other side of Vietnam [in-country] yet. For the first time I was seeing the family's responses and how they coped with these morbid injuries. This experience was an introduction to the reality of the brutality of war.

Then I arrived in South Vietnam as an army nurse.

I stayed a year in-country Vietnam and spent more than half of my time at the Ninety-first Evacuation Hospital, III Corp.[10] The Ninety-first Evacuation Hospital was located close to a fishing village near Tuy Hoa Air Force Base.[11]

My first duty was as an "in-country" air evacuation crew member. I would jump on a C-130 and fly with the crew when they transported patients. At Tuy Hoa, there were three squadrons of F-100 fighters and also several squadrons of C-130 Hercules. The C-130 crew would take off at Tuy Hoa Air Force Base, and then we would go to Da Nang to pick up a medical team. From there we would start hopping all over the place picking up patients at Camp Evans, Hue, Quang Tri, and Hue Phu Bai. Then we would bring them back to Da Nang and unload the patients and the medical team there. Finally, by the end of the day, we would fly back to Tuy Hoa, and I could be back to my hospital.

When I first began making these air evacuation flights, they were very fast. The crew had to load patients very quickly, as the C-130 was a favorite target of the VC and NVA's mortars. They wanted to stop the U.S. air evacuation and destroy cargo capabilities. We could only load the patients who were physically at the end of the runway before we touched down. We could not wait for them to be brought out. The aircraft commander briefed us, saying, "We are just going to load on the ones that are on the flight line and then close the cargo doors." That is the way it was many times. Even though the first mortar rounds were close, the VC or NVA had to adjust their target. The second set would be more accurate, but with the third set we would be gone. Needless to say, every crew member worked quickly.

After each pick-up, we lifted the patients and secured the litters in the stanchions. These flights were low and fast. There was a lot of up and down. There was not enough time for the aircraft to reach a flight altitude where the air was cooler. The C-130 Hercules aircraft was a literal oven. The fuselage was extremely hot. The air crew even flew the plane with the large manhole on the flight deck open. So the crew in the back would take off their wringing wet shirts and continue with their duties. I had many really neat experiences doing that in-county air evacuation.

The person who impressed me the most was my commanding officer, Lt. Col. Annie Ruth Graham, at the Ninety-first Evacuation Hospital at Tuy Hoa. As an army nurse in both World War II and Korea, she was a totally fascinating person. Speaking with a true Southern drawl, she thought we were all her little chickens. We needed her mothering, and she provided that for us. Unfortunately, she had a stroke while stationed at the Ninety-first. I flew with her to Japan as her flight nurse. We made an emergency flight in a C-135 tanker out of Tuy Hoa and flew straight to Japan. She died four days later in Japan. She never regained consciousness. I must interject here that the United States is the only country I know that would and did use one huge super jet aircraft to transport one patient to a hospital half-way around the world. There were many times that a C-135 would transport one burned soldier from Vietnam directly to San Antonio to receive specialized treatment at the Fort Sam Houston Army Hospital burn unit.

I spent some time at a surgical army hospital in I Corps and in the Mekong Delta serving the Ninth Infantry Division and the navy.[12] This army hospital was located on the Mekong River at Can Tho.

I spent a little time at Hue. The 101st Airborne Division was treated at this surgical hospital. It was located at Camp Evans. This was as far north as we could get, just eighteen miles from North Vietnam.

While in-country, one of my most humorous experiences involved the theft of my brassieres. We would hang our clothes outside to dry while in Vietnam. One particular day, I had washed and hung my clothes out to dry. I really don't know if it was the marines or the 101st Airborne Division, as they were both in the area. Anyway, all of my underwear disappeared! That placed me in a bad fix, because there were no places to shop to get more bras. Sometime later as I boarded a C-130 aircraft there she was! One of my long lost bras proudly draped across the fuselage with a big sign that said, "Lest We Forget!" I confess that I needed the brassieres really bad, but I did not claim it. I said to myself that I would just pass this one up.

Well, the story didn't end there. I went on R&R to Japan. While visiting Japan, my friend and I were in a beauty shop getting our hair fixed. We had already gone to the base store looking for some underwear, but the Japanese girls are really small. Therefore, there was not a whole lot of offering for me. The sales lady said, "Well, we had two in your size, but someone just came and bought them." Shortly after I went back to the hotel someone knocked on the door. I opened the door to an American woman. She said that "I'm the one who bought those brassieres. I overheard you in the beauty shop. I want you to have these." I wanted to pay her. But she refused to take my money. This woman was some general's wife and she was very gracious. Actually, I have never known a general that is not very gracious. He usually has a good woman behind him. So I wound up with a couple of brassieres from some general's wife.

While in Vietnam, I had to prepare my medical corpsman with what he was supposed to do if we had a rocket or mortar attack at night. The postulated reports were kind of like a weather forecast: "You may have incoming [rockets] tonight." Many times we were alerted of impending attacks. I told my corpsman to place a blanket over this patient as he was in traction. This one was going on the floor and to place his mattress on top of him. All of their IVs were placed down by their side. I went through every single patient and told him exactly what we were going to do. I briefed him about these procedures, because it was only the two of us working together. When an incoming attack occurred, we needed to be on the same page.

After running him through the procedures, he looked me squarely in the eye and replied to me in a slow Southern drawl: "Ma'am, I sure hope you can do all that by yourself, because I am going to be over here behind this refrigerator." He was very serious! I thought back on that incident and said to him, "Well, okay!"

Another funny story involved one of our nurses who was pregnant,

2nd Lt. Judy Crausbay Hamilton
receives her medal in 1967.

and her husband was back in the States. She was delighted to be pregnant, as she thought this would be her ticket home. She went to the military radio station, which had acronyms like MARS. The radio station would shoot up a beam when the satellite was going over and catch the satellite, which would bounce back and be picked up in the States. A ham radio operator in the States would pick up the signal and then call that person's home. Once communications were established, the two parties would talk. This method was the only way you could communicate home back then.

Our pregnant nurse was calling to tell her husband the good news. The operator told her: "Alright, you're ready to go ma'am . . . go ahead and tell him." The nurse said: "Honey, I'm pregnant!" The message didn't go over and therefore they could not understand her on the other end of the line. Finally, the operator told her that "there is a problem with the tone level in your voice. Here, let me give it a go."

So now the male operator was saying: "Honey, I'm pregnant!" He was literally screaming this message over the airwaves. Suddenly the line became quiet. Then another operator's voice came over the radio, saying: "You guys will just do anything to get out of Vietnam, won't you?"

The male operator at our MARS sounded like one of our soldiers saying he was pregnant! This happened way before the television series *M*A*S*H*. I have reflected back on that story and thought it would have made a great scene for Corporal Klinger.

I spent one memorable day and night at a Special Forces camp. I wanted to see some of the Central Highlands and how the Montangnards, the tribal mountain people, lived. I had a friend who was an air force FAC [forward air controller]. He dropped me off at this Special Forces camp. This was a Green Beret "A" Camp. The captain in charge took me to a village, which looked like something from a *National Geographic* documentary. The huts were all on stilts with bamboo thatch roofs. The women were topless with a baby hanging off of their breasts. They all chewed beetle nut, as their smiles showed black teeth. At first, they were all very frightened of me as I looked so different to them. They would not come out of their huts or even stick their heads out. It seemed like nobody was home.

After passing by one hut, a young girl came running out of a hut screaming at me in Vietnamese, "Lieutenant!" Then she started talking in English to me. I found out that she was one of many children wounded and sent to our hospital during the Tet Offensive. Around thirteen years old at that time, the girl was crippled with rickets and could not walk very well. Therefore, I traded my boots for her "Jesus shoes," which were sandals made of tires. The young girl was able to hobble around in my sturdy boots. With her as my guide, the villagers began to let down their guard and even welcomed me inside of their tiny huts. Most of the villagers warmed up to me, while some still shied away from me. I think it was because of my blonde hair.

I also wanted to go further into the village. The captain told me that we were not allowed in the village because the Viet Cong troops were sleeping during the daytime. They did not bother the Special Forces at night. In return, the Special Forces did not bother them during the day. I was told not to pass this post.

At night, I found out that these Green Berets were in a quandary as there was actually not a place for me to sleep. All of their quarters and operations were under the ground in well-fortified bunkers. However, there had to be one guy on the radio at all times. This radio was located in a commons area where they ate and showered. The captain agreed to take the radio, so I could use his private quarters. While trying to sleep in the underground quarters, I felt something drop on the covers. I turned on the flashlight and saw several giant bugs scurry out into the darkness. I wrapped my sheet around myself and sat outside. It was really peaceful and quite lovely. Then I realized that sitting out in the open in the middle of the Central Highlands, wrapped in a very white sheet under the very bright moonlight, was not a good idea. So I went back to the captain. He told me to sleep on the sofa out on the veranda on a screened-in porch. When I tried to sleep, the rats started coming out from the sandbags surrounding the terrace. Those rats were doing a tight rope act on the electrical wires above me. These rats were as large as kittens. I kept turning my flashlight on and chasing away the rats.

The best thing that happened to me in Vietnam was giving nursing care to the American soldiers, marines, and seamen. To be their mother, sister, girlfriend, or whatever they needed to see when they woke up. Many of them did not realize they were not talking to their girlfriend, sister, or their mother. The next best thing would be the camaraderie that I had with my peers. There were no false pretenses. We all bonded quickly. We would sit up at all-night parties waiting for somebody's baby to be born in the States. The other people would be just as drunk and rejoicing as the daddy was. I remember guys coming back from R&R, and meeting with their wives and family. Everybody got excited about everybody else's excitement. We shared each other's joy. I remember people reading their letters out loud to everyone and everyone sharing their care packages.

The best lesson I learned from the military service was that you must agree with the mission before you commit yourself to the service. I did not even know what the mission was. I would have still gone as a nurse, even though I do not now, and did not then, agree with President Johnson's foreign political policies. I had not an intimate knowledge of how his policies would much later have an effect on my life. I lost all faith in the political system of my country. I did not agree with how President Johnson and other politicians handled the war in Vietnam. The generals did not direct the battles, the politicians did. If the politicians had allowed the generals to lead, we would have won the war. Our men were very restrained. Their very lives were compromised in one battle after another. They were restricted to "taking one hill after another." They were rightfully angry.

So I would say to the soldier, "Agree with the mission." Learn what the mission is before joining the armed forces. If you cannot deal with combat and everything combat entails, then do not join. During the Vietnam War, even the cooks had to use their weapons on different occasions. If an individual cannot agree with the mission, then they do not need to sign up. Once a person has joined the armed service, they should be prepared to give it 100 percent every day.

I have no regrets when reminiscing over the time I served in the military. It was some of the worst times and the best times of my life. Sometimes in the night hours I am wakened with latent grieving for the many, too many American sons and daughters sent to war in the jungles and rice paddies halfway around the world. They sang that hit song of the 1960s: "We Gotta Get Out of This Place." Sadly, it was the last thing they ever did.

Chapter 17

Life and Death of an
ARVN Doctor

Dr. Nguyen Canh Minh didn't have much choice during the French Indo-china War of 1946–1954 and the Vietnam War of 1960–1975.[1] His country became a battleground where two political ideologies competed in order to show their superiority. The Vietnamese people were only chessmen on a board, who unfortunately transformed the struggle between two superpowers into their own bloody civil wars. All the Vietnamese youth approaching military service age were drafted in both South and North Vietnam. The war between two peoples in one nation, brother against brother, friend against friend, and sometimes even father against son, was very destructive for family bonds and the nation as a whole.

As a field doctor, Minh risked his own life several times to rescue others in South Vietnam. As a medical group commander, he worked with different U.S. advisers in the army hospital and had quite different experiences. Dr. Minh's view on the ARVN officer corps was also different from the war-time stereotype. After the Communist takeover of the South, he was sent to a "reeducation camp," or a prison camp, in the North for more than four years.[2] In these POW camps, all of the prisoners had to do manual labor work to produce enough food for themselves and to send a surplus to the Communist government. They had to accept the Communist ideology by studying the propaganda materials and confessing their own "crime" against the Communists in the war. They were punished if they failed to work hard or to criticize themselves. Many of the POWs died in these camps. Dr. Minh witnessed some life-or-death situations in his prison camp. While in camp he made up his mind to leave Vietnam and come to America.

After his release from the prison camp, he took three of his children with him, traveling by foot for a week to flee Vietnam. After crossing the Vietnamese-Cambodian border, they continued their long march for another three weeks, traveling by foot for five hundred miles and crossing the "killing fields" of Cambodia, which was also under Communist control at that time. After their long march of four weeks, they finally entered Thailand. Two years later, the broken family reunited in America.

Dr. Nguyen Canh Minh

Medical Group Commander, Army Hospital at Can Tho, Fourth Tactical Zone, ARVN (South Vietnam)

I was born in 1930 in Hue, the capital city of South Vietnam from 1945 to 1955. I had three brothers and three sisters. When I was in high school in Hue, the First Indochina War, or the French Indochina War, broke out in 1946. To fight against the Vietnamese Communist forces [Viet Minhs] in the North, the French government and our Emperor Bao Dai signed an agreement to establish a Vietnamese National Army [VNA] in 1949. I went to a college in 1947 and finished my B.S. degree in biochemistry and physics within four years.

When I graduated from college in 1951, the Vietnamese government had enforced a compulsory service for all South Vietnamese youth.[3] The army was mostly equipped, trained, and commanded by French military. The French had established a training system for the VNA officer corps. Youths who had a high school diploma could sign up for military training at the national military academies as officers.

Since I joined the army with a college degree, I was sent to the VNA Medical School at the Hanoi Medical University in 1951. Many of the medical instructors were French military surgeons and doctors who had field experience in World War II. During the four years [1951–1954] of my medical school, I studied a French medical curriculum at the Medical University in Hanoi, which had been under the French occupation from 1946 to 1954. The French professors and doctors emphasized basic knowledge, systematic training, and professionalism. Patient and skillful, they helped us learn a lot of foundation and general education subjects.

In 1952, I met my future wife, Nhon, at the university, where she studied medical education for her teaching degree. She was also from Hue.

We had so much in common. After two years of dating, with our families' permission, we got married at Hue in 1954. After the French army lost their battle at Dien Bien Phu in the spring of 1954, the French government decided to negotiate for a settlement in Indochina. The Geneva Peace Agreement was signed in July 1954. While the French troops evacuated from Vietnam, the Viet Minh troops withdrew to north of the 17th parallel, and the VNA troops regrouped in the South.

In 1955, the Republic of Vietnam (RVN) was founded with Saigon as its capital city. The VNA was renamed the ARVN in the same year as South Vietnam's national army. Having replaced the French in South Vietnam to fight against the Communist expansion, the United States began to help the ARVN with its reorganization and improvement. The army received military advisers, financial aid, and weapons and equipment from America to defend South Vietnam against a perceived Northern invasion by the NVA from the North.

After 1954, my family was separated between the North and the South. My oldest brother stayed behind in the North and served as a post office cadre for the Communist government. Two brothers moved down to the South with the ARVN. My second eldest brother served as an instructor in the ARVN National Police Academy. My youngest brother worked as an airplane electrical engineer in the ARVN Air Force at Da Nang. If you entered the service, you lost your freedom. You had to relocate with your service and unit. Military rule was very tough, and you had to endure military discipline.

The army moved its medical school from Hanoi to Saigon and renamed it the Medical University of Saigon. I moved with my newly wed wife to Saigon so that I could continue my medical studies for three more years [1954–1957]. At the Medical University of Saigon, we now had American doctors in our classroom with their medical expertise and field experience in the Korean War. Their teaching style and training approach were different from the French. The American instructors introduced the cutting-edge technology and showed us how to use new medical equipment. We had a lot of hands-on opportunities, which really helped me later in the hospitals. I was trained as a general practitioner at the Medical University of Saigon. After my graduation from the university in 1957, I received an additional six months' training for field surgery by the ARVN.

I began my medical service in the ARVN in 1958 and continued my service for seventeen years, until 1975. For the first three years, from 1958 to 1961, I headed a small medical team as medical captain performing physicals for an ARVN recruiting office. We traveled to every district of the Mekong Delta to draft Vietnamese youth approaching military service age. At the beginning, the service age was twenty years of age. Later, this age was reduced to eighteen. During wartime, I believe that everyone should serve his country through the compulsory service system.

After my promotion to medical chief as a major, I became chief of a medical group for medical and sanitary inspection of the ARVN troops from 1962 to 1965. I had an American adviser for our group. We usually flew in a helicopter from base to base for the routine inspection of infantrymen's physical and living conditions. Our job was to prevent an epidemic breakout, food poisoning, and any potential health problem which may cause noncombat casualties or lower our troops' combat effectiveness and morale.

My first scary life-and-death experience occurred at this time. One day, I and my U.S. adviser flew a helicopter to an army camp for a routine sanitary inspection. During this flight, our chopper had a mechanical failure and went down with heavy smoke. We crashed in an unsafe zone, but we were all okay. Only two things could happen to us: either the ARVN or the U.S. chopper would rescue us, or the Viet Cong would kill us. It depended on who would arrive first. The crash site was at the bottom of a hill and near a forest. I suggested hiding in the forest. But the American adviser refused, saying that we should wait at the crash site so rescuers could find us. We should give them one hour. After that, we could move into the forest. Everybody checked their weapons and was ready to defend our position. Fortunately, a U.S. Marine chopper showed up only twenty-five minutes after our crash and before the Viet Cong could reach us. I appreciated the American adviser's experience and advice, which saved our lives.

After 1965, the battles became more intense between the ARVN-U.S. forces and PLAF-NVA forces in the South. My inspection team was reassigned as a medical evacuation group which flew wounded ARVN soldiers from the front line in the Fourth Tactical Zone to a nearby hospital in the Mekong Delta. We had several helicopters, and we flew almost every day to transport the wounded soldiers. During these years, I received a Courageous Combatant Medal from the ARVN high command for risking my life to serve wounded soldiers.[4]

During these years, I worked with different U.S. advisers who were very professional and helpful. Nevertheless, I didn't like some of them. Ignorant

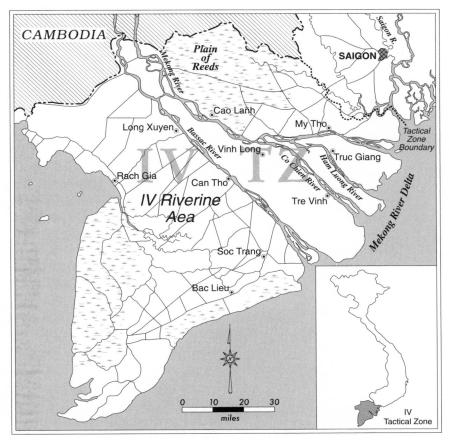

ARVN Fourth Tactical Zone and the Mekong Delta, 1964–1975

and self-centered, they didn't want to talk to you, because they believed they already knew everything about you and your problems. One of them caused the worst thing to happen to me during my service.

After another promotion, I became a residential doctor at a big hospital of the army in the city of Can Tho. My wife was happy about my transfer and liked this big city.[5] I worked in the Can Tho General Hospital and treated wounded soldiers, including gunshot, mine explosion, and other injuries. As a large regional hospital, the Can Tho General Hospital served both military and civilian patients at that time. We had two separate systems in the hospital: one side of the hospital served the civilians; and the other side was the army hospital. We had two separate clinic buildings, two in-patient facilities, and two supply/storage buildings.

In the army hospital, we were very busy. We received many wounded soldiers every day. The residential doctors had to work two shifts, day and night. Even when I was not on duty, I was still on call. The army hospital was so big that we had more than one thousand beds in the military in-patient facilities. This two-in-one hospital really caused confusion. People always looked for places, and many times they walked into wrong buildings. The Army Hospital administration always asked about why a civilian was in a military clinic building, or why a military surgical doctor was in a civilian supply/storage building. That was exactly what would happen to me. As an army residential doctor, I also knew several civilian doctors, so I visited them from time to time and had lunch with them when I was off duty. I walked in and out of the civilian clinic and supply/storage buildings quite often.

One day in 1967, a newly arrived American adviser to the hospital civilian administration accused me of stealing medical supplies from the civilian supply/storage building and selling them to Viet Cong. It was totally false, but a serious accusation. I was in a very dangerous situation in which I could be arrested as a traitor and even executed as a Viet Cong sympathizer. I defended myself by writing many letters to prove my innocence. The U.S. adviser ignored the facts and used the stereotype measurement to judge me as another corrupt ARVN medic and to cover up a large number of their missing medicines and supplies.

My supervisor, as an American adviser to the military administration at the hospital, came to my defense and explained everything to the hospital heads. He also wrote a report to the U.S. Medical Service and Advisory Headquarters in Saigon. Later, they cleared my case and transferred the U.S. adviser who had falsely accused me to another hospital in early 1968. I remember the date because it happened just before the Viet Cong's Tet attacks. On Mau Than, New Year's Eve, or Tet in 1968, the city of Can Tho was unexpectedly attacked by the PLAF and PAVN as part of their nationwide offensive campaign.

I know a typical American viewed the ARVN officer corps as incompetent, corrupted, and bureaucratic. However, as far as I know, there were many good, honest, and well-trained Vietnamese officers in our command. Among these were Gen. Ngo Quang Truong, commander of the Fourth Army Corps in 1966–1969, and Gen. Nguyen Khoa Nam, the last commander of the Fourth Tactical Zone until 1975.[6] Both of them were honest, hard-working, and efficient commanders. They made good fighting plans for the Fourth Corps. They never allowed their families to take advantage of their high-ranking positions for personal interests.

In 1969–1972, I was promoted to the commander of the ARVN Seventy-fourth Medical Group in the Fourth Tactical Zone. I oversaw most of the medical activities in the zone and worked with U.S. advisers closely on plans, joint activities, and problems.

Every three months, accompanied by a couple of American medical advisers, we went to inspect our Viet Cong POW camps. There were two major camps on the islands off the coast. One of them was on Con Dao, or Poulo Condore Island, located about eighty kilometers east of Saigon, under the command of the Second Tactical Zone. The other camp was on Phu Quoc Island, about 120 kilometers from Can Tho, offshore under the Fourth Tactical Zone command.[7] The Phu Quoc was the largest POW camp, holding about 30,000 Communist prisoners. The contrast between the way the ARVN treated the POWs with the way the Communists were dealing with prisoners was stark. As the zone medical chief, I inspected the POWs' health conditions and camp sanitary situations on a regular basis. After each visit, I reported to the zone command about the problems and made improvement suggestions. As we know, the Viet Cong and PLAF did not have any medical routine inspection or treatment. They didn't even have any facilities for ARVN and American POWs. They just placed captives anywhere in a village, a cave, or even holes in the ground, anywhere that was convenient for them to conceal the POW camps.

In 1972, I retired from the service. I received the National Honor Medal for serving the nation during a time of war. After my retirement, I still worked in the same hospital, the Can Tho General Hospital, as a physician in the civilian clinic. I also trained some doctors and nurses in the hospital. In 1974, the war situation was getting worse every day. Many people worried about the future of South Vietnam. I talked to my wife and we decided to send two of our nine children to America to attend college.

In April 1975, the Communist forces took over the South. In the summer, the Communist government sent soldiers to my house and arrested me because I had served in the ARVN during the war. They sent me all the way from the South to a "reeducation camp" in the far North, close to the Vietnamese-Chinese border. I spent more than four years in the camp.

My "reeducation center" was in a mountainous region northwest of

Hanoi, known as Son La Prison Camp. It contained about six thousand ARVN officers imprisoned, including sixty physicians, pharmacists, dentists, and medical service corpsmen. The Son La Prison Camp was in a big forest and far away from any village or town. It was guarded by the NVA soldiers and there was no way to escape. You couldn't survive in the wild forest.

We had to work hard as manual laborers in the prison camp to support ourselves. After we arrived in 1975, the camp officials told us that they would supply 75 percent of our food and other basic needs for the first six months. We should produce the rest of our daily needs. Then, after the first six months, they would reduce their supply and give us only 50 percent of our basic needs for the second six months. By the first anniversary, a year later, they would supply nothing, and we had to provide 100 percent of our food, cloth, tools, housing, and other needs.

After my arrival in 1975, I worked in the rice field with many others to feed this large prison population. Some of the prisoners worked in the vegetable gardens or chicken farms to produce various vegetables and meat for the camp security troops and officials. We were lucky to have some chicken meat in our meals several times a year during the holidays. We got a haircut twice a year. And we were not allowed to write to our family for the first year.

In 1976, I worked with a construction team to build more shelters for the growing prisoner population and repaired the only dirt road through the forest, along with several bridges. We walked into the forest every day, cutting down the big trees and dragging them back to the camp. We didn't have any truck or machine. All we had were small hand tools like those in your garage [in America]. It was hard and dangerous to cut down the big trees and to cut them into useable timbers. We had no hard hats, no gloves, no working shoes, nor any protection. Prisoners got injured every day. Several teammates were killed by falling trees in the forest and by accidents during construction in the camp.

Later, about 1977, the camp officials chose twelve of the sixty medical professionals to set up a dispensary to treat their fellow inmates in case these POWs were injured or hurt. I was one of the twelve people. We got some rudimentary surgical instruments and outdated medicine. We never had enough medicine to treat injured prisoners. And we could not send any seriously injured prisoner to a hospital for further treatment. One time, a prisoner's arm was cut by a rice reaping hook. We didn't have any

Dr. Nguyen Canh Minh (front center) and other physicians at the prisoner camp in 1976.

medicine or instruments to stop his bleeding. He suffered serious pain. We just watched him bleed to death later that evening. The camp officials and guards were there, too. I knew they had a good supply of medicine and an army nurse in their quarters. But he was taking care of the Communist officers and soldiers, not any of the prisoners. By that time, I had made up mind that I had to leave Vietnam. I couldn't live under the Communist authorities. There was no freedom for the people, no respect of human life, and no safety under the Communist control. If possible, I would leave this country to look for a better place to live for my children, my wife, and myself.

In late 1978, the security troops increased. They were armed with machine guns and mortars. There were some rumors that China and Vietnam had problems along their border, and that there would be a war between the two Communist countries. In early 1979, for several weeks, we could not go outside the camp to work in the rice field or in the forest. We could only stay inside the camp. We could hear some heavy artillery gunshots, but it seemed far away.

In the summer, the camp headquarters began to release the prisoners. I was released in October 1979. Many of the prisoners didn't make it, including several of my friends in the medical team. After being released from the prison camp, I didn't go back to Can Tho. I knew that the local Communist authorities were waiting for me and would give the released prisoners a hard time. I stopped at Saigon, now renamed as Ho Chi Minh City. In November, I met my wife and children in Saigon. We made the important decision to leave Vietnam and to go to America. We had two children studying in American colleges at that time.

How would we go to America? Our plan was to walk out of Vietnam by foot. We would cross the border and enter Cambodia first. Then we would cross Communist-controlled Cambodia and enter Thailand, which was still a free country in Southeast Asia. In Thailand, we could contact our children in America. Hopefully we would come to America from there.

In December 1979, my family split again. I took three of seven children with me, said good-bye to my wife, and began our long journey to America. We walked west toward Cambodia. We traveled through three provinces [states] along the Mekong River. We pretended to be local people by not carrying any luggage. We walked for one week and reached the Vietnamese-Cambodian border. At night, we passed the NVA guards, crossed the border, and finally entered Cambodia.

In Cambodia, we continued our long march by foot. We had to cross the country to reach Thailand. We were still very careful traveling through Cambodia because the Vietnamese Communist troops occupied that country at the time. And Cambodia was under a radical Communist government which had turned the country into the "killing fields" at that time.[8] We saw the dead bodies everywhere; and we also saw a lot of Vietnamese refugees in Cambodia. If the soldiers and local authorities found out you were Vietnamese, they would send you back to Vietnam. We tried not to say any Vietnamese word when there were people around us. Two of my three kids were sick in Cambodia. I found some herbs in the mountains to treat their fever and sickness. We walked five hundred miles for three

Dr. Nguyen Canh Minh in 2007.

weeks to cross Cambodia. In that year, my wife sent two of the four children she had out of Vietnam among the "boat people."

Finally, on December 26, 1979, after the long march of four weeks, we crossed the Cambodian-Thai border. In Thailand, we found the International Red Cross and settled in one of the Red Cross refugee camps. I contacted my wife, asking her to leave Vietnam by following my route to Thailand. In 1980, my wife arrived in Thailand with our other two children. We also contacted our son and daughter in America.

On January 1, 1981, we arrived in the United States. It took us more than a year to come to America. In 1986, after passing a medical exam, I got a job in medical research at the Wisconsin Medical Center, Milwaukee, Wisconsin. I worked there for the next thirteen years. After moving to Chicago, I worked in orthopedic research at Rush Hospital until my retirement.

Chapter 18

A Korean Captain
and His Hospital

We met for the first time at an international symposium on the Asian-Pacific Rim in 1991. As the conference organizer, Dr. Walter Byong I. Jung brought in American governors, Asian ambassadors and consuls, university presidents, and many scholars from Asia. With a widely recognized reputation in academic exchanges and a Ph.D. in urban development, Dr. Jung taught at state universities in the United States for more than twenty years and published many books in America and Korea. His favorite topic, however, was Vietnam. When I was invited to his home for dinner, I found out that he and his wife, Young, met in the Vietnam War. Capt. Walter Jung served in the Ninth Infantry Division of the South Korean Army, or the Army of the Republic of Korea (ROK), from 1966–1967, while his wife was an ROK Army nurse.[1]

Captain Jung told me that the South Korean government began to send its troops to Vietnam in March 1965. As the "ROK Military Assistant Group, Vietnam," the early arrivals consisted of medical support, engineers, and security troops. In November, the ROK Army sent its Capital Infantry Division and a marine brigade to South Vietnam to join the American operations. In 1966, the ROK doubled its troops in Vietnam by sending its Ninth Infantry Division and more marines.[2]

According to Captain Jung, many Korean soldiers, tough and well trained, were no-nonsense fighters. They were the bulwark in keeping the pivotal Highway 1 in central Vietnam reasonably free of the Viet Cong menace. That does not mean the enemy fighters were soft or inferior; on the contrary, they were tremendously motivated and remarkably resourceful, though they were poorly armed and supplied. For every rice field and mountain ridge in central Vietnam, two armies contested bitterly. Neither the ROK Army nor the Viet Cong won every battle and encounter. As part of the Ninth M.A.S.H. command of the Ninth Division, Captain Jung managed the hospital security, medical supply, logistics, and transportation. His stories about how to deal with a Viet Cong POW major's psychological tactics and hospital escape, a hostage situation, and local nurse recruitments are very interesting.[3]

Capt. Walter Byong I. Jung

Ninth Mobile Army Surgical Hospital (M.A.S.H.), Ninth Infantry Division, Army of the Republic of Korea (South Korea)

I was born in South Korea in 1942. When I was eight years old, North Korea invaded the South, and the Korean War broke out in 1950. It was the first time that I had ever seen American soldiers. I remember that, friendly and funny, they were handing out candies and gums to the Korean kids. I really liked these soldiers who had come all the way from America to Korea to help our people fight the war against the Communist invasion. I never thought that I would fight side by side with American troops in the Vietnam War fifteen years later.

When I was in college, I enrolled in the ROTC program. In 1964, I was commissioned a second lieutenant of the South Korean Army (ROK Army). Thereafter, I was posted for the 1103rd Field Engineering Group, serving as a specialist in river crossing operations. In 1966, I transferred to command the First Combined Motor Pool of the Second Army Corps. Later that year, I received the order that our motor pool unit would be reassigned to the White Horse Infantry Division headquarters, which was leaving for South Vietnam in August.[4]

On August 11, 1967, we were aboard a large transport ship for Vietnam. We arrived in Nha Trang, a provincial capital in central South Vietnam. As a member of the new replacement group, I spent two more days for the paperwork at the Logistics Command headquarters. I received the new orders.

According to my new orders, I and two medical officers headed to the Ninth Mobile Army Surgical Hospital [M.A.S.H.], located in the vicinity of Tuy Hoa, the capital city of Phu Yen Province. The Ninth M.A.S.H. supplied medical services for all the Korean soldiers in the region. Our hospital facilities were along the coast, facing the ocean, or the South China Sea in the east. I'd walk down to the beach from my office within five minutes. We had the Twenty-eighth Regiment of the White Horse Division on our right, or the south side, with its base along the shore. A little to the north, the giant Tuy Hoa U.S. Air Base sat with many artillery units and firebases nearby.[5] I was happy to be stationed side by side with American forces. Having felt safe, I just wondered if the Viet Cong or Viet Minh could ever get me or my hospital. I would learn about this within no time.

I had a good sleep during the first night, or at least half of the first night. It might have been a pure coincidence. My very first night in Tuy Hoa was like Viet Cong's premeditated welcome ceremony for us new arrivals.

"Get up, get up, Lieutenant Jung!" Lieutenant Kim, my brand-new roommate, desperately shouted, while shaking violently my nearly comatose body. I don't know how long it took for me to finally grasp the essential reality that I was at one of the Korean Army's forward bases in South Vietnam. Justifiably, Lieutenant Kim was highly agitated by my unmilitary-like response, though he surely remembered that I had arrived at the base just that afternoon and before a few glasses of whisky.

Under Lieutenant Kim's incessant encouragement, I finally got up from the canvas bed and timidly asked, "What's going on?" "We are under the enemy attack! You have to follow me now." Kim's explanation was rushed and short. Well, that was all he knew at the moment. Within a minute, we came out into the night, where a rather colorful battle was under way. Although the night was confusingly noisy, I followed him in full speed, under only partial illumination supplied by the battle itself. I couldn't ask any questions, but figured we were heading toward the compound's eastern fence, over which the South China Sea slept. Running on the strange land I didn't know anything about, it was challenging and dangerous. At the moment, I had no combat gear: no helmet, no rifle, not even a pistol. I should have assigned those items to myself when I reported that afternoon. But I decided formally to take over the supply department the next day, leaving myself unarmed in the war zone just for the first night.

As soon as we reached the edge of the compound, Kim pushed me into what appeared to be a personal foxhole. Alas, it was in name only. Apparently the foxholes were dug quite awhile ago, but the company forgot to maintain them to be functional. My foxhole barely covered the lower part of my body. I was half exposed even in the foxhole. It was painfully clear to me that the hospital commanders did not expect to use the foxholes at all.

Sitting in the half-exposed foxhole with my empty hands, I observed the night battle for the very first time. I was a forced spectator of the night's aerial battle, but I felt neither fear nor curiosity. Boldly, the Viet Cong initiated the confrontation by launching a few artillery rounds into the Twenty-eighth Korean Regiment base. Predictably, the allies of the area, the U.S. and ROK forces, responded to the provocation with their mighty firepower: the sky was full of colorful tracers and burning flairs. The air was thick with sounds of flying and exploding artillery shells. Phantom fighters repeatedly bombed nearby Homba Mountain, while helicopter gunships were busy patrolling the shore, sporadically firing their machine guns toward fishing boats, warning them not to get too closer to the shore and thus the allied bases. It was a three-dimensional operation with full color and soundtrack. I hoped that forceful display of the allied firepower should have sufficiently impressed the enemy to realize the futility of attacking the allied bases. The battle situation was over within an hour, however. Soon, the base recovered the calm and poise; all were ordered to go back to their living quarters, except of course sentries.

First thing in the morning, I opened the company warehouse and secured my personal weapons: a rifle and a pistol. I thought it would be scandalous for me again to face an enemy attack without personal arms. As expected, all units in the zone of the regimental combat group were ordered to assemble for the area commander's speech.

Colonel Lee, a thin but rather tall man, appeared upset and at the same time amused by the attack of the night before. "The enemy dared to attack our base. We can't tolerate that, no matter what." He ordered every unit to rebuild its combat bunkers and foxholes at once, and that all activities other than extreme essentials should be cancelled until the defense works were completed.

As ordered, we mobilized all available hands for this urgent project for the next five consecutive days, building new command bunkers and numerous combat bunkers along the base's entire fence. All bunkers were stocked with ammunition. The remnants of old foxholes were all cleared. During these days, the enemy artillery blasts continued every night. Interestingly, the enemy artillery attacks lasted for five consecutive nights—a few rounds of artillery blast between eleven and one, at midnight. Our artillery battalion was always quick and effective in directing counterattacks, allowing the enemy only a short window of opportunity for their attacks. Although they sure were irritating distractions, the base inhabitants suffered no deaths and only a few light wounds.

The Twenty-eighth Korean Regiment had suffered perhaps the most painful defeat on September 25, 1967. In advance, the regimental headquarters informed the area units of the upcoming operation, a company-strength thrust into the contested territory. Late that afternoon, we sent off the convoy trucks full of soldiers heading to the interior. Nobody showed any undue concerns over the convoys, as it had become a rather daily routine for our soldiers to go out and chase the enemy away. We were expecting them to come home the next morning with POWs or even some kills. In that region, we were yet to encounter the enemy who could outfight our men.

Unfortunately, the operation didn't pan out as the regiment commanders anticipated; in fact, the convoy was ambushed by the enemies waiting for them. Our wounded soldiers began to arrive at the hospital about two hours after the troops left the base. Our landing site was full as helicopters waited in the air to unload the wounded. When nurses in the wards informed me of bed shortages, I ordered to transfer any and all metal beds to the wards, even from the BOQ [Bachelor Officers' Quarters]. Still we were short of beds and space to put the wounded soldiers, as our wards were overflowing. Standing in front of our emergency room entrance, Colonel Kim and I were barely able to hide our emotion. I was wondering if the regiment was all destroyed.

My position was the hospital's S4, chief of supply department, which was responsible for the hospital's logistic administration and other relevant works. A second-year first lieutenant, I served for a field engineering group and a medical battalion, where I commanded a large motor pool, prior to my transfer to the M.A.S.H. in South Vietnam. Directing the hospital's supply department was not particularly challenging, as the hospital was a relatively small unit with 130 personnel; all supply depots were found nearby. But my actual duty was much more extensive than that of a typical unit: I had to run the mess hall and the motor pool, and to oversee the company's combat preparations. I also was responsible for maintenance of all the hospital's physical assets. Even securing the power supply fell under my domain. I was the designated fall guy for almost anything that went wrong in the hospital.

I spent most of my time maintaining the hospital's 24-hour operation or carrying out a number of other works. We had a couple of small-scale construction works in the compound almost always. Although the design and material support came from the U.S. Army contractors, the P&E

[power and electric company] workers were all Vietnamese, for whom I had the responsibility of supervising. As one might imagine, they were far from enthusiastic in their works. Therefore, I had to drop by to the work site often. They were having lunch hours seemingly too many times, making me angry.

The most risky and unique work for me was to recruit Vietnamese girls for the hospital's kitchen and laundry department. I worked with the local officials: they selected the village, and I would set up the schedule. For each visit, they never failed to remind me that I was entering a potentially hostile zone. At the time, we had to assume that there were Viet Cong sympathizers in most villages. They could easily kill me and my men during our visit. Yet I chose not to arm ourselves, a three-man team plus a driver and an interpreter. My logic was that our safety should be the vehicle: an army ambulance with prominent Red Cross emblems on sides and back. However, if the enemy chose not to honor the sanctity of the assumed medical mission, we were to be sitting ducks regardless of whether we had weapons or not. My message was that we were on a peace mission if not a medical mission per se.

As we entered the village, we were met by the village officials. Usually I found ten to thirty young girls already assembled on the court of a rather spacious home, more often than not the home of a village chief. I would greet them and present a cigarette to each girl, using both hands, while my interpreter followed me a step behind with his lighter's flame on so the girl's could smoke. To my astonishment, most girls accepted my little gesture eagerly. After the greetings, I asked their ages and education—that is, if they could read and write. I also explained the nature of the work and the selection process to the whole group. Then I told them that they would hear our decisions from the county office. Only after we had returned to our patrolled zone did we feel the mission was accomplished.

About three months after I arrived, the hospital received an administrative order to set up a ward for the Communist POW [Viet Cong and NVA captive] patients. I was assigned the new task to establish a twenty-bed ward.

The first POW patient group arrived shortly with eleven or twelve men, all young local Viet Cong fighters. To my surprise, many of them didn't show any gunshot wounds. They followed our orders and soon started to salute me whenever I stopped by their ward. I instructed them to help themselves with their meals. They would bring their meals from the kitchen to their ward, and returned utensils when they were finished. It was a simple chore that eliminated the need for our soldiers to serve them.

This rather strange but mutually accommodating coexistence underwent a radical change when one of the most important POWs the Twenty-eighth Regiment ever captured was transferred to our hospital. A Communist major in the regular North Vietnamese Army [NVA], he was a vice commander of a battalion. As soon as he arrived, the POW ward underwent a total transformation. The POWs refused to self-serve their meals. I had to assign our soldiers to do the work. I was quite upset. Their rather pleasant, if strange, salute to me also vanished. My sergeant in charge informed me that the POW major told the Communist POWs what to do. The major had turned my POW ward into his own little kingdom overnight.

I decided to confront the culprit myself. The sly major was by no means surprised by my visit. Calmly he faced me with a long laundry list of demands. But first he accused me of violating the provisions of the Geneva Convention, which I didn't remember at all. Anyway, that was how he justified their refusal of self-help meals. He was not happy with my POW ward. His material demands were quite extensive and included bars of soap, toothpastes, and writing papers. I promised him that I would look at the issues, but reminded him that some supplies were limited even to my soldiers. His most troublesome demand, again using the Geneva Convention as the justification, was going to the beach and bathing in the sea. They had been given periodic showers, a generous gesture on my part, considering our less-than-adequate water supply. I rejected his beach bathing outright; I had no way to guard them securely in the South China Sea.

Once his demands were all presented, he initiated his ideological argument promptly. He denounced the South Korean Army for interfering in Vietnam's internal affairs.

"You, South Koreans, have no business in Vietnam. No business at all. We are not your enemy in any way and in any historic period. You are here as battle fodder for the American imperialists. So you should go back to your country immediately." Apparently, he didn't care about the fact that I was only a first lieutenant, who had little voice in such a national or international decision. But since he provoked me first, I had to respond. I told him that "You got it all wrong. We are here as a part of the allied forces to protect the democratically elected government of South Vietnam from the Communist attacks. In fact, you are the aggressor. You are trying to destroy the legitimate government in Saigon. This is the war against aggressors and the international Communists. Moreover, we will prevail. Just watch us. We will wipe out your Viet Cong collaborators and North Vietnamese forces in the South." He didn't believe it and asked me, "You mean that the U.S. imperialists will win this war?" "Absolutely, we will win!" "No, no. Neither Americans nor Koreans will win this war. Matter of fact, you yourself will not return to your home safely. Believe me!"

My confrontation with the major was intense and far reaching. But in a way, I enjoyed the verbal battle with the die-hard Communist. I visited him regularly, not because I desired to hear his rambling harangues, but because I had to check the ward's security status myself. It quickly became apparent that his favored response was "don't know" on almost any subject related to military operation. Though tempted, I did not apply any physical measures on him to extract military information. Through frequent contacts, however, I was able to collect a few pieces on his background. A Hanoi native, he graduated from the North Vietnamese Military Academy. As an officer who had earned his superior's trust, he conducted himself flawlessly even under such a dire circumstance. Once he surprised me with a confession that his superiors in Hanoi warned him to avoid, if possible, any battle contacts with South Korean forces. The reason was that the South Korean soldiers were all martial art experts. He was sure of this by watching us practicing martial arts every morning on our drill ground.

The NVA major did not look like a wounded man at all. Yet he was highly skillful in producing some phony symptoms, and thus succeeded in prolonging his hospital stay. The longer he stayed, the more trouble I would have. I ordered my sergeant to infiltrate the POW group. Shortly, I managed to secure one reliable information source, a Viet Cong informer. Promptly he gave us extremely detailed information on the ward itself and particularly on the major's conduct. Behind our back, the major was holding secret tribunals for Viet Cong POWs, doling out punishments to those who did not follow his orders to the letter. Apparently, he commanded the group with an iron fist. In a couple of weeks, the informer spilled the biggest surprise: the major was planning an escape. I was shocked by the possible fallouts if his plan was carried out. I immediately upgraded the ward's security by posting two sentries at all hours. But I knew well that the sentries, no matter how many, should not be a guarantee against his escape attempt.

One night, when I was on duty, the informant sent an emergency note:

the major would escape that night. I immediately called the military police with an ultimatum. The MPs shortly arrived to take custody of the troublemaker. I was watching the transfer from the front of the ward. The major saw me, but he did not acknowledge my presence. However, he did not hide his hatred over my spoiling his plot. I never forgot his steady, penetrating glance to me, one filled with the most poisonous and hateful hostility I ever witnessed. Though he was an enemy, I secretly admired him for his exemplary conduct as an officer throughout his captivity, including his bold escape plot. Indeed, I did not think that any other officer would conduct himself in his POW captivity the way that this North Vietnamese officer did.

It was a rather calm Sunday on a late January afternoon when I received a frantic call from a master sergeant. I rushed to the last patient ward and saw a small crowd of Korean men, about five to six patients, standing against the wall. As I reached the crowd, I saw that a young Korean patient, half angry and half deranged, was threatening the crowd with two live grenades, and that their safety pins were already removed. The hapless patients and our security guards were completely immobilized by this disgruntled Korean man and his two grenades. He wanted to talk to me. I was facing a hostage situation by one of our own Korean soldiers.

The patient, later identified as Private Kim, somehow learned that I was the hospital logistic chief running the central kitchen. To my astonishment, he started to ramble about the quality of the hospital's meals, and directly blamed it on me. Like the other men, I found myself promptly incapacitated by fear of the two live grenades. I was not able even to attempt repudiating his totally inaccurate criticism, in a sense, but accepted his blame. I decided not to do anything to provoke this unstable soldier. His incomprehensible harangue went on for a while to further offend me. But perhaps bored by my total silence, the private shifted his attack back to another complaint, that the doctors didn't care about his illness, and that the doctors did not give him any medicine. Our doctors later stated Private Kim did not need any medicine since he was here for a routine observation. Two doctors came, but they did not argue with Kim either. His impromptu hostage taking continued with his periodic threat to blow up the grenades, thus taking the lives of those standing next to him.

I felt completely powerless; I was unable to do anything at all. I had no idea how to defuse the explosive, potentially lethal, situation, although clearly I was the one who should take a decisive step. Even those military policemen with their helmets and armbands were not able to utter a single word. We stood there listening to Kim's increasingly incoherent rambling, while our eyes were all glued to the two grenades.

Against my desperate attempts to contain the potential danger, about ten soldiers from the engineering company of the Logistics Battalion walked in and joined the hapless congregation, making the potential casualty pool even bigger. Like everybody present, the new men were curious about the situation and quickly found that the agitated man was holding live grenades.

But one of the men from the engineering company started talking and walking toward Kim. "Hey, what in hell are you doing? Are you crazy or something," said this corporal. He sounded more dismayed than fearful. Everybody turned their heads to the man, for it was the first time someone other than the private uttered words. He looked plain, with no particular characteristics. Kim appeared even more startled than his hostages as the corporal slowly approached him, seemingly disregarding the grenades.

"You stop there! These grenades have no pins. Don't you know?" But Kim's threat didn't do anything to the corporal. It seemed he didn't care at all. "You are even more stupid than I thought. If you want to go, just go by yourself. Nobody will stop you. But don't take all these innocent people." Kim was unable to give a response to the man. In silence, he was blankly looking at the man, who stood just a step from him. It was a most astonishing scene. The corporal said to him that "You really shouldn't have done this. Let's go there and get rid of those terrible things. You just follow me this way." The corporal led the way and amazingly Private Kim followed him, offering no resistance whatsoever, still holding his two live grenades. They talked, but we couldn't hear. Probably we all were too stunned to hear anything. It took only several minutes for the two men to reach the beach. Soon there were two muffled grenade explosions with spouting water columns in the South China Sea.

The hostage situation was finally defused without a casualty—but by a humble corporal. I, the hospital's on-the-job combat commander, helplessly staged a show of shameful humiliation. The incident clearly demonstrated a plain truth that real courage has nothing to do with either rank or level of education. It has everything to do with one's big, warm heart. Needless to say, I had a difficult time in reporting the incident to the commanding officer.

Among my various duties, the most dreadful one was related to the

Dr. Walter B. Jung in 2001.

Korean soldiers who made the ultimate sacrifice on the battlefield.[6] It was a duty I did not even know existed until I assumed the position. As the hospital's property officer, I was in charge of soldiers' bodies while they remained in the hospital morgue awaiting their long journey back to their hometown in South Korea.

With profound anguish, many times I performed the duty of sending a letter and a package of his belongings to his parents. I still remember their most meager possessions: folded and worn letters from home, photos of parents and girlfriends, and a few dollars of military notes. It was the most sad, painful thing I did in South Vietnam. I even had to process a handsome second lieutenant who went to Vietnam on the same ship I was on. He was killed by a sniper shot. His medical report showed that he was hit on the precise midpoint of his forehead by a Viet Cong.

The war that was fought both in the front and in the rear refused to exclude anything from its target list. So our base was on the receiving end of the enemy's periodic artillery showers. But shells did spare the hospital compound. Even the infamous Tet Offense somehow avoided offending our Red Cross emblem.[7] Had there been a divine intervention? I am not sure. But it could have been.

Part Five

Logistics Support

Chapter 19

"Loggie's" War

Napalm, Fuel, Bombs, and Sweat

Lt. Col. Terry May told me about 1st Lt. Bill Nelson's war story and what hap-pened after his Vietnam duty.[1] After his discharge, Nelson resumed a teach-ing career, transitioned into higher education, and along the way earned two master's degrees and a Ph.D. Then Dr. Nelson served as associate vice president at a major metropolitan university and prepared students for their future. He believes that the military offered him substantial education and experience, and he still thinks frequently about his tour as a "loggie" in the Vietnam War.

The Vietnam War has sometimes been described as a logistician's war. Nearly everything consumed by U.S. forces there, from ammunition for the war-fighters to envelopes for the unit administrative clerks, was at the end of incredibly long supply lines stretching back sixteen time zones and ten thou-sand miles to the United States. The ratio of support troops to combat sol-diers has been estimated as ranging from 6–1 to 12–1.[2] Many stories have been documented about the war experiences of U.S. veterans who saw com-bat in Vietnam. Less common, however, are stories from the veterans who were part of keeping those supply lines going. These troops—the logisticians—were responsible, daily, for accomplishing the miracles needed to feed, arm, fuel, and otherwise supply as many as a half million-plus service personnel stationed in Vietnam at the height of the war. In the informal vernacular of the U.S. military, these troops are sometimes referred to by others and them-selves as "loggies" (log-ees). It is a term of pride and endearment attached, even today, to an absolutely pivotal component of the American military war-fighting infrastructure. This is the story of one such Vietnam War loggie.

*First Lt. William Nelson's story reveals how the U.S. Army placed extraordi-
nary responsibility on its junior officers, particularly in a combat zone. His
story also suggests that the ARVN troops lacked combat effectiveness, which
increased the casualties of the American troops, and highlights some differences in living conditions between the U.S. Army and Air Force.*

1st Lt. William (Bill) Nelson

155th Transportation and Terminal Company, Cam Ranh Bay, U.S. Army

I'd received my commission as a second lieutenant in 1965 through the
Army ROTC program at California Polytechnic University, San Louis
Obispo. Then I went on an educational delay, taught high school for two
years in California, and entered active duty in June 1967.

I volunteered for Vietnam duty soon after my completing the U.S.
Army's Transportation Officers' Basic Course at Fort Eustis, Virginia. That
twelve-week orientation course on all aspects of the army's Transportation Branch was designed to prepare us for platoon-leader duties. But we
couldn't have anticipated, then, just how unusual our army future would
be. The reason I volunteered was to get a better assignment. I could have
gone to Korea for thirteen months and be in charge of a truck company
without combat pay. However, my assignment officer said, "Or you can be
in Cam Ranh Bay." I thought you could get shot in Korea, too. And it's cold
there. I told him I thought I'd be better off in Vietnam. So that's how I got
to South Vietnam.

I did have a lot of consternation and concerns. I was married nine
months before I went, so I was concerned not only for what I was facing; whether it was going to be a life-threatening situation I was getting
into; and what the effect would be on my wife, because we had just gotten
married. I knew very little about the enemy forces at the time. Only that
I guessed they were a serious foe. You could get yourself killed. It was an
enemy to take seriously, one that could not be trusted. One that could not,
in many cases, be identified. The VC didn't wear a uniform. How did you
distinguish between the military and the civilian? That was my concern.

On March 19, 1968, I arrived in South Vietnam. My assignment was at
Cam Ranh Bay, about two hundred miles north of Saigon.[3] I was assigned
on the ammo pier at Cam Ranh Bay as a ship and shore platoon leader on

the ammunition pier of the 155th Transportation and Terminal Company. I drew a unique job, filling a critical and little-known function: Military Stevedore Officer, responsible for supervising the off-loading, storing, and moving inland of a wide variety of key war-fighting material arriving on ships and barges at Phan Rang, on the South China Sea coast. This included ammunition, bombs, napalm, jet fuel, artillery projectiles, small arms, plus general cargo and equipment. The army places extraordinary responsibility on its junior officers, particularly in a combat zone. At age twenty-four and as a lieutenant, I was commanding a military port facility.

We had a rigorous duty schedule in the intense tropical heat. Our soldiers worked awfully hard. I worked with some *very* good people. We worked seven days a week, twelve hours a day, from midnight to noon. That was one shift. The other shift was noon to midnight. And we rotated those every two weeks. The reason for that was that it got so hot. When you're down in the hold of a ship, you've got steel all around, and when you're moving canisters or bombs, you work awfully hard.

Three months later, on July 5, 1968, after I was promoted to first lieutenant, I was selected to command the Phan Rang Outport, down the coast from Cam Ranh Bay.[4] I was there until DEROS [rotation to the States]. Our basic mission was to off-load LSTs, LCUs [large, military cargo watercraft], barges; off-load ammunition and general cargo from those vessels, store it, and ship it via truck convoy to the Phan Rang Air Force Base, about a thirty-minute drive away.[5] Part of that [mission] was to accept a ship that carried aviation gas and jet fuel.

We had a buoy that accepted that ship; we tied it up to the buoy. We didn't have a port deep enough to bring it in to the barge pier. So, we'd go out in a LARC (lighter, amphibious, resupply, cargo; a sixty-three-foot wheeled amphibian craft with a five-ton carrying capacity), tie it up, and hook it (large rubber hose) up to a pump on the compound there. And then it was pumped on top of the ground, in about a six-inch pipe, to the Phan Rang Air Force Base. And that was another big part of our mission.

As Outport Commander, I had main control over a small documentation unit, and then it was a contract operation with Alaska Barge and Transport, which later became PAC [Pacific Alaska Columbia]. These were American civilians. They did most of the off-loading. They technically worked for me, but obviously there was a contract there, and they had a project director. I also had a truck platoon attached to me, out of an army compound adjacent to the Phan Rang Air Force Base. They did, indirectly, report to me. Also, we had an infantry company that patrolled the perimeter with dogs. I was part of the First Log (Logistical Command), with my commander at Cam Ranh Bay. I reported directly to that commander.

Duty there was also dangerous. The Viet Cong frequently mortared this important facility. We were always scared that the bombs (in storage on the compound) would blow up. Many times the beach was hit, the Outport was hit by the VC with some NVA commandos. One day, the VC blew up 150 tons of napalm on the beach. And they killed a [U.S.] dog handler and his dog during that attack.

Many things would happen there. Either our trucks would get pinned down, or the pipeline would be blown [by the Viet Cong, or VC]. Our compound was by the beach, and then there was a road, a pipeline following the road, and then a banana grove. It was about a quarter to a half-mile away. The pipeline would be blown two to three times or so a week. Usually there's a big fire by the banana grove when the VC blew the pipeline at night. My troops had to run to the pumps, on the other end of the compound, and turn them off so it [the fire] would burn itself out. We wouldn't do anything further at night, because they would pin you down with small arms fire. There was no sense in going out at night. So, my soldiers would go out in the morning to fix the pipeline. We never got shot at in the morning, at least that I can remember. It was always at night. So they went out the next morning, to replace two or three lengths of pipe. One day, when they got there with their wrenches and big pry bars to fix that pipe, the VC had put a grenade under it. When they moved the pipe, the grenade went off and killed two of them.

That truck company I was talking about had deuce-and-a-halfs (two and a half-ton trucks), and they had jeeps with machine guns on them. They were [operational] twenty-four hours a day. Well, they'd get shot at in that doggone banana grove. One night they got pinned down. They called back for support. The infantry could not leave because they were responsible for the perimeter. They didn't have a response team. So I got my guys together and we were ready to go. When I got to the gate, our own guards said, "You can't go." They [the guards] reported that the MACV (Military Assistance Command, South Vietnam) troops nearby were going. A half hour later they were finally gone, and (by then) it was all over. Twelve guys from the truck company were killed. Going to these and other funeral ceremonies was the worst part of my duties in Vietnam.

I didn't know why the South Vietnamese troops couldn't get there sooner. It's either a combination of a lack of training, lack of discipline, or lack of commitment. I don't honestly know. A lot of that would have had to do with their MACV advisers, their U.S. advisers, and how they saw the South Vietnamese (soldiers) that they were managing and directing. A couple of times I experienced their military action. It showed they didn't come through. I'm sure that they did some good things, but I can't point to that because I didn't have the opportunity to observe it. So, in some ways what I just said is a little contradictory to what I observed in them as individuals. Because, if you're hard working and you're committed to what you're doing, that ought to transfer over to the military. Maybe it did, and maybe I just didn't see it.

All I know is, we were hit that night, and we needed to respond because the VC hit the pipeline. Not only that, they hit the convoy, and we had to go out and help. They [the South Vietnamese military] were supposed to do it, and a half hour later they were on the way. And they were just next door, just a couple hundred yards away, and it took them a half an hour to get organized to go do it.

The enemy was not always the only threat, however. Tropical storms could be devastating. One time we had a typhoon. I attended one of the intelligence briefings at the [Phan Rang] air base. They said, "You got to move. The surf is going to get so high you'll be flooded out." I came back and told everybody. And I said, "No way could we move. We can't leave all these bombs and napalm sitting here." So we decided to stay. Luckily, the typhoon got downgraded to a tropical storm. It destroyed part of our barge pier. What really hurt us was that the storm took out the road to the air base. That was the only direct route to the base. So I figured out another route, through this little village, then through Phan Rang and into the base. We had to be able to keep moving our stuff (bombs, etc., to the airbase). So we put the bombs on the trucks to go that way.

Then I get this doggone MACV major who calls me down on the beach, and he said, "You can't do that." "Why? Who's gonna stop me?" And he told me that "the Province Chief is gonna stop you. He's already complaining. He's like the mayor of Phan Rang and he doesn't like these bombs coming through his town." So what I had to do from that time on, until the road was fixed, was to move general cargo that wouldn't blow up.

The life at the air force base seemed different. They had an officers' club at Cam Ranh Bay, entertainers' visits, and many other fun things. I don't know whether to call it respect or envy, about how the air force lived. They lived pretty well.

Another most vivid memory from my service in Vietnam comes from the middle of a November 1968 night. A barge loaded with five hundred tons of napalm broke loose from its mooring buoy and drifted some two-plus miles down the shoreline into unfriendly territory. I got a call from the PAC project director, and he said, "We got a problem. We got a barge that's gone adrift." What had happened was that in the process of switching barges at the barge pier, with a tugboat, one of the barges, full of napalm, got loose. By the time that they found they could not get it back—they'd already been playing around with that barge for a couple hours trying to get it back—so here about midnight I got this call, "Can we get the LARC and go out and see what we can do?"

So we did. It was way down the beach, eight or ten miles down the beach. It was stuck up on the sand. We got pretty close to it and could see that there were possibly unfriendlies up on the barge. Well, the problem was a barge full of napalm, maybe five hundred tons. We went back to get ropes and weapons. When we got back, some Vietnamese people were moving or stealing stuff off the barge. When they saw us, they ran away. I don't know if they were the VC, or maybe just some local people getting some plywood. They stole some nose cones, but they did not steal any napalm. We were able to retrieve everything that was explosive. We didn't know if we could pull the barge off the sandbar. So we hooked up the barge to the LARC, turned it around and got it [the line] taut and cranked it [the engine] up and pulled that doggone barge off the beach. We pulled it far enough so that the tug could get up close and get on to it.

I guess the important thing is that, first of all, if we had lost that darned barge that would've been terrible. But if they would have got that napalm, what could they have done with all that napalm? But still, we were able to keep it out of the hands of the enemy. I guess that has to be real important. We received a commendation from the PAC for that.

I was pretty lucky, not wounded and not hurt. I was treated well. I had the opportunity to fulfill a position that really was for a captain, and I was a first lieutenant. So I had the opportunity to do some things in the military that I would never have had the opportunity to do in a similar position in civilian life. The kind of responsibility I had, on my own. I was cultivated to stay in when a colonel, Colonel McQuinn, came down from Cam Ranh and spent the day with me; a nice guy and everything, trying to talk me into staying in. The fact that he came down and spent a full day with me was pretty darned important to me. Even though I was the Outport Commander, I was still just a first lieutenant. I did not stay because my objective was to become a teacher, and I had volunteered for five months after we were married to go to Vietnam.

I got back from Vietnam on March 13, 1969. I processed out at Fort Lewis, Washington. The first thing I did after I went through the processing was calling my wife and said, "I'm out of the service. I'll be on whatever the next plane is." My wife, my mother, and my brother came to the airport when I arrived. It was really great. I wore my uniform to Los Angeles.

To appreciate what you have was the biggest lesson. What my wife and I had before I went, and what she and I have had since. And, the fact that you can always go an extra mile, and always do more than you think you can. I probably think that way because even though I had a good deal [in Vietnam], it was twenty-four hours a day.

I'm very proud of my service in Vietnam.[6] I think what I was able to do provided a great benefit to the recipient of my responsibilities. I feel quite good about that. We were very important in terms of providing munitions to the air force and the army. I had a satisfaction of getting things done. I felt a concern for safety. I felt frustration in trying to deal with political realities. I had an emotional longing for home: my wife, my mother, and my brother. And I felt a strong tie with the men who reported to me. We depended on each other. And that was very important to me. I remember my wife said, "You sure talk about your men a lot." I was better attuned to that culture in Vietnam than I was Stateside. That allowed me to function better, I think, in that situation than a comparable situation in the States. That has to do with leadership style, and that's still my leadership style today. That was one of the factors that caused me to decide to get out of the army when I got back. That probably drove my decision, a lot.

Take advantage of everything you can. There's a great deal that the military has to offer, from education to experience, the whole bit. Just take it seriously and make it a good experience. And it is an honorable experience. I was in the service slightly less than two years, and it had such an important impact on my whole life.

Chapter 20

Support and Survival in Thailand

M.Sgt. David Graves served in the U.S. Air Force during the Vietnam War. He told me that his motive for enlisting and serving in the military can be described by one word: honor. He had to join the services because of personal honor and his family heritage of service to this great nation. He showed me records of both of his great-great grandfathers' service in the U.S. Civil War. His father fought in World War II in the Pacific, and his uncle fought in the Korean War. He believed that it was just his turn to go.

Master Sergeant Graves tells his story about the U.S. Air Force support and assistance in Thailand.[1] During the Vietnam War, the U.S. armed forces had a large number of support troops in Southeast Asia and offshore to assist the war effort in Vietnam. In 1968, about 100,000 men in the surrounding countries supported U.S. operations, including Thailand, the Philippines, Taiwan, Guam, and Okinawa, Japan. Little has been written about the men and women who served as support troops in these countries and areas.

M.Sgt. David Graves

Ninety-fifth Squadron, U Tapao Air Base, Thailand, U.S. Air Force

I actually began my military career in the U.S. Navy Reserve. There were about eighty of us who joined the reserves in our high school senior year. I went to boot camp in the summer of 1961 in San Diego, California, straight out of high school, for thirteen weeks. Some of us stayed in the reserves, some went into the navy, and I went to college for one semester. For the first part of my college experience, I remained very attentive and made the Dean's Honor Roll. Before the start of the second semester, however, I enlisted in the U.S. Air Force.

It had always been my dream to be in the air force, and I took my boot camp in February 1962 at Lackland Air Force Base in Texas for five weeks. I then continued my training at Keesler Air Force Base in Mississippi for technical school and what they called phase two basic training. By this time, my papers from the navy caught up with me and showed I'd already had thirteen weeks of basic training and five weeks in the air force, for a total of eighteen weeks of basic training. So I took this information to the first sergeant and asked him if I needed any more basic training. He agreed that I didn't, so I did not have to go through phase two of basic training. I was only required to be put through technical school, where I trained in light ground radio, including facsimile machines, single sideband ground/ air stations, and man-portable equipment. I trained to perform service and repair on all kinds of ground communications equipment.

Out of technical school, I was assigned to the air force security service, which is still a sensitive subject that I'm not supposed to discuss much. When coming back to the U.S., I was stationed at Scott Air Force Base in Belleville, Illinois, for two and a half years in the communications field.

In the fall of 1965, the U.S. was becoming more involved in the war in Vietnam, and my enlistment was due to expire in February 1966. I had a gut check that required me to choose whether I was going to be a civilian or if it was really my turn to serve my country in a more direct manner than what I'd ever considered before. The last day in September 1965, I took a reenlistment in the air force specifying that I wanted to go to Vietnam. This is simply where I felt I was needed. Vietnam was where I needed to go. It turns out that instead of being assigned directly to Vietnam, for whatever reason, I was sent to Thailand after I received training in Oklahoma City, Oklahoma, with the Federal Aviation Administration [FAA] at Will Rogers Field. I was part of a project that was joint Air Force and FAA, named project MAT 322. This project was responsible for installing FAA civilian control towers in Southeast Asia. Whenever a tower was ready to be put together overseas, the project team came together to complete the tasks.

I went to Thailand, arriving at Bangkok in May 1966. My squadron was not located at my base at U Tapao, Thailand, close to Sadehip, because it was still under construction.[2] I thought I'd get several days in Bangkok, which was a beautiful city. But instead the colonel said that the first mobile COM out of Clark Field to the Philippines would include my base. We were sent to install original communications on the air base. I was one of the first hundred people at U Tapao, an airfield that became operational for KC-135s and B-52s by February 1967.

An interesting story I came across during my squadron's mission included one Thai boy. We laid a lot of landlines and cut a lot of ends off of a lot of wire, sometimes a thread and sometimes three to six inches of wire. Consequently, we'd have a lot of scavengers that would come around where we'd dump our refuse each day. I remember one boy, who was probably around thirteen years old and had a peg leg, like Long John Silver. I wondered about this kid. You can't imagine a family of six on a Honda 50cc machine, but I guarantee you the Thais could get by real well on one. They'd strip the insulation off of this copper wire and sell it by the pound to the dealers in copperware, and that's how they made their existence. The first newspaper that came out at our air base (actually it was just a mimeographed sheet), there was a story about this young man. He'd been working the rice paddies with his dad one day, and a banded krate, one of the deadliest snakes in the world, bit him on the leg. His dad proceeded to take his machete and immediately removed his leg above the knee, which saved the boy's life. Krates are one of the most aggressive of all the pit vipers, and we had several pit vipers to look out for in Thailand.

I was totally a support troop, and yet there were tens of thousands of us in Thailand that supported the war in a direct manner by supporting the aircraft and tankers that took care of North Vietnam. Our stories may not be as exciting as the combat veterans', and I certainly admire them above anybody, but I have come to realize that we did play a very important role in the war.

One of the worst memories I have of my service involved a first sergeant. He was truly a gentleman, nice and knowledgeable, and very well liked and respected by those around him. We all got called together one morning and were told that our first sergeant checked himself into a room in Sadehip, which was the nearby town, took a government-issued .45, and killed himself. The informers wouldn't give us any details and wouldn't go any further about the suicide, but that event will continue to stick out in my mind.

I found the Thai people to be very energetic, very outgoing. The Thais actually built the base at U Tapao. There was a Thai captain who was the head engineer. I got to know him very well and respected him a lot. The man was a genius at what he did. On the other side, I remember a book written about the Americans before we became really involved in Vietnam

M.Sgt. David Graves in 2004.

called *The Ugly American*. It was written about an American who went into Thailand and believed that he was a little better than the people that lived there and that the Thais were second-class people, someone to push around, someone to talk ugly to. We never learned their language, and as far as I know, there were very few Americans that really could speak fluent Thai, and still are as far as I know. At the time I could speak a little Thai, but I wasn't in Thailand long enough to learn anything about their language.

For me, I was fortunate enough to make a career out of what I learned in the military.[3] I worked with communications and electronics work the entire time I was in the air force. I worked either in communications or electronic countermeasures, which was very interesting. When I got out of the air force, I got hired at Tinker Air Force Base in the test equipment lab and worked there until the FAA hired me back. The lesson I learned was that, if possible, try to learn a good trade while serving in the military because it can benefit you your whole life. I really liked the way my service turned out, because I was able to use my service time to benefit myself as well as my country. I was fortunate because when I came home in 1967, all of the big antiwar protests were not in full swing yet. I saw some people with signs, but they basically didn't bother me and I didn't bother them. But I didn't care what they thought anyway, I would have done what I thought was best anyway and it didn't matter what somebody else thought. Freedom is not free. It is very expensive. Somebody had to die for us to be here today, a lot of somebodies.

Chapter 21

Three Great Escapes

Many Americans came to believe that the RVN government suffered from corruption, factionalism, personal connection and loyalty, and mismanagement in the 1960s. At the local levels, including both province and township, the governments had similar (if not worse) problems. Mr. Nguyen Vung, a former army officer, describes how bribery, kickbacks, and illegal deals took place in the provincial government and why so many officials were involved in these scandals and corruption.[1]

Vung believed that there was a tripod of power—Americans, RVN government, and ARVN, tied together by the American cold war policies and commitment to the Vietnam War. In this triangle relationship, even though U.S. aid and involvement played the most important role, Americans needed a coalition that included the South Vietnamese government and military working together to win the war. Under American supervision, a military-government bureaucracy was established. It sought to use political power and mutual interests to avoid the South's collapse and Communist penetration. Thus, personal networks and loyalty were very important to maintain the system. As a result, corruption seemed inevitable since individuals in the government worked for their boss, not the Vietnamese people or the public. They also intended to profit from their service in exchange for supporting the system. Mr. Vung tried to stay away from the problems and maintain a moral standard for himself.

Nguyen Vung

Chief, Construction Project, Traffic and Transportation Department, Gih Dinh Provincial Government (South Vietnam)

On September 10, 1933, I was born in an educated family in Hanoi. My father, Nguyen Khang, graduated in 1927 from the University of Paris, France, with a bachelor's degree in Economics. He could speak French, Spanish, Vietnamese, and Chinese languages. After his return in 1931, he worked as the chief of the Taxation Department in the Northern Colonial Administration of the French Indochinese Union.[2] He supported the French government and its colonial policy. After the Japanese occupied Vietnam in 1942, my father quit his job and opened a small shop selling ceramic products in Hanoi. I had one younger brother. Our parents combined modern Western and traditional Vietnamese cultures together. We followed my parents, and everybody listened to my father. He taught us traditional calligraphy, Asian classics, Christianity, and French literature. I remember his saying, "Family first, to keep family in your heart."

After the Pacific war suddenly ended in August 1945, the Viet Minh took over Hanoi and established a Communist regime in the North. My father closed down his shop, because the Communist revolution targeted the wealthy people and business owners in the city. Hanoi was in turmoil of both radical revolution and social disorders.

In 1946, the French came back to Vietnam and retook Hanoi. They offered my father the same job as he had for the colonial government before World War II. My father declined their job offer. He realized that a large number of the Viet Minh stayed in Hanoi as underground Communist agents after the French takeover of the city. The returning French government had no control of the people and society, nor protection of its employees.

The Viet Minh organized anti-French movements and received popular support. The Communist agents assassinated many pro-French Vietnamese, even their family members. These collaborators either had worked or cooperated with the French government. Hanoi actually became a battleground, with the French control in daytime and the Communists at night. A lot of violence occurred at night in the city, such as robbery, rape, and murder. My father did not want to work for the French government because he wanted to protect his family.

My parents told me to stay at home after six o'clock in the evening. My father said to us so many times that "You could get killed if you stay out-side after the sun goes down." After he reopened the ceramic shop in early 1947, his shop was robbed three times at night from February to August that year. I and my younger brother survived our middle and high schools during these turmoil years. Then I went to the University of Hanoi in 1950. I graduated in the summer of 1954 and received my bachelor degree in architecture engineering.

On September 8, 1953, my uncle, Nguyen Dong, a Catholic priest, was killed by a gunman on his way back from his church after a night of Bible study. The whole family was shocked by my uncle's death. My father believed that it was a planned assassination and a Communist terrorist act against pro-French Catholic churches. Although my father loved Hanoi, he decided to move to the South for the family's safety.

In March 1954, my father closed the store and moved the family from Hanoi to Hai Phong as the first step to leave the North. In May, they continued the southward journey by boat from Hai Phong to Saigon. Then our family settled in Hoa Hung.[3] I came down to the South in the summer after my graduation from the University of Hanoi. That was the first escape by my family from the Communist-controlled North.

After the Geneva Conference in the summer, the Communists controlled North Vietnam and the Republic of Vietnam was founded in the South. In the fall, a new Southern Republican Vietnamese government was founded in Saigon. My father worked in the Planning Department, Gih Dinh Province, Republic of Vietnam, from 1954 to 1965.[4]

At that time, the ROV government began to draft all the youth for military service. I joined the ARVN as an engineering officer. From 1955 to 1957, I worked for the army's defense work at the Long Binh Airport.[5] I got married in 1956 and moved to Thu Duc, Gih Dinh Province [present-day's Ho Chi Minh City].[6] I found an office job in the provincial government while I still served as an army reserve officer.

From 1957 to 1973, I worked at the Transportation Department as the chief of construction projects. I was involved in many projects, including many building auctions, project bidding, and construction contracts. Many contractors and companies tried to get one of these government construction deals. In order to get their contracts, many of them brought gifts to my home, or offered cash to my family. With my father as my role model, I didn't accept any bribery or personal favor. I didn't like corruption. I told them that I had a salary, and I worked for the government. I said to every-

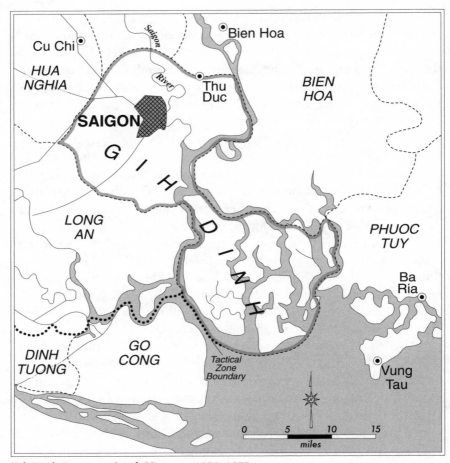

Gih Dinh Province, South Vietnam, 1955–1975

body, "If I can help, I will. It depends on the fairness and project, not personal relations or kickbacks." My father saw what I was doing. He was very proud of me. I was not just following his steps, but also setting up the good example for my own kids. My first daughter was born in 1957.

But the corruption as a common practice had been part of the governmental system. Many of my colleagues believed that they were underpaid, and that they didn't have any retirement or any future since the war didn't go very well in the 1960s. Their only hope was to save some money to buy a passport and a foreign visa, in order to send their family members overseas. Then they could leave Vietnam and join their family later in case the

South lost the war. I saw my officemates making under-table deals, playing personal favors, signing illegal contracts, stealing the construction materials, and even transferring government funds to private accounts.

I understood why some of them had to do this. They got their jobs in the government through some kind of personal connection. When they were in the office, they needed to return the favor to those, usually a higher ranking official, who had helped them get the appointment. They were willing to be used as somebody's tool to serve other people's interests in order to keep the job. Some had spent a fortune for the lucrative job. After in the office, they rushed to cash in to get their money back. It was a corrupted system, in which the government offices served personal interests, rather than the nation's or its people's interests. It was based upon bureaucratic-military cooperation through personal networks and loyalty. It became worse after Pres. Ngo Dinh Diem was assassinated with his brother in a military coup in 1963.[7]

After 1965, we were very busy because many new construction projects were coming. Then the government corruption continued and reached its high level. They made the illegal deals right on the table, not under it like they had done before. They brought the large amount of cash to the office, not to the home as they did before. My colleagues didn't cancel what they were doing. They didn't pretend anymore. They even worked together. After work, they usually went together to the restaurants, bars, and hotels, having parties, ballroom dancing, and an escort service paid by their contractors. There was no more professionalism, not even any moral or ethical value in our office in the 1960s.

I knew I couldn't stop it, but I didn't want to be part of it. They always asked me to go out with them. I always said no. They felt embarrassed and became uneasy with me. They didn't understand that, educated and idealistic, I was still working or fighting for a just society. If we were not better than the Communists, what were we fighting for? Some thought I was stupid, and others considered I was a threat to what they had been doing.

In order to avoid any unnecessary problem in our working place relations, I enrolled in a MBA degree program at Phu Tho University. The program offered evening classes in management and administration. My officemates didn't understand why I needed to go to school every evening after work during the wartime. I just didn't want to be involved in their activities, not see their problems without saying anything. Two years later, I got my MBA degree from Phu Tho University. My father was so proud of me. He knew that it didn't matter what happened around me or in the war, I was still his son, the honest, hard-working person. My father died of cancer in 1966. I never forgot what he said to me, "Family first and keep your family in your heart."

After the American government withdrew its troops from South Vietnam in 1973, the war situation was getting worse every day. So was the working condition in our office. More people tried to make money, or make a living, out of this war. I really had enough of the corruption and bureaucracy in the government. I resigned from my position in 1973.

Through a friend's recommendation, I got a teaching job at Phu Tho University. I taught architecture, building design and construction, and some other classes as a university instructor. Even though this job didn't pay that much, it became the best two years in my entire professional career. At least I could find some fresh air in the polluted world where the war, politics, and corruption worked together. I could enjoy the academic freedom without worrying about the bureaucratic red tape or political accusation.

My teaching career, however, didn't last long. On April 30, 1975, the Communist forces took over the capital city, and the ROV president issued his orders to all the ARVN troops to lay down their weapons and surrender to the NVA and PLAF at their locations. At first I believed that I was lucky to have quit the government job before the fall of Saigon. I might not have to go to jail for my service since I had retired.

The Communist government, however, announced that all the military personnel, government officials, and those who had cooperated with the Americans had to do their time in prison. Soon I was arrested and sent to jail. But I was still lucky to stay in prison for only two years, instead of five to seven years, since I had retired from the active service in the army.

While I suffered a lot in jail, my wife and children encountered hardships. After I was arrested, my house and properties in Hoa Hung were seized by the Communist government. My wife had to take our children to live with one of her relatives. My elder daughter and son were expelled from their universities because their father had served in the enemy forces and government. They joined my wife, working as manual laborers to support the family.

I was released from the jail in June 1977. After my release, I talked to my wife about our family future. It became apparent that there was not much left for us in this country under the Communist authorities. As a former enemy official, there was no trust, no good job, but a "bad profile" for me for the rest of my life. My problems would have a negative impact on my kids as well. They didn't have much future either. We needed to leave Vietnam.

Through a friend's connection, I found a boat owner who was willing to sail refugees out of the country. We had to pay him up front three ounces of gold for each person to get on his boat. We sold everything and put together only nine ounces of gold, enough for three persons. Who was leaving Vietnam first? It was a painful but realistic decision. We decided that I would take my eldest son and eldest daughter with me. They might be old enough to survive out of the country. My wife stayed in Vietnam with the other five kids.

In December 1977, I took two children with me, leaving our home. We got on a small fishing boat at the beach with three hundred people. It was very crowded with men, women, and kids, seated against each other like sardines in a can. The boat owner warned us that there was no talk, no move, and no baby cry. Escaping from the country was illegal. If the Communist patrol gunboat found us, they would open fire and kill us all in the sea. Nervous and quiet, we didn't say anything while the boat left the beach and sailed into the ocean in the middle of the night. This was my second escape from Communist-controlled Vietnam.

At dawn, we were told that we had left the territorial waters of Vietnam and that we were in the international waters now. Everybody was so happy, hugging each other and laughing loudly, as if we had gotten our freedom. It was actually not yet.

All the boat owner did was to take the refugees to the international waters [high sea, outside of the twelve-mile territorial waters of Vietnam]. Then, we, the "boat people," just waited there. We had to wait for an international cargo ship to come to our rescue. According to international navigation law, all the ships should rescue the wrecked boat and the people on board. Hopefully, the rescue ship would take us to a free country.

We waited for one day. The weather was nice, and the South China Sea was quiet. I checked on my kids, who were in as good a spirits as the others. Day two, some little babies became sick due to the hot weather and cried a lot. Day three, some of the boat people were running out of food and water. They begged others to help their small kids. Nobody wanted to help because they didn't know how long we had to wait in the ocean. I offered a little help. I could tell from their eyes that my children didn't blame me for giving away our own water and food. Instead they were proud of me.

It proved later that I was wrong. Days four and five, there was no ship showing up at all. The people became impatient and worried. Some women became crazy when their babies were very sick. They wanted to return, but the others insisted to wait. The boat owner said that we would sail back to Vietnam on the seventh day, if there was no ship or rain.

The sixth day was the worst day for all the boat people. We had no more food and, more importantly, no water. I worried about my daughter, since she had the fever for days. The medicine we took with us didn't work at all. She just needed some water, which we didn't have. One woman passed out when her sick baby died. They just wrapped the body in some newspapers and threw her into the ocean. More kids were sick. Some adults were sick, too. Some guys started a fight over a bottle of water. One of them was cut badly by a knife. Again, there was again no ship or rain.

"A ship, a ship!" I was awaked by cheers early on the morning of the seventh day. It was a cargo ship! It was so big, beautiful, and coming our way. The boat owner launched an emergency signal. Everybody shouted and waved, with tears in many people's eyes. I held my daughter up and let her share this moment. She smiled without saying any word.

While the ship was getting closer, the cheers suddenly came to a stop. The enthusiasm was freezing down to a chill. We saw the Soviet flag on the top of the ship! It was a Soviet ship. The Soviet Union, as a Communist country, had supported the Vietnamese Communist government during and after the war. "Are they firing on us?" my son asked me quietly when the ship approached our boat. It was worse. The Soviet captain sent his sailor/soldiers to our boat and took all of us back to Vietnam.

We were back in Vietnam! Nevertheless, although fleeing the country was a crime according to the Communist government, it was during its second year of reconstruction, when it didn't have facilities or manpower to contain the boat people like they would do later after 1978. We left the harbor and accepted the boat owner's offer, that he would make a second try without additional charge.

Most of us were back on his boat for the second time. Some didn't make it. We brought with us a lot of food and water this time. On the third day of our second sail, a container ship from Panama rescued us and took us to Malaya [now Malaysia]. We were so lucky since we saw and heard a lot of "boat people" died in the storms, were robbed or raped by pirates, or committed suicide in the oceans. They never had a chance to reach the land of freedom.

The Malayan government had set up several refugee camps on three islands since a large number of Vietnamese boat people were arriving daily. The Malayan officials worked with the U.S. refugee agents in the camps. We were registered, had physical checkups, and also filled out the applications for humanitarian organization programs sponsored by the U.S. government to help the South Vietnamese prisoners of war.

In 1978, my application was approved by the U.S. government, and I came to the United States of America. My third escape was a happy journey with my two kids to the United States. We settled in California. To support my kids, I worked a full-time job in an electrical company and a part-time job in the evenings and weekends. I also tried to improve my English by going to a Catholic church language school for immigrants. In 1982, my son finally graduated from a college in California. I was so glad that I could bring to my children a better life. But I still worried about my wife and other five kids in Vietnam. In 1997, I eventually made a trip back to see my wife and other children. They have been always in my heart.[8]

Chapter 22

Chinese Railroad Engineering Operations

Col. Hou Zhenlu and his regiment had been busy working in Vietnam for five years, from 1965 to 1970, as China's railroad engineering troops. They fought hard to keep rail transportation moving as Beijing supplied Hanoi throughout the Vietnam War. From 1965 to 1973, China shipped to Vietnam 1.86 million small arms, 60,000 artillery pieces, 16 million artillery shells, 1.1 billion rounds of ammunition, 15,000 vehicles, 552 tanks, 320 armored vehicles, 155 airplanes, 148 naval vessels, 180 surface-to-air missiles, and many other weapons and pieces of equipment, including communication and command equipment, medical instruments, missile radars and launchers, engineering equipment, and repair and rebuilding facilities. All of these weapons and equipment could arm 2 million men.[1] China also took care of most of the NVA's logistics, including food, clothing, fuel, and many other supplies. According to one of the agreements signed by the NVA and the PLA, for example, the Chinese would provide each Vietnamese soldier 800 grams of rice, 80 grams of meat, 30 grams of fish, and other food items every day. The Chinese also agreed to provide three sets of uniforms and three pairs of shoes for each Vietnamese soldier every year. The estimated value of the Chinese aid during these years was about $5 billion.

During the U.S. Operation Rolling Thunder, a massive bombing campaign against North Vietnam, railroads were the primary targets for U.S. air strikes. As the American attacks intensified, they cut major rail lines and made Hanoi desperate for help. According to Chinese intelligence, U.S. air raids paralyzed the five main railroads in North Vietnam, totaling 1,100 kilometers. Rail shipping totaled only one hundred tons a day in April 1965, much less than the minimum of three thousand tons a day needed for North Vietnam. The Chinese report suggested building three new east-west railway lines linking the two major north-south railroads; moving the train stations out of the cities, where they were vulnerable to U.S. air strikes; and replacing all the outdated Vietnamese rails with new standard rails. Without these urgent improvements, the report warned, the existing Vietnamese railroads would not be able to deliver Chinese and Soviet military aid to the front lines.[2]

Upon Ho Chi Minh's request in May 1965, Mao Zedong agreed to send the Chinese railroad engineering troops to North Vietnam to keep the railways open. On June 9, 1965, the First Division of the Chinese railroad engineering troops began to enter North Vietnam, and numbered 30,000 men by July. As a regiment commander in the First Division, Colonel Hou's story explains the plans and operations of the Chinese troops, their problems, and their learning experience in China's longest foreign war.[3]

Col. Hou Zhenlu

Sixtieth Regiment, First Railroad Engineering Division, Railroad Engineering Corps, PLA (China)

I was born in 1925 in Shandong Province, China, and joined the Chinese Communist army during World War II. Fighting against Japan's occupation, I served as a private and later as a sergeant in the PLA. In the Chinese Civil War of 1946–1949, I became a lieutenant and participated in the Shanghai offensive campaign in the spring of 1949. When China sent its troops to the Korean War, my unit, the 174th Regiment, Fifty-eighth Division, Twentieth Army, Ninth Army Corps, was part of the second wave, which entered Korea in November 1950, fighting against the UN/U.S. forces. Later that month, we engaged with the U.S. First Marine Division at the Chosin Reservoir, one of the bloodiest battles in the Korean War. In 1952, I was promoted to captain. When we returned back to China in 1953, the PLA high command told us that we had won the Korean War, and taught America a hard lesson. They won't bother China anymore. We won't have to fight another war against America. I never thought, nobody did, that China would fight America again in the Vietnam War twelve years later.

In 1958, when the PLA established the Railroad Engineering Corps, I was transferred to the PLA-REC and promoted to major. My battalion as a railroad construction unit participated in the construction of the railways in 1959–1962, preparing a cross-strait campaign against Taiwan and other enemy-held offshore islands. In 1963, however, we began to receive information on the war situation in Vietnam. In 1964, we heard some rumors that China might send its troops to Vietnam to support the Vietnamese Communists fighting American forces.

It became official in early 1965 when the PLA high command started its mobilization of the troops for the Vietnam War. On April 17, the CCP Central Military Commission [CMC] issued the orders to establish the "Chinese Volunteer Forces for Aiding Vietnam and Resisting America." Following the CMC orders, the General Staff established three forces of the Chinese Volunteer Forces the next day.[4] Among the others was the "Chinese People's Volunteer Engineering Force" [CPVEF], including the PLA's railway engineering, civil engineering, and communication troops. The CPVEF had five divisions, with the railway engineering troops as the First Division.[5]

Having selected the best engineering units from eleven railway engineering divisions in the PLA Railway Engineering Corps, the First Division included eight railway engineering regiments, one railway prospecting team, and a dozen antiaircraft artillery battalions, about 30,000 troops,[6] with Gen. Long Guilin as the commander, Guo Yenlin the political commissar, and Li Qingde the deputy commissar. My battalion was part of the selected troops in the First Division. Our main tasks were to construct and improve the railways, train stations, bridges, and tunnels in North Vietnam; build warehouses, telephone lines, underwater cables, and communication centers for the NVA commands; construct antiaircraft defense, antiflood works, and commanding headquarters for the NVA troops; protect them from U.S. bombing; and repair them in case of any damage to guarantee railway transportation and communication between China and Vietnam.[7]

On April 27, the Chinese government signed the first agreement with the North Vietnamese delegation in Beijing regarding the dispatch of Chinese troops to Vietnam to construct new railways and repair railroads north of Hanoi. According to this agreement, China would also supply Vietnam with transportation equipment and all the construction materials needed for railway building and repairs. Thereafter, more agreements followed, including one hundred projects for new railways, train stations, and distribution centers construction and reconstruction. In total, the Chinese would maintain 554 out of 1,100 kilometers, almost one-half of the railways in North Vietnam.[8]

From June 23, 1965, the CPVEF's First Division, about 30,000 troops in two groups, began to cross the borders from Youyiguan in the east and Hekou in the west. Youyiguan is a Chinese border city in Guangxi Province, about 180 kilometers from Hanoi. After entering Vietnam, our group in the east traveled south along the Youyiguan-Hanoi line. The western group traveled south along the Lao Cai-Hanoi line. Lao Cai is a Vietnamese city in Bao Thang, across the border from Hekou, Yunnan Province, about 230 kilometers to Hanoi. Both deployed their troops along the two major rail lines and began their reconstruction and repair works in North Vietnam.

We were regular Chinese troops as engineering units, but not wearing PLA uniforms. We wore blue worker uniforms with no Chinese badges during the mission in Vietnam. By March 1966, China had dispatched 130,000 troops to Vietnam.[9] Later, the CPVEF became part of the "Chinese Supporting Forces" [CSF], which included all of the Chinese railway engineering, civil engineering, antiaircraft artillery, and logistics divisions in Vietnam. Unlike the artillery divisions, which were rotated back to China after twelve to eighteen months in Vietnam, our railway engineering division stayed for five years, until June 1970.

Continuous U.S. air raids remained our major issue. The division command categorized the U.S. air strikes into three different phases. The first phase that began in July 1965 and lasted until June 1966 became known as "intermittent bombing." The U.S. airplanes bombed each target with a short intermission of seven days. According to the division statistics, during these twelve months, the U.S. Air Force launched 99 air raids with 576 waves, totaling 2,165 sorties, against 355 targets along the 554-kilometer Chinese sections of the railways. The U.S. airplanes dropped 2,178 bombs, 327 of which hit the targets, about 15 percent. The second phase, from July 1966 to May 1967, was categorized as the "continuous bombing." The U.S. airplanes raided and bombed almost every day without any break. The air raids totaled 323 in these eleven months, with 2,891 waves, including 9,262 sorties. The U.S. airplanes dropped 5,992 bombs against 815 targets, and 960 bombs, or 16 percent, hit the targets. The third phase, from June 1967 to March 1968, the "bombing in waves" phase, was the heaviest of all the years. The air raids averaged twice a day, in some cases five times a day. The

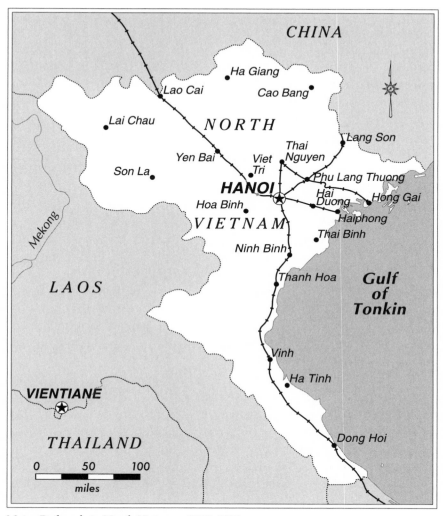

Major Railroads in North Vietnam, 1965–1973

U.S. Air Force launched 545 air raids with 1,744 waves, totaling 12,000 sorties against 1,369 targets. The airplanes dropped 18,000 bombs, and 2,241, about 12.4 percent, hit the targets. For the Chinese sections, about 180 out of 554 kilometers of the railways were destroyed or damaged, more than 30 percent.[10] The U.S. air strikes against the Chinese troops were much heavier than we had experienced during the Korean War.

As Korean War veterans, our commanding officers asked the troops to build the headquarters in the caves along the mountain ranges. All the troop living quarters had to be away from the worksites, warehouses, and rail lines. Each battalion had its own air-defense team with antiaircraft artillery and machine guns. Each company had its own outposts and warning system connected with the division warning network. As our antiaircraft defense capability increased, the U.S. bombing hit target percentage reduced from 15.9 percent in 1965, down to 14.6 percent in 1966, 13.3 percent in 1967, and 9.5 percent in 1968.[11]

The U.S. bombing almost cut off the two major rail lines, the Hanoi-Youyiguan (or He-You, the eastern line) and Hanoi-Lao Cai (or He-Lao, the northwestern line) railroads. When the Chinese railway engineering troops arrived in late June 1965, many parts of the railways were severely damaged and not functioning. Moreover, the tracks were French-built meter gauge [1,000 mm] rails, and hard to be replaced. The division command decided to reconstruct these two old railways with the standard track gauge [1,435 mm] by adding the third rail to the meter gauge tracks. We called the new railways the "three legs tracks," which could double the shipping capacity by using both Vietnamese and standard locomotives and cargo cars. Meanwhile, the rail transports continued without interruption during the railway makeovers.

On July 7, reconstruction began. Our division concentrated its troops on one part at a time. Thus, their antiaircraft defense teams could guard the section from air raid and sabotage. After finishing one section, then the troops moved on to another. The most difficult task was reconstructing bridges. These two lines had 196 bridges, including 61 large- and medium-size bridges, totaling 5,262 meters, over many rivers in the North. The bridge battalions had to reconstruct each bridge before the additional third rail could be added.

By December 23, 1965, our division had completed reconstruction of 363 kilometers of two rail lines by spending 757,500 work days. The reconstruction significantly increased shipping capacity. In our eastern section, the Hanoi-Youyiguan line almost doubled its annual transport capacity, an increase from 1.4 million tons to 2.8 million tons. The reconstruction also improved these two railroads by adding dozens of new train stations, bridges, and tunnels.

Our division headquarters also designed a new strategic, standard gauge railroad between Kep and Thai Nguyen to serve as an east-west circuitous supplementary link between the Hanoi-Thai Nguyen and Hanoi-Youyiguan north-south lines. The new railway line, fifty-five kilometers long and serving as a wartime railroad, traversed mountains and forest. The First Division had to construct four tunnels, totaling 4.7 kilometers, four train stations, and several bridges along the Kep-Thai Nguyen [or Ke-Tai, central] line. Our division began the construction in October 1965 and finished it on December 2, 1966, with a total of 1.5 million work days. The construction established a rail network north of Hanoi. According to Chinese statistics, when the last unit of the division left Vietnam in June 1970, the division had completed 117 kilometers of new railway lines and established twenty new railway stations.

According to the agreements, the Chinese railway engineering force maintained, repaired, and improved the four major railroads north of Hanoi, including Hanoi-Youyiguan, Hanoi-Lao Cai, Kep-Thai Nguyen, and Dung-Thai lines, totaling 554 kilometers. Our division also built numerous emergency bridges, detour lines, bypass links, totaling ninety-eight kilometers. We also constructed many defense works and underground warehouses along the four major railroads to guarantee the shipment and communication despite the heavy U.S. bombing. We had built thirty-nine new rail bridges, fourteen tunnels, and laid eight kilometers of underwater cable.

Our railway engineering troops provided emergency repairs to all the damage north of Hanoi along the four major railroads after each bombing. We applied lessons learned during the Korean War with rushed repairs on the damaged railways during and after the U.S. air raids. According to our division's estimates, from June 1965 to October 1968, the American airplanes dropped 288,000 bombs along these railways. In the peak month of June 1967, the American planes dropped 9.6 tons of ordnance per kilometer of these railways, and 2.5–6.3 tons per meter of the major railway bridges. Chinese antiaircraft defenses and their railway repair were inextricably intertwined.

Heavy bombing forced the division command to modify its original plan to keep all the railroads working. The new plan focused on keeping the northern lines open. On August 11, 1967, the U.S. Air Force heavily bombed the Long Bien Bridge (or Paul Dewey Bridge), one of the most important railway bridges north of Hanoi. The French-built 1,681 meters-long bridge was seriously damaged by the bombing. Some Soviet experts estimated a minimum of three months to repair the bridge and reopen to the rail traffic. The NVA headquarters requested our division to repair the bridge. The division sent one bridge battalion and an engineering company, totaling one thousand troops. Despite frequent air raids, the Chinese troops worked day and night and completed their repair within eighteen days. On September 30, the rail traffic resumed over the bridge. Later the bridge was bombed again and was out for 186 days. However, since the bridge battalion had built one temporary bridge and two ferries to cross the river, the railway transport was interrupted only for four days.

Between August 1965 and February 1969, the First Division had accomplished 1,178 repair missions for damaged railways and facilities, disarmed 3,100 time-delay bombs, rebuilt 157 kilometers of destroyed railway tracks, built 39 new rail bridges, constructed 14 tunnels, laid 8 kilometers of underwater cable, and repaired 1,420 kilometers of railroad telephone lines. I was promoted to colonel in 1969 in the Vietnam War.

The First Division, like other Chinese divisions, however, still suffered casualties from continuing U.S. air raids. We lost 297 officers and men to the air strikes. During a railway repair job right after an air raid, for instance, the Fifth Regiment lost more than twenty officers and soldiers to an undiscovered time bomb. In the meantime, 1,634 men were wounded by bombing, including the commander. On August 21, 1966, General Long, commander of the First Division, rode in a jeep with his staff, guards, and translator. U.S. aircraft attacked his vehicle while they were on their way from the headquarters to a worksite along Route 1. His staff and driver were killed, and Long was wounded. His guard, also wounded, took him to a nearby NVA field hospital and saved his life. On August 24, General Long returned to China and was hospitalized for a year.[12] Our troops stayed in Vietnam until 1970.

Conclusion

Perspectives on the War

The cold war globalized the Vietnam War, leading a number of countries to send forces to support either the Communist North or the anti-Communist South. For both sides, the international contributions became part of their efforts for victory. By 1968, Communist military cooperation had made the PLAF and NVA stronger and more capable of attacking the U.S. and ARVN units in the South. In the meantime, however, China demonstrated the limits to its cooperation when its army suddenly terminated military operations and withdrew all of its troops from Vietnam. Chinese leaders never considered military cooperation a separate issue from their relationship with the Russians. The stories reveal how the American escalation put more pressure on the Communist coalition and worsened relations between Beijing and Moscow.

Hanoi recognized the competition between Moscow and Beijing for the leadership in the Asian Communist movement. Each claimed a position as a key supporter of the Vietnamese Communists' struggle against the American invasion. The Vietnamese welcomed both Chinese and Soviet troops into North Vietnam, increasing the competition between the two Communist giants. American intelligence never fully understood the nature and seriousness of the Sino-Soviet rivalry. Intelligence chiefs had predicted a possible improvement in the relationship between Moscow and Beijing during the Vietnam War. In September 1965, a Special National Intelligence Estimate (SNIE) argued that with rapidly increasing demands for air defense in North Vietnam, "China will need Soviet support and protection. Greater Soviet involvement might reluctantly be desired to deter the U.S. This is an additional factor likely to promote a constructive resolution of previous Sino-Soviet frictions over the speed, scope, and method of aiding Hanoi and bolstering South China bases."[1] It is evident in these chapters that the Chinese and Soviet air defenses in North Vietnam against America's Rolling Thunder air campaign did not improve their relations. Chinese and Russian officers never united to support Vietnam, which instead became another battleground between the two contesting Communist states.

To obtain the maximum material support for its war effort, the DRV tried to maintain a neutral position in the Sino-Soviet rivalry. The serious competition between the Chinese and Soviets generated more material, financial, and military technology with which the PLAF and NVA could modernize their forces. According to the stories, one of the primary advances in Viet Cong military organization was the establishment of local units based on village structure to mobilize the peasants in the South. Even though the Viet Cong was rich in manpower, the peasant soldiers were illiterate and poorly trained. The PLAF's command structure was chaotic, and often favored personal relationships and local interests. In the mid-1960s, however, the Viet Cong incorporated many new factors into their military organization, including Russian and Chinese arms and Northern officers to train the peasant soldiers. In addition, the PLAF troops gained battlefield experience. By the Tet Offensive of 1968, the PLAF and NVA had experienced some important transformations in terms of command, organization, operation, logistics, and training in South Vietnam. Some of this book's accounts reflect how the PLAF and NVA changed from a peasant, guerrilla army into a regular army by expanding its operations. The Viet Cong command shifted from local to regional defense, from small- to large-scale operations that became more offensive and aggressive in nature. As the war progressed, more and more local troops joined major operations with North Vietnamese troops.

Another important factor was that large numbers of the Northern Communist troops, including some of the best NVA units, infiltrated into the South through the 1960s. A few chapters reinforce evidence that these troops were trained and armed by the Chinese and Russians. Many of their officers were seasoned veterans of the French Indochina War and familiar with the South. The NVA command eventually replaced the PLAF command in South Vietnam in the late 1960s, and after the Tet Offensive the PLAF was integrated with the NVA. Between 1963 and 1975, the NVA and PLAF mobilized more than 8 million Communist troops against the United States, ARVN, and their allies. They suffered an estimated 4 million casualties, including 1 million military deaths.[2]

The Vietnamese Communist forces had previously fought in wars against Japan and France, but they knew little about American forces. The combat experience the NVA gained against the U.S. forces bolstered the Vietnamese military modernization in accordance with the Chinese and Russian models. After the conclusion of the Tet Offensive, the NVA high command began to emphasize the role of technology and firepower. In the early 1970s, the NVA increased the number of special units, such as artillery, tank, engineering, and missile regiments, with available Soviet military resources. Eventually, they were moving away from their traditional people's war and instead engaged in mobile warfare and strategic attacks with stronger fire support and better infantry training. The Vietnam War thus began Vietnam's military modernization. In this respect, the United States turned out to be a "useful adversary" in the Vietnam War.[3]

The Communist military coalition, however, did not survive the Paris peace negotiations that began in May 1968. On November 17, Chinese chairman Mao Zedong suggested to Vietnam's Premier Pham in Beijing that some of the Chinese troops withdraw back to China.[4] After further discussions between the NVA and the PLA, the Chinese troops began returning to China in March 1969.[5] By July 1970, all of the Chinese AAA troops had withdrawn. One of the Vietnamese leaders later recalled that "I know the [VWP] Party had long ago decided to form an alliance with the Soviet Union. The movement in this direction started way back in 1969, and the passing away of Ho Chi Minh paved the way for officially making the decision. However, there was no open declaration, because Chinese assistance was still needed."[6]

The Vietnamese Communists' victory was a direct result not only of international Communist military support, but also of the political and social circumstances in the South. The South Vietnamese stories tell us that the military cooperation between the United States and ARVN did not intend to militarize the Southern population. Instead, it intended to protect the population by separating them from the war and relocating the peasants from their villages. Unfortunately, many Vietnamese peasants did not want to leave their homes and the land they had farmed for generations. The increasing rural resistance by the peasants undermined the grassroots support for the South Vietnamese government and ARVN troops. More and more peasants and their families turned to the Viet Cong for help and fought against ARVN troops.

American soldiers in South Vietnam were often critical of the performance of the ARVN. Even though the majority of the South Vietnamese were not sure about the Communists' taking over, they desperately wanted an end of the American War and some long due political reforms. They did not fully support their government. As a result, judging from these recollections, the RVN failed to act as a nation with the same degree of patriotic mobilization as the North. It appears that failure in nation-building cost the South Vietnamese state its legitimacy. With America's increasing support from the late 1950s, the RVN had a chance to promote major reforms short of revolution; its failure contributed to the rise of the NLF and PLAF in the South in 1960. For the South Vietnamese, the most important problems of the war were not military, but connected to political and economic developments.

The RVN government's refusal to reform and its brutal suppression of the peasant and student movements alienated many ARVN soldiers and shook their loyalty. Moreover, the young recruits, as seen in earlier chapters, were further disillusioned by their commanding officers' corruption, mismanagement, and, worst of all, failure against the Communist insurgency. Religious diversity and urban-rural gaps further separated the men from the officer corps. Lacking enthusiasm and low in morale, the ARVN veterans stated that they felt like they were fighting a war for their commanders, government, and the Americans, rather than themselves and the Vietnamese people. The Americanization of the ARVN in the early 1970s led to its dependence on the U.S. forces. Most of the veterans agreed that the ARVN troops needed a strong fighting spirit, and that having one could have brought about a different result for their country. However, the corruption in the bureaucracy and battlefield failure proved the ARVN could not protect its government and South Vietnam from further attacks by the PLAF and NVA. Its assumed failure and incompetence influenced the Johnson administration's military escalation of the Vietnam War in order to help the hopeless South Vietnamese.

If the South Vietnamese Army had problems in the early 1960s, so did the American armed forces that came to its rescue. From the beginning, the U.S. policy was aimed to support the government and ARVN in their fight against the Communist aggression. Nearly 80 percent of U.S. aid was military support through the 1960s. The U.S. spent at least $180 billion in Vietnam, Cambodia, and Laos.[7] Nevertheless, from 1963 to 1973, the American military found itself engaged in a "limited war" against a "total war" of the Communist world. According to the veterans, the U.S. forces utilized military technology and firepower, especially air power, in most battles. This allowed them to both minimize casualties and draw on the vast industrial and technological capacity of the United States.

American air power forced the PLAF and NVA to take to the jungle, hills, and mountains, and they found tremendous difficulties supplying their troops due to frequent air raids and bombing. During most of the 1960s, the Communist troops had to employ hit-and-run guerrilla tactics, harassing the Americans and ARVN to make the war as costly as possible for their enemies, while protecting their bases and population. This defensive strategy prolonged the war and eroded the morale and fighting spirit of the American troops.

As Vietnam's terrain differed from that of previous wars, so did the soldiers. Early in the conflict, the U.S. Army fielded the best-trained and -equipped force in its history. Units initially deployed together. Having trained together Stateside, they possessed the cohesion needed in combat. According to our stories, however, as the war escalated, it became an army of replacements. This resulted from one of the war's most controversial legacies, the rotation system. Unlike the soldiers of World War II, who only went home upon death, severe wounds, or the end of the war, the soldiers in Vietnam served a one-year tour of duty. The policy resulted from a desire to limit U.S. casualties.[8] Though sound in theory, the policy affected unit cohesion. An infantry unit conceivably underwent a complete change in a ten-month time span. With the constant rotation of troops in and out of Vietnam, combined with injuries and deaths, a different group of soldiers fought each year of the war. One consistent complaint among veterans concerned the lack of *esprit de corps*. Pride and a sense of belonging are key components of effective military units. Without sustained membership in the units, however, this proved difficult to obtain.

At home, the prolonged war fueled political instability and an antiwar movement. All of the U.S. veterans mentioned that, after the Tet Offensive, a majority of Americans began to question the U.S. war policy toward Vietnam. More and more American people believed that the U.S. government had made a mistake in sending troops to Vietnam. Soon the public disaffection grew into political crisis in the government. In March of 1968, President Johnson announced that he would not seek reelection. The presidential candidates from both parties promised their voters that, if they won, they would bring the war to an end. After the failure of the Vietnamization effort by the Nixon administration in 1969–1971, the U.S. government decided to end its military cooperation with the ARVN and RVN government through a peace settlement with the Communists. In early October 1972, Secretary of State Henry Kissinger and the North Vietnamese negotiators finally reached an agreement that provided for U.S. withdrawal sixty days after a cease-fire, the return of American POWs, and some political arrangements in the South. On January 27, 1973, the North Vietnamese and American governments signed the Paris Accord. The last American troops were pulled out of South Vietnam by March. More than 58,000 Americans had died in the long war, and over 313,000 more had been wounded.[9] Many Americans at home seemed more relieved that it finally had ended than worried about what would happen to South Vietnam thereafter.

During the Paris peace negotiations in 1968–1973, Moscow further strengthened its military and economic assistance to Hanoi. From 1969 to 1971, the Soviet Union signed seven economic and military aid agreements with North Vietnam.[10] After the American withdrawal in 1973, the Soviet Union continued its material and military support to North Vietnam, which was winning the war against the South. On April 30, 1975, the NVA streamed into Saigon and claimed victory in the long civil war. After the war, Moscow's continuing commitment to Vietnam further drained Soviet resources. In the meantime, the Soviet threat and conflicts pushed the Chinese leaders to improve their relations with the United States. Their strategic needs eventually led to the normalization of the Sino-American relationship in the 1970s. In terms of the impact it had upon East Asia and the global cold war, the Sino-American rapprochement dramatically shifted the balance of power between the two superpowers. While policymakers in Washington found it possible to concentrate more of America's resources and strategic attention on the Soviet Union, Moscow's leaders, having to confront the West and China simultaneously, seriously overextended the Soviet Union's strength and power.

Notes

Introduction

1. The two-day tour of Ho Chi Minh City (formerly Saigon), Vietnam, took place in May 2006. Mr. Huynh Van No was our local guide.

2. Interviews by the author in Ho Chi Minh City, Vietnam, in June 2006. Staff Sergeant No belonged to the First Battalion, Third Regiment, ARVN An Giang Provincial Command, in the Vietnam War.

3. Interviews by the author at St. Paul, Minnesota, in February 2003. Lt. Nguyen Yen Xuan served in C Company, Second Battalion, Airborne Division, ARVN, in the war.

4. Each chapter includes a list for further reading on the specific topic, such as the ARVN, NVA, Viet Cong, U.S. Rolling Thunder, or the Chinese forces, in the endnotes. It provides some information on recently published personal memoirs, oral history, and scholarly books.

5. For the details of the Soviet aid, see Li Danhui, "The Sino-Soviet Dispute over Assistance for Vietnam's Anti-American War, 1965–1972," http://www.shen-zhihua.net/ynzz/000123.htm, 4–5. Her source is Foreign Trade Bureau, "Minutes of Meeting between Chinese and Vietnamese Transportation Delegates," July 26, 1965, International Liaison Division Records, *PRC Ministry of Railway Administration Archives,* Beijing, China.

6. Li, "The Sino-Soviet Dispute over Assistance for Vietnam's Anti-American War, 1965–1972," 1–2.

7. Ilya V. Gaiduk, *The Soviet Union and the Vietnam War* (Chicago: Univ. of Chicago Press, 1996), 59.

8. Guo Ming, *Zhongyue guanxi yanbian sishinian* (Uncertain Relations between China and Vietnam, 1949–1989) (Nanning: Guangxi renmin chubanshe [Guangxi People's Press], 1992), 103.

9. Chen Jian and Xiaobing Li, "China and the End of the Global Cold War," conference paper for the "Fifth Cold War Conference Series: From Détente to the Soviet Collapse" at the First Division Museum at Cantigny, Wheaton, Illinois, October 12, 2005.

10. Chen Jian and Xiaobing Li, "China and the End of the Cold War," in *From Détente to the Soviet Collapse: The Cold War from 1975 to 1991,* ed. Malcolm Muir Jr., 121 (Lexington: Virginia Military Institute, 2005).

11. For more detailed discussions, see Niu Jun, "Mao Zedong's Crisis Conception and Origins of the Sino-Soviet Alliance's Collapse," in *Lengzhan yu zhongguo* (The Cold War and China), ed. Zhang Baijia and Niu Jun, 273–296 (Beijing: Shijie zhishi chubanshe [World Knowledge Publishing], 2002).

12. China had provided a total of 6.7 billion yuan in foreign aid by 1963. The

foreign aid consisted of about 2 percent of China's annual national expenditure. National Bureau of the Foreign Economy and Liaison, *Report on the Current Foreign Aid and Request for More Foreign Aid in the Future* (Beijing, China), September 1, 1961.

13. Up to 1967, the military and economic aid from the Communist states had totaled 1.6 billion rubles (Russian currency), or about $1.6 billion. Russian aid was valued at 547 million rubles, 34.2 percent of the total, while the Chinese aid was worth 666 million rubles, about 41.6 percent. See Gaiduk, *The Soviet Union and the Vietnam War,* 58, 264 n. 4.

14. Shuguang Zhang, "Beijing's Aid to Hanoi and the United States-China Confrontations, 1964–1968," in *Behind the Bamboo Curtain: China, Vietnam, and the World beyond Asia,* ed. Priscilla Roberts, 271 (Stanford, Calif.: Stanford Univ. Press, 2006).

15. Zhang Aiping et al., *Zhongguo renmin jiefangjun* (The Chinese People's Liberation Army) (Beijing: Dangdai zhongguo chubanshe [Contemporary China Press], 1994), 1:274, 276. Also see Han Huaizhi, *Dangdai zhongguo jundui de junshi gongzuo* (Contemporary Chinese Military Affairs) (Beijing: Zhongguo shehui kexue chubanshe [China Social Sciences Press], 1989), 1:70, 540, 557; and Xiao Shizhong, "An Important Military Operation to Put Out Flames of War in Indochina," in Military History Research Division, China Academy of Military Science, ed., *Junqi piaopiao: xinzhongguo 50 nian junshi dashi shushi* (PLA Flag Fluttering: Facts of China's Major Military Events in the Past Fifty Years) (Beijing: Jiefangjun chubanshe [PLA Press], 1999), 2:451.

16. Qu Aiguo, Bao Mingrong, and Xiao Zuyue, eds., *Yuanyue kangmei: zhongguo zhiyuan budui zai yuenan* (Aid Vietnam and Resist America: China's Volunteer Forces in Vietnam) (Beijing: Junshi kexue chubanshe [Military Science Press], 1995), 12.

17. Gaiduk, *The Soviet Union and the Vietnam War,* 16–18.

18. Jung Chang and Jon Halliday, *Mao: The Unknown Story* (New York: Knopf, 2005), 357.

19. Spencer C. Tucker, *Vietnam* (Lexington: Univ. Press of Kentucky, 1999), 133.

20. Interviews by the author in Chengde, Hebei Province, China, in July 2006. Maj. Guo Haiyun was the chief of staff, Second Battalion, First Regiment, Sixty-fourth AAA Division, of China's PLA in the Vietnam War.

21. One noted oral history book, for example, *Patriots: The Vietnam War Remembered from All Sides,* does include one Russian story (about two pages), told by Sergei Khrushchev, son of the Soviet leader Khrushchev. Nevertheless, Sergei lived in Moscow through the war. See Christian G. Appy, *Patriots: The Vietnam War Remembered from All Sides* (New York: Viking, 2003), 87–89.

22. Interviews by the author at the International Conference on "Intelligence in the Vietnam War," Texas Tech University, Lubbock, Texas, in October 2006; the other interviews were by the author in Silver Spring, Maryland, in September 2007.

23. For the English publications based upon the Communist sources, see David W. P. Elliott, *The Vietnamese War: Revolution and Social Change in the Mekong Delta, 1930–1975*, concise ed. (New York: M. E. Sharpe, 2007); Qiang Zhai, *China and the Vietnam Wars, 1950–1975* (Chapel Hill: Univ. of North Carolina Press, 2000); Gaiduk, *The Soviet Union and the Vietnam War*; and John Colvin, *Volcano under Snow: Vo Nguyen Giap* (London, England: Quartet Books, 1996).

24. For example, Robert Cowley, ed., *The Cold War: A Military History* (New York: Random House, 2005), and Appy, *Patriots*.

25. The term "Viet Cong" was used by President Diem to label the NLF (National Liberation Front), meaning "Vietnamese Communists," to discredit it. The South Vietnamese Communists and the NLF never used the term "Viet Cong" to describe themselves. The PLAF was the armed force of the NLF. For their publications on NVA and PLAF in English, see Col. Dinh Thi Van, *I Engaged in Intelligence Work* (Hanoi, Vietnam: Gioi Publishers, 2006); Gen. Hoang Van Thai, *How South Viet Nam Was Liberated* (Hanoi, Vietnam: Gioi Publishers, 2005); and Gen. Phung The Tai, *Remembering Uncle Ho: Memories in War Years* (Hanoi, Vietnam: Gioi Publishers, 2005).

26. Fredrik Logevall, "Bringing in the 'Other Side': New Scholarship on the Vietnam War," *Journal of Cold War Studies* 3, no. 3 (fall 2001): 77–93; Mark Bradley and Robert Brigham, "Vietnamese Archives and Scholarship on the Cold War," *Cold War International History Project,* Work Paper 7 (Washington, D.C.: Wilson International Center for Scholars, 1993).

27. For more details on the Western Way of War, see Victor Davis Hanson, *Carnage and Culture* (New York: Anchor Books, 2001), 20–23.

28. Xiaobing Li, *A History of the Modern Chinese Army* (Lexington: Univ. Press of Kentucky, 2007), 53, 55, 66–67.

29. During their stay at the refugee camp in Indonesia in 1978, Tran located Sunny's mother in De Ridder, Louisiana. Tran and Sunny came to America in 1979.

1. A Buddhist Soldier Defends a Catholic Government

1. Interviews by the author in Ho Chi Minh City, Vietnam, in June 2006.

2. For further reading on the ARVN, see Andrew Wiest, *Vietnam's Forgotten Army: Heroism and Betrayal in the ARVN* (New York: New York Univ. Press, 2007); and Robert K. Brigham, *ARVN: Life and Death in the South Vietnamese Army* (Lawrence: Univ. Press of Kansas, 2006).

3. John F. Kennedy's words quoted in Hoang Ngoc Thanh and Than Thi Nhan Duc, *Why the Vietnam War? President Ngo Dinh Diem and the U.S.: His Overthrow and Assassination* (Tuan-Yen and Quan-Viet, Vietnam: Mai-Nam Publishers, 2001), vi.

4. For further reading on the "Strategic Hamlet Program," see Philip E. Catton, *Diem's Final Failure: Prelude to America's War in Vietnam* (Lawrence: Univ.

Press of Kansas, 2002); and Richard A. Hunt, *Pacification: The American Struggle for Vietnam's Hearts and Minds* (Boulder, Colo.: Westview, 1995).

5. George Donelson Moss, *Vietnam: An American Ordeal,* 6th ed. (Upper Saddle River, N.J.: Prentice Hall, 2010), 383–384.

6. Historically, Vietnam was overwhelmingly Buddhist. It is estimated that 66–70 percent of the population were Buddhists, 7 percent Catholics, plus others like Confucianists and Daoists in South Vietnam during the 1960s. See D. R. SarDesai, *Vietnam: Past and Present,* 4th ed. (Boulder, Colo.: Westview, 2005), 82–84, 108.

7. According to some statistics, from the late 1950s to early 1960s, more than 60 percent of the ARVN troops were Buddhist soldiers. See Marilyn B. Young, *The Vietnam Wars, 1945–1990* (New York: HarperCollins, 1991), 167.

8. The ARVN troops were organized at three different levels. The first level was the national force, which equaled about 45 percent of the total troops. The best troops, they numbered 400,000 men in 1968, including thirteen divisions. The second tier was at the regional or provincial level, and represented about 20 percent of the ARVN. Supporting the national units, they stationed in their own provinces under one of the four regional commands. The third tier was at the local or village level, the so-called Popular Forces, or People's Forces. They were farmer-soldiers working to defend their own village and protect the local population from Viet Cong harassment. Mostly in rural areas, they were the least trained and equipped units of the ARVN.

9. The "Strategic Hamlet Program" was designed by the South Vietnamese government to fight against the Viet Cong's "people's war." Viet Cong infiltrated into the villages to mobilize the farmers and collect materials for their guerrilla warfare. In order to stop the Viet Cong's harassments, this program began in 1962 to relocate the villagers into fortified hamlets for their protection and separation from the Communist troops.

10. After the Communists won the war in 1975, Huynh spent seven years in jail because of his military service in the ARVN. He lost his teaching job in the middle school as an English instructor. In the late 1990s, he became a bi-lingual tour guide working for a travel agent in Ho Chi Minh City.

2. Surviving the Bloody Jungle

1. Interviews by the author at St. Paul, Minnesota, in February 2003.

2. The Twenty-third and Airborne divisions which Lt. Nguyen Yen Xuan served belonged to the national forces of the ARVN.

3. Moss, *Vietnam,* table B, 384.

4. For further reading on the ARVN and the South Vietnamese government, see Mark Moyar, *Triumph Forsaken: The Vietnam War, 1954–1965* (New York: Cambridge Univ. Press, 2006).

5. Lieutenant Xuan's family lived in a small town near Ban Me Thuot, Darlac Province.

6. The ARVN Airborne Division was established in December 1965 as one of the best combat divisions. It had an independent command under the direct control of the Joint Chiefs of Staff (JCS).

7. As part of the ARVN general reserve, the Airborne Division moved around all over South Vietnam as reinforcement for other ARVN units. Nevertheless, its headquarters was at Tan Son Nhut.

8. Lieutenant Xuan complained about the lack of American supplies and material support. After 1973, in fact, the U.S. government continued to provide the ARVN with huge financial aid and massive technological support.

9. After the fall of Saigon on April 30, 1975, RVN president Duong Van Minh issued a surrender order to all the ARVN troops.

3. Electronic Reconnaissance vs. Guerrillas

1. Interviews by the author with a graduate student research assistant at Garland, Texas, in May 2003.

2. The two novels were published in Dallas, Taxes, in 1999 and 2002, and the third volume, a poetry collection, was published there in 2000.

3. For further reading on the intelligence during the Vietnam War, see Michael Hiam, *Who the Hell Are We Fighting? The Story of Sam Adams and the Vietnam Intelligence Wars* (Hanover, N.H.: Steerforth, 2006); John Prados, *Safe for Democracy: The Secret Wars of the CIA* (Chicago: Ivan R. Dee, 2006); and Harold P. Ford, *CIA and the Vietnam Policymakers: Three Episodes, 1962–1968* (Springfield, Va.: Center for the Study of Intelligence, Central Intelligence Agency, 1998).

4. For further reading on the military intelligence in the Vietnam War, see George Allen, *None So Blind: A Personal Account of the Intelligence Failure in Vietnam* (Chicago: Ivan R. Dee, 2001); Timothy Castle, *One Day Too Long: Top Secret Site 85 and the Bombing of North Vietnam* (New York: Columbia Univ. Press, 1999); and Sharon Maneki, *The Quiet Heroes of the Southwest Pacific Theater: An Oral History of the Men and Women of CBB and FRUMEL* (Washington, D.C.: Center for Cryptology History, National Security Agency, 1996).

5. Lieutenant Nhieu did not know at that moment that only a small number of the naval officer-students could go to America for their further training.

6. The naval base at Saigon provided basic training for new recruits of the River Force. The naval troops at the base were also responsible for handling operations in the Rung Sat "Special Zone," a maze of rivers and swamps south of Saigon.

7. In 1970, the U.S. Navy began its ACTOV (Accelerated Turnover to the Vietnamese) as part of the Vietnamization program. It included training of Vietnamese naval officers by the U.S. Navy both in South Vietnam and in the United States.

8. The ARVN Navy consisted of the Sea Force, or Fleet Command, and River Force. The River Force had twenty-eight bases along the major rivers at Saigon,

My Tho, Vinh Long, and Can Tho. It successfully controlled key waterways in the South during the war.

9. After 1971, the U.S. Navy transferred 571 naval vessels to the ARVN Navy, which began to assume the coastal operations from the U.S. Navy. The United States also transferred to the ARVN Navy complete control of the high seas surface patrol operations.

4. Communist Regulars from the North

1. Interviews by the author in New Orleans, Louisiana, June 2004, when Sgt. Tran Thanh visited his granddaughter, Connie Tran. There were four meetings/interviews through bi-lingual translators between Vietnamese and English. Connie and Tran Li provided the translations.

2. For further reading on the NVA, see the NVA official history, Merle L. Pribbenow, trans., *Victory in Vietnam: Official History of the PAVN* (Lawrence: Univ. Press of Kansas, 2002); Michael Lanning and Dan Cragg, *Inside the VC and the NVA* (New York: Ballantine Books, 1992); and Douglas Pike, *PAVN: People's Army of Vietnam* (Novato, Calif.: Presidio Press, 1986).

3. For more details on the NVA, also see Sandra C. Taylor, *Vietnamese Women at War: Fighting for Ho Chi Minh and the Revolution* (Lawrence: Univ. Press of Kansas, 2003), and Bao Ninh's historical novel from the NVA perspective, *The Sorrow of War* (New York: Riverhead, imprint of Penguin Group, 1996).

4. The military death total includes both NVA and Viet Cong. For more details, see Moss, *Vietnam,* table C, 384.

5. The Vietnamese Communist Party was founded on February 3, 1930, with Ho Chi Minh as its chairman. In October 1930, it became the Indochinese Communist Party (ICP). At its Eighth Plenum in May 1941, the ICP formed the "Viet Nam Doc Lap Dong Minh Hoi" (League for the Independence of Vietnam), well known as the "Viet Minh" during World War II in 1941–1945 and the First Indochinese War in 1946–1954. The ICP ceased to exist in 1945, but came back in 1951 as the "Dang Lao Dong Viet Nam" (Vietnamese Workers Party). In 1976, it changed its name back to the Vietnamese Communist Party. See Tucker, *Vietnam,* 89–90, 191.

6. The NVA missile troops developed fast in the 1960s with help from the Soviet Union. The NVA had twelve antiaircraft missile regiments in the early 1970s. See Douglas Pike, *Vietnam and the Soviet Union: Anatomy of an Alliance* (Boulder, Colo.: Westview, 1987).

7. In October 1964, the NVA sent more infantry troops to South Vietnam and directly engaged with the U.S. and ARVN forces. Nguyen Nhi, *Con Gai Nguoi Gac Den Bien* (Daughter of the Service Man) (Dallas, Tex.: Vhnt Publishing, 1999), 211–219.

8. The DRV government at first kept secret North Vietnam's infantry movement to and engagement in South Vietnam. Entering the South publicly at the

time might have risked a U.S. invasion by its ground troops. Not until much later did the DRV publicly recognize that the NVA had entered the South to assist the People's Liberation Armed Forces (PLAF) of South Vietnam in the war. Young, *The Vietnam Wars*, 160–161.

9. Among the major offensive campaigns was the attack on Ban Me Thuot in the spring of 1975.

5. People's War against Americans

1. Interviews by the author at TP Longxuyen, An Giang Province, Vietnam, in June 2006. Tran Li was the translator.

2. For further reading on the NVA mobilization, see William J. Duiker, *Vietnam: Revolution in Transition*, 2nd ed. (Boulder, Colo.: Westview, 1995); and Duong Thu Huong's historical novel from the Communist Vietnamese perspective, *Novel Without a Name* (New York: Penguin, 1996).

3. The "people's war" is one of the military strategies for a weak army to fight a stronger opponent, or a foreign invading force, by mobilizing the entire population to engage in the war. For its definition and the PAVN experience, see Gen. Vo Nguyen Giap, *People's War, People's Army* (New York: Bantam, 1962).

4. The Ho Chi Minh Trail began to play a major role in the North's infiltration and transportation to the South in the spring of 1965. Hoang Khoi, *The Ho Chi Minh Trail* (Hanoi, Vietnam: Gioi Publishers, 2002), 51–52.

5. For further reading on the NVA's deployment and operation in South Vietnam, see John Prados, *Vietnam: The History of an Unwinnable War, 1945–1975* (Lawrence: Univ. Press of Kansas, 2009); and Mark Atwood Lawrence, *The Vietnam War: A Concise International History* (New York: Oxford Univ. Press, 2008).

6. Captain Hao's father was born in 1924 and served in the People's Army of Vietnam (PAVN or NVA) from 1953 to 1979 as an officer, rising to the rank of a two-star general. He had retired from the NVA and lived in Hanoi when the author interviewed his son, Captain Hao, at Longxuyen, An Giang, in June 2006.

7. From 1965 to 1968, the NVA and PLAF had set up a joint command to coordinate their military operations. After the spring of 1968, the PAVN took over the command of the Communist military operations in South Vietnam.

8. Before the Tet Offensive campaign, the PLAF had carried most of the fighting in the South. During the Tet, the PLAF troops suffered such heavy casualties that the NVA took over the major operations thereafter.

9. The Battle of Ia Drang was the first major engagement of the U.S. ground forces in South Vietnam. From November 14 to November 18, 1965, the U.S. Army's First Cavalry Division (Airmobile) fought against a large number of the NVA-PLAF troops in the Ia Drang Valley. The U.S. troops suffered 534 casualties, including 234 dead. The NVA-PLAF casualties were estimated to be over 2,500. For more details, see Lt. Gen. Harold G. Moore and Joseph L. Galloway, *We Were*

Soldiers Once . . . and Young: Ia Drang—The Battle That Changed the War in Vietnam (New York: HarperCollins, 1992).

10. Plei Me (also called Plei Mei), about forty-four kilometers southwest Pleiku, was a strategic point in the Central Highlands. The siege of the ARVN camp by the PLAF-NVA troops led to the U.S. First Cavalry Division's first major battle in the Ia Drang Valley. See Michael P. Kelley, *Where We Were in Vietnam: A Comprehensive Guide to the Firebases, Military Installations and Naval Vessels of the Vietnam War, 1945–75* (Central Point, Oreg.: Hellgate Press, 2002), 5–411.

11. Pleiku, a city about 225 miles northeast Saigon, was an important strategic point in South Vietnam during the war. It had a U.S. Air Force base, airport, hospital, and ammo depot, the U.S. Army's Fourth Division headquarters, and the ARVN's II Corps headquarters. See Kelley, *Where We Were in Vietnam*, 5–412.

6. No Final Victory, No Family Life

1. Interviews by the author at My Thanh, Vietnam, in June 2006. Tran Li was the translator.

2. For more details about the regrouping of the Southern carders to the North, see Stein Tonnesson and Christopher E. Goscha, "Le Duan and the Break with China," in *Behind the Bamboo Curtain: China, Vietnam, and the World beyond Asia*, ed. Priscilla Roberts, 453–486 (Stanford, Calif.: Stanford Univ. Press, 2006).

3. Ho's words quoted in Gen. Phung The Tai, *Remembering Uncle Ho*, 148.

4. For further reading on NVA and PLAF officers, see Pribbenow, trans., *Victory in Vietnam*, and Dang Thuy Tram, *Last Night I Dreamed of Peace*, trans. Andrew X. Pham (New York: Harmony Books, 2007).

5. Dang Cong San Viet Nam (Vietnamese Communist Party Committee), *Dang Vien Cao Nien Tuoi Dang* (Generals of the Vietnamese Communist Party) (Long Xuyen, An Giang, Vietnam: Dang Bo Thanh Pho, 2002), 155.

6. By the end of 1952, the NVA had six infantry divisions and one artillery division, the 351st Division. For more details about the Chinese military assistance to Viet Minh in the French Indochina War, see Li, *A History of the Modern Chinese Army*, chapter 7.

7. General Huynh then served in the U Minh Artillery Training Department at the NVA No. 9 Quan Khu Artillery Training Center.

8. Dang Cong San Viet Nam (Vietnamese Communist Party Committee), *Dang Vien Cao Nien Tuoi Dang* (Generals of the Vietnamese Communist Party), 32.

9. Ibid.

7. Russian Missile Officers in Vietnam

1. As a veteran of China's Ministry of Public Security in Beijing, Anthony Song worked in the Foreign Affairs Bureau's Soviet Union and Eastern Europe

Division for more than ten years in the 1980s–1990s. He was in charge of approving and issuing Chinese travel documents to the diplomats and military missionaries from the former Soviet Union and its satellite states. He had many friends and stayed in touch with them after he retired from the Ministry of Public Security. Song has lived in Boston, Massachusetts, with his family since 2000.

2. Interviews by the author in Kyiv, Ukraine, in July 2005. Anthony Song was the translator.

3. For further reading on the Soviet involvement, see Gaiduk, *The Soviet Union and the Vietnam War*.

4. The title of the book is *War Experience in Vietnam, 1965–1973*, published in Moscow in 2006. It includes personal accounts of Soviet officers who served in Vietnam during the war, though none of them mention the word "Vietnam" in their stories. Rather, they use "that country."

5. Since the collapse of the Soviet Union, a large portion of the archives of the former Soviet government have become accessible, including the Presidential Archive (known officially as the Archive of the President, Russian Federation, or APRF), the archives of the Soviet Foreign Ministry, and documents of the Communist Party Central Committee. However, many key documents in the archives of the General Staff of the Soviet Armed Forces are still waiting for declassification.

6. For example, Gaiduk has employed the American archives, including the Presidential Papers in the Johnson Library and the National Security Archives at Washington, D.C., on this topic for his well-written book *The Soviet Union and the Vietnam War*, 60–61.

7. The sources in Chinese indicate that the 1965 Moscow-Hanoi agreement requested that the Soviet Union send four thousand Russian military personnel that spring, including five hundred air force technicians and logistic officers who would station in China, north of the Chinese-Vietnamese border. Beijing rejected the proposal and refused any Soviet military establishment inside China. Then Beijing helped to ship most of the Soviet military aid and personnel by rail through China in 1965–1968. The first group of Soviet officers, totaling 282, crossed the country and arrived in North Vietnam in April 1965. Later, Beijing and Moscow reached several agreements on the Soviet personnel transfers, including a maximum of 400 each time and that they were not to carry weapons. Among the important Chinese archives are the International Liaison Division Records, the PRC Ministry of Railway Administration Archives, and the PRC Ministry of Foreign Affair Archives, Beijing, China.

8. Director of Central Intelligence, "SNIE 10-11-65: Probable Communist Reactions to a U.S. Course of Action, September 22, 1965," in National Intelligence Council (NIC), *Estimative Products on Vietnam, 1948–1975* (Washington, D.C.: Government Printing Office, 2005), 294–296.

9. The Soviet leaders, including Leonid Brezhnev, the Soviet general secretary himself, made offers several times in late 1964 and early 1965 to send Soviet personnel or volunteers to Vietnam, if the war circumstances warranted this and

Vietnam requested it. However, in early 1965, during a meeting with Ilia S. Scherbakov, the Soviet ambassador to North Vietnam, DRV Deputy Foreign Minister Hoang Van Loi disclosed that, while the Vietnamese people expressed their gratitude for the Soviet offer of volunteers, as yet they did not need any, though they would request them later if this became necessary. Their conversations are quoted in Gaiduk, *The Soviet Union and the Vietnam War,* 38.

10. During 1965–1973, the Soviet Union had trained more than ten thousand Vietnamese officers in missile equipment, air defense, aviation engineering, and other military technology areas. For details, see Li Danhui, "Cooperation and Conflicts between China and the Soviet Union during the Vietnam War," in Li Danhui, ed., *Zhongguo yu yindu zhina zhanzheng* (China and the Indochina Wars) (Hong Kong: Tiandi Tushu [Heavenly Earth Books], 2000), 129–130.

11. The U.S. Air Force lost another F-111 on April 22, 1968.

8. The Dragon's Tale

1. Interviews by the author in Harbin, Heilongjiang Province, China, in July 2002.

2. Between 1955 and 1963, Chinese military aid totaled 320 million yuan. Yuan is the Chinese currency, or Renminbi (RMB). It had an exchange rate of 3:1 with U.S. dollars back then. Thus, 320 million yuan RMB equaled roughly $106 million at the time.

3. For further reading on China's involvement, see Chen Jian, *Mao's China and the Cold War* (Chapel Hill: Univ. of North Carolina Press, 2001); and Zhai, *China and the Vietnam Wars.*

4. In 1958, Mao launched the Great Leap Forward as a new economic policy to industrialize China. The policy failed and China experienced a serious economic depression on a gigantic scale in 1959–1962. The resulting famine claimed more than 20 million lives. The Chinese government, however, blamed it on the bad weather and called it a three-year "natural disaster." For more details, see John K. Fairbank and Merle Goldman, *China: A New History,* enlarged ed. (Cambridge, Mass.: Harvard Univ. Press, 1998), 372–382; and also Jonathan D. Spence, *The Search for Modern China,* 2nd ed. (New York: Norton, 1999), 552–553.

5. The People's Liberation Army (PLA) is the name for all Chinese armed forces, including army, navy, air force, and missile troops. See Xiaobing Li, Allan R. Millett, and Bin Yu, trans. and eds., *Mao's Generals Remember Korea* (Lawrence: Univ. of Kansas Press, 2001), 25–30, 66.

6. All Chinese military services were divided into nine regional commands from the 1950s to the 1980s. The PLA armies and divisions were under a certain regional command. Each command was named after the city where its headquarters was located. They were PLA Shenyang Regional Command (Northeast China), Beijing Regional Command (North China), Jinan Regional Command (East China), Nanjing Regional Command (Southeast China), Fuzhou Regional

Command (Southeast China Coast and the Taiwan Straits), Guangzhou Regional Command (South China), Kunming Regional Command (Southwest China), Wuhan Regional Command (Central China), and Lanzhou Regional Command (Northwest China). See Fang Zhu, *Gun Barrel Politics: Party-Army Relations in Mao's China* (Boulder, Colo.: Westview, 1998), 86–108.

7. For more information on the PLA's political instructor/commissar system, see Paul H. B. Godwin, "Change and Continuity in Chinese Military Doctrine: 1949–1999," and Xiaobing Li, "PLA Attacks and Amphibious Operations during the Taiwan Strait Crises of 1954–55 and 1958," in *Chinese Warfighting: The PLA Experience since 1949*, ed. Mark A. Ryan, David M. Finkelstein, and Michael A. McDevitt, 23–55, 143–172 (New York: M. E. Sharpe, 2003).

8. For China's involvement in the Vietnam War, see Qiang Zhai, "Reassessing China's Role in the Vietnam War: Some Mysteries Explored," in *China and the United States: A New Cold War History,* ed. Xiaobing Li and Hongshan Li, 97–118 (New York: Univ. Press of America, 1998).

9. After the Gulf of Tonkin Incident in August 1964, the United States escalated its intervention in South Vietnam. At the same time, it shifted its war efforts increasingly against North Vietnam, the Democratic Republic of Vietnam (DRV). The United States' heavy bombing against the North in 1964–1965 made the DRV desperate for help. In April 1965, Le Duan, first secretary general of the North Vietnamese Communist Party, and Gen. Vo Nguyen Giap, defense minister of the DRV, rushed to Beijing to ask China to increase its aid and send troops to Vietnam. On behalf of the Chinese leadership, Liu Shaoqi, president of the People's Republic of China and vice chairman of the CCP, replied to the Vietnamese visitors on April 8 that "it is the obligation of the Chinese people and party" to support the Vietnamese struggle against the United States. "Our principle is," Liu continued, "that we will do our best to provide you with whatever you need and whatever we have." In April, China signed several agreements with the DRV government delegation concerning the dispatch of Chinese support troops to North Vietnam. In May, Ho Chi Minh paid a secret visit to Mao Zedong and asked Mao to help the DRV repair and build twelve roads in the area north of Hanoi. The Chinese leader accepted Ho's request.

10. The NVA command disliked the rotation policy. The Vietnamese believed that the Chinese did not shoot down enough American airplanes to protect North Vietnam. Thus, they invited the antiaircraft missile troops from the Soviet Union. They knew that the Soviet Union and China were rivals in the Communist camp, competing for the leadership of the worldwide Communist movement as well as influence over Vietnam. Each claimed itself to be a supporter of the Vietnamese Communists' struggle again the American invasion. So the Vietnamese brought both Communist armies into North Vietnam, increasing the competition between the Chinese and Soviet Communists. The Chinese high command ordered its troops to intensify their training so as to shoot down more American airplanes than the Soviets could.

11. Vietnam has fifty provinces, which were divided among the South and North during the war. Hao Binh was a northern province southwest of Hanoi. See Tap Ban Do Hanh Chinh, *Viet Nam* (Vietnam Administrative Atlas) (Hanoi, Vietnam: Nha Xuat Ban Ban Do [Ban Do Cartographic Publishing House], 2005), 14.

9. Chinese Response to the U.S. Rolling Thunder Campaign

1. Maj. Gen. Qin Chaoying (PLA, ret.), secretary general of the China Society of Strategy and Management (CSSM), provided me with a long list of Chinese Vietnam War veterans for my interviews and research during our meetings at CSSM in Beijing in the summer of 2005.

2. Interviews by the author in Chengde, Hebei Province, China, in July 2006.

3. Le Duan quoted in a conversation with Zhou Enlai, Deng Xiaoping, and other Chinese leaders in Odd Arne Westad, Chen Jian, Stein Tonnesson, Nguyen Vu Tungand, and James G. Hershberg, eds., "77 Conversations between Chinese and Foreign Leaders on the Wars in Indochina, 1964–1977," Cold War International History Project, Working Paper No. 22, (Washington, D.C.: Woodrow Wilson International Center for Scholars, 1998), 95.

4. An August 1966 SNIE (Special National Intelligence Estimate) still believed that "For some time Chinese military personnel have been present in North Vietnam; current strength is estimated at 25,000 to 45,000. They include AAA troops, engineers, construction crews, and various other logistical support groups" (Director of Central Intelligence, "SNIE 13-66: Current Chinese Communist Intentions in the Vietnam Situation, August 4, 1966," in National Intelligence Council (NIC), *Estimative Products on Vietnam, 1948–1975*, 349).

5. Interviews by the author in Chengde, Hebei Province, China, in July 2006.

6. Mao, "Faith in Victory Is Derived from Struggle," conversations with a party and government delegation from the DRV on October 20, 1965, in Ministry of Foreign Affairs and Party Archives and Manuscript Research Center of the CCP Central Committee, comps., *Mao Zedong on Diplomacy* (Beijing: Foreign Languages Press, 1998), 435.

7. Chen Pai, *Yuezhan qinliji* (My Personal Experience in the Vietnam War) (Zhengzhou: Henan renmin chubanshe [Henan People's Press], 1997), 22.

8. For further reading on the Chinese military operation in the Vietnam War, see Ryan, Finkelstein, and McDevitt, eds., *Chinese Warfighting*; and Li, *A History of the Modern Chinese Army.*

9. For more details of China's arms purchase from the Soviet Union, see Mshl. Xu Xiangqian, "The Purchase of Arms from Moscow," in *Mao's Generals Remember Korea,* trans. and ed. Xiaobing Li, Allan R. Millett, and Bin Yu, 143–145 (Lawrence: Univ. Press of Kansas, 2001).

10. The PLA experienced several reorganizations during the Cultural Revolution of 1966–1976. See Li Ke and Hao Shengzhang, *Wenhua dageming zhong*

de renmin jiefangjun (The PLA in the Cultural Revolution) (Beijing: Zhonggong dangshi ziliao chubanshe [CCP Historical Document Press], 1989), 370–371.

11. Also see Mshl. Xu Xiangqian, "The Purchase of Arms from Moscow," in Li, Millett, and Yu, trans. and eds., *Mao's Generals Remember Korea,* 144–146.

12. Gen. Yao Fuhe, commander of the Sixty-fourth AAA Division, "Battles of Bravery and Wisdom," in Qu Aiguo, Bao Mingrong, and Xiao Zuyue, eds., *Yuanyue kangmei: zhongguo zhiyuan budui zai yuenan* (Aid Vietnam and Resist America: China's Supporting Forces in Vietnam) (Beijing: Junshi kexue chubanshe [Military Science Press], 1995), 17.

13. Li Ke and Hao Shengzhang, *Wenhua dageming zhong de renmin jiefangjun* (The PLA in the Cultural Revolution), 292–294.

14. Chen Pai, *Yuezhan qinliji* (My Personal Experience in the Vietnam War), 21.

15. The American statistics of U.S. airplanes lost in North Vietnam are different from those in Communist sources. According to the Chinese sources, from 1965 to 1968, the Chinese antiaircraft troops engaged in 2,153 battles, shooting down 1,707 American airplanes and damaging 1,608. American official sources say that the United States lost 918 aircraft in 1965–1968 (Moss, *Vietnam,* 236).

16. Chen Pai, *Yuezhan qinliji* (My Personal Experience in the Vietnam War), 68–69.

17. Gen. Yao Fuhe, commander of the Sixty-fourth AAA Division, "Battles of Bravery and Wisdom," in Qu Aiguo, Bao Mingrong, and Xiao Zuyue, eds., *Yuanyue kangmei; zhongguo zhiyuan budui zai yuenan* (Aid Vietnam and Resist America: China's Supporting Forces in Vietnam), 19.

10. Russian Spies in Hanoi

1. Maj. Gen. Robert J. Kodosky, Col. Konstantin Preobrazhensky, and other former KGB agents attended the International Conference on "Intelligence in the Vietnam War" at the Vietnam Center at Texas Tech University, in Lubbock, Texas, on October 20–22, 2006.

2. Interviews by the author in Silver Spring, Maryland, in September 2007. Both of us spoke Chinese and English during the interviews.

3. For further reading on KGB and Soviet military intelligence during the Vietnam War, see Cowley, ed., *The Cold War,* Christopher M. Andrew and Vasili Mitrokhin, *The Sword and the Shield: The Mitrokhin Archive and the Secret History of the KGB* (New York: Basic Books, 1999); and Gaiduk, *The Soviet Union and the Vietnam War.*

4. For more details on the KGB organization, see Andrew and Mitrokhin, *The Sword and the Shield,* 318–364.

5. In February 1965, Soviet premier Alekei Kosygin visited Hanoi and signed an agreement with the Vietnamese government to increase Russian military aid. Thereafter, the Soviet Union intensified its military assistance and involvement in the Vietnam War. For more details, see Gaiduk, *The Soviet Union and the Vietnam War,* 59, 61–62.

6. In fact, the Soviet intelligence service began to train and help the Chinese

Communist agents in the 1930s and 1940s. The CCP back then was an underground and antigovernment Communist movement. In 1949, the CCP founded the PRC, a Communist state.

7. Col. Nikita Karatsupa served in the KGB provincial offices in the 1950s and in the headquarters office in the early 1960s. Because of his achievements and success, he was awarded the highest Soviet decoration, the Golden Star of the Hero of the Soviet Union, in 1965. Then Colonel Karatsupa came to Hanoi for his new assignment. His case shows that the KGB had given its intelligence in Vietnam the top priority and sent its best agents to Hanoi.

11. Long Days and Endless Nights

1. Interviews by the author with a graduate student research assistant in Moore, Oklahoma, February 2004.

2. For further reading on the U.S. Army in the Vietnam War, see Ingo Trauschweizer, *The Cold War U.S. Army: Building Deterrence for Limited War* (Lawrence: Univ. Press of Kansas, 2008); and James F. Dunnigan and Albert A. Nofi, *Dirty Little Secrets of the Vietnam War* (New York: St. Martin's Press, 1999).

3. For the "16F40 MOS," 16F is the air-defense artillery, 40 is the rank of sergeant, and MOS (Military Occupational Specialty) stands for his field of training.

4. The quad fifties were a group of four mounted .50 caliber machine guns. The M-42 duster is a self-propelled armored vehicle with a pair of 40 mm cannons.

5. Tuy Hoa is a coastal city on QL-1, midway between Qui Nhon and Nha Trang and about ninety kilometers south of Qui Nhon. One of the major U.S. Air Force bases was located outside the city and included the U.S. Army antiaircraft artillery support units. See Kelley, *Where We Were in Vietnam,* 5–525.

6. Two Bits was a landing zone with an airfield about two kilometers from the intersection of QL-1 and Hwy. 514. Landing Zone English was originally known as Area Dog and LZ Dog, along the west side of QL-1, about three kilometers northeast of the An Lo River. Landing Zone Uplift, at Deo Nhong Pass, was along QL-1, about eight kilometers northeast of Phu My. Kelley, *Where We Were in Vietnam,* 5–172, 5–526, 5–528.

7. QL-19 is the highway running east and west that goes from Quin Nhon to Pleiku through the Mang Yang Pass and An Khe Pass. See Tap Ban Do Hanh Chinh, *Viet Nam* (Vietnam Administrative Atlas), 54.

8. Sgt. David McCray earned the National Defense Ribbon, Vietnam Service Medal, and Vietnam Campaign Medal with three campaign stars, along with a Good Conduct Medal.

12. And Then They're Gone . . . Just Like That

1. Interviews by the author with a graduate student research assistant in Edmond, Oklahoma, in March 2006.

2. For further reading on President Johnson's policy, see James H. Willbanks, *Abandoning Vietnam: How America Left and South Vietnam Lost Its War* (Lawrence: Univ. Press of Kansas, 2008).

3. "The Arizona Territory" is the nickname for the An Hoa Basin, the area between the rivers in Dai Loc and Duc Districts. The name reflects the area's wild west characteristics and danger, like that in early Arizona. It was noted for its dense foliage, booby traps, mines, and ubiquitous enemy forces. For more details, see Kelley, *Where We Were in Vietnam*, 5–20.

4. Hill 65 is along Route 4, about twenty-eight kilometers southwest of Da Nang. It covered Thuong Duc Corridor approaches to Da Nang. See Kelley, *Where We Were in Vietnam*, 5–224.

5. Munson pointed out the connection between the Vietnam War and the collapse of the Soviet Union during the interviews. "While that relationship seems obvious to me, it hasn't occurred to many others. I'm dissatisfied with the fact that here we are, thirty-plus years later, and it's a matter of public acceptance that the war was wrong, and we lost. I don't believe either one of those things. Certainly we lost politically. Also, the North captured the South. The troops who were there allowed neither of those things. One of my friends had a hat embroidered with the words: 'Vietnam: 1970–1971. We were winning when I left.' We weren't losing—we just left. That had nothing to do with us veterans. None of us were fans of the war, believe me, and we didn't like being there, but the war was what my country was asking me to do. This was the one [war] that occurred during my generation. Without necessarily understanding it all, we were part of it, did a pretty good job, and both got and gave full measure."

6. Munson received the Navy-Marine Corps Medal for rescuing the helicopter pilot. Munson also earned the Navy Achievement Medal with Combat "V" (for valor) device, Combat Action ribbon, Vietnam Cross of Gallantry, Vietnam Service Medal, and Vietnam Campaign Medal. Munson is now a retired Marine officer and successful investment representative with a nationally prominent company.

13. No John Wayne Movie

1. Interviews by the author with a graduate student research assistant after Lt. Gary Doss's presentation at Edmond, Oklahoma, in November 2003.

2. Moss, *Vietnam*, tables C, D, and E.

3. Da Nang was one of the six autonomous municipalities of the Republic of Vietnam. It became the northern commercial center and the second largest southern city after Saigon. In the 1960s, the city had one of the major U.S. Air Force bases and many other American military facilities, such as an Air Force heliport and hospital; an Army base, depot, and ammunition supply points; and a Navy base, seaport, hospital, and support facility. For more details, see Kelley, *Where We Were in Vietnam*, maps 7, 44, and 45, and pages 5-129–130.

4. Chu Lai is not a Vietnamese name. Rather, the U.S. Marine officers named

it per Chinese Mandarin pronunciation. Chu Lai base site, about fifty-five miles southeast of Da Nang, is near today's Nui Thanh, Quang Nam Province. In 1965, the U.S. Marine Corps built an airfield there. See Tap Ban Do Hanh Chinh, *Viet Nam* (Vietnam Administrative Atlas), 48; and Kelley, *Where We Were in Vietnam,* maps 7 and 43, and page 5-108.

5. Ky Ha was one of the U.S. Marine air facilities. Marine Air Group (MAG) 36 flew helicopters from Ky Ha to protect the Da Nang Air Force Base and provide logistics, transport, and rescues to marine units. Kelley, *Where We Were in Vietnam,* page 5-283; Tap Ban Do Hanh Chinh, *Viet Nam* (Vietnam Administrative Atlas), 48.

6. Originally it was called "Archie's Angels," for their first commander, Col. Archie Clapp. After Colonel Clapp left the group, the name was changed to "Ugly Angels" after a wounded marine heard the beating rotor of a Sikorsky coming to save him and exclaimed, "That's the ugliest angel I've ever seen."

7. In fact, the U.S. armed forces employed helicopters in the Korean War of 1950–1953. Despite some limitations, the helicopter played a major role in that war. They were used for battlefield observation, air-sea rescue, transport of men and supplies, and for the evacuation of the wounded. Because of the film and television series *M*A*S*H,* there is no more enduring image of the Korean War for most Americans than a helicopter landing at a MASH unit with wounded soldiers. For more details, see Richard Peters and Xiaobing Li, *Voices from the Korean War: Personal Stories of American, Korean, and Chinese Soldiers* (Lexington: Univ. Press of Kentucky, 2004), 41–42, 105, 106.

8. At Ky Ha Marine Air Facility, MAG-36 flew H-34 helicopters.

9. Doss returned to the United States in 1967 and continued to serve in the marines through January 1970. In recent years, he volunteers with the YL-37 Group Foundation (a Marine veterans organization) as a spokesperson and former public relations officer.

14. More Than Meets the Eye

1. Interviews by the author with a graduate student research assistant at the University of Central Oklahoma, Edmond, Oklahoma, in August 2002–February 2003.

2. For further reading on U.S. intelligence in the Vietnam War, see Hiam, *Who the Hell Are We Fighting?;* James L. Gilbert, *The Most Secret War: Army Signals Intelligence in Vietnam* (Washington, D.C.: Government Printing Office, 2003); and Ford, *CIA and the Vietnam Policymakers.*

3. The conference on "Intelligence in the Vietnam War" at the Vietnam Center at Texas Tech University, in Lubbock, Texas, on October 20–22, 2006, was cosponsored by the National Center for the Study of Intelligence and Texas Tech University. For more details on the conference, see www.intelligence.vietnam.ttu.edu.

4. Ford, *CIA and the Vietnam Policymakers,* ix.

5. For further reading on veteran families, see Donna Moreau, *Waiting Wives* (New York: Atria, 2005); Jessica Redmond, *A Year of Absence: Six Women's Stories of Courage, Hope and Love* (New York: Elva Resa, 2005); and Larry H. Addington, *America's War in Vietnam: A Short Narrative History* (Bloomington: Indiana Univ. Press, 2000).

6. After military retirement he served as assistant vice president for academic affairs at the University of Central Oklahoma, Edmond, Oklahoma. Besides his story, May also interviewed other Vietnam veterans in Oklahoma, two of whose stories are included in this volume. He made an important contribution to this collection. Lieutenant Colonel May passed away on December 27, 2003.

15. Medevac and Medcap Missions and More

1. Interviews by Lt. Col. Terry May in 2000, who contributed Peterson's story in 2003.

2. For further reading on the U.S. Marine Corps air force in the Vietnam War, see Andrew Wiest, ed., *Rolling Thunder in a Gentle Land* (New York: Osprey, 2006), Robert F. Dorr, *Marine Air: The History of the Flying Leathernecks in Words and Photos* (New York: Berkley Caliber Books, 2005); and Ronald B. Frankum Jr., *Like Rolling Thunder: The Air War in Vietnam, 1964–1975* (Lanham, Md.: Rowman and Littlefield, 2005).

3. Monsoons are seasonal winds that affect the weather and rainfall of Southeast Asian countries like Vietnam. Between May and September, the monsoon winds go southwest, bringing most of the annual rainfall to the region. In December–February, the monsoon winds go northeast. See D. R. SarDesai, *Southeast Asia: Past and Present* (Boulder, Colo.: Westview, 2003), 7.

4. The USO brought many famous entertainers to Vietnam to entertain the American troops. Some of the entertainers came from Hollywood and others from Broadway.

5. U.S. Marines Air Group (MAG) 16 stationed at the Da Nang Air Base during that time. It provided transportation and air support to the First Marine Division. See Kelley, *Where We Were in Vietnam*, 5–129.

6. The Marble Mountain is about three miles southeast of the Da Nang Air Base. See Kelley, *Where We Were in Vietnam*, maps 44 and 45.

16. Drowning Tears with Laughter

1. Second Lt. Judy Crausbay Hamilton was invited many times to talk to the students in the History of the Vietnam War, the Cold War in Asia, Modern Southeast Asia, and other history classes at the University of Central Oklahoma.

2. Interviews by the author with an undergraduate student research assistant in Edmond, Oklahoma, February 2004.

3. Judy Crausbay Hamilton received the Meritorious Service Medal from the

U.S. government in February 2006 to honor her service as a U.S. Air Force flight nurse and a U.S. Army nurse during the Vietnam War.

4. For further reading on American women in the Vietnam War, see Lynda Van Devanter, *Home before Morning: The Story of an Army Nurse in Vietnam* (Boston: Massachusetts Univ. Press, 2001); Olga Gruhzit-Hoyt, *A Time Remembered: American Women in the Vietnam War* (Novato, Calif.: Presidio Press, 1999); and Keith Walker, *A Piece of My Heart: The Stories of 26 American Women Who Served in Vietnam* (Novato, Calif.: Presidio Press, 1999).

5. Ron Smith, 101st Airborne, from Gainesville, Texas, to Judy Crausbay Hamilton, on June 17, 1994. Quoted from the original letter from Hamilton's collection.

6. Peggy Durham, "Cityan Earns Flight Experience 'Hard Way,'" *The Oklahoma Journal* (February 7, 1967), 2–3.

7. Ibid., 6.

8. National Guard Bureau, "Guard Aero Med Team Meets Unexpected Crisis," *The National Guardsman* (March 1967): 11–14.

9. Maj. Gen. L. E. Weber then was the Adjutant General of the Air National Guard. The quote is from the original letter of General Weber to Judy Crausbay Hamilton on February 9, 1967.

10. The Ninety-first Evacuation Hospital was a semi-mobile army hospital with 325 beds. It was located at Tuy Hoa from December 1966 to July 1969, and then it relocated at Chu Lai from July 1969 to November 1971. According to some works, it was under the command of I and II Corps. For example, see Kelley, *Where We Were in Vietnam*, 4–10.

11. Tuy Hoa, as a coastal city, had one of the major U.S. Air Force bases in South Vietnam. The 101st Airborne and its headquarters were stationed at the Tuy Hoa Air Force Base.

12. Can Tho is about one hundred kilometers southwest of Saigon. It was the largest population center of the Mekong Delta and was the center of all U.S. operations in the areas under IV Corps command.

17. Life and Death of an ARVN Doctor

1. Interviews by the author with Dr. Jessica Sheetz-Nguyen in Oklahoma City, Oklahoma, in March 2007.

2. After the Vietnamese Communists won the war, all the officers and soldiers who served in the ARVN during the war were sent to jail for five to seven years. Dr. Nguyen Canh Minh was jailed for four years because he served in the ARVN hospital.

3. The Vietnamese National Army totaled 150,000 men by 1950, including three infantry divisions.

4. Dr. Minh received many medals, honors, and awards. He considers the Courageous Combatant Medal to be his best.

5. The city of Can Tho, about sixty miles southwest Saigon, was the largest population center of the Mekong Delta. As the center of all U.S.-ARVN operations in the Mekong Delta, it hosted the headquarters of the U.S. IV Corps and ARVN Fourth Tactical Zone.

6. Lt. Gen. Ngo Quang Truong was commander of the Fourth Corps from August 21, 1970, to May 4, 1972. Maj. Gen. Nguyen Khoa Nam was its commander from October 30, 1974, to April 30, 1975, when the ARVN surrendered to the PAVN after the fall of Saigon.

7. Phu Quoc Island is the largest island in South Vietnam, about thirty-one by sixteen miles. As the major ARVN POW camp, in 1968–1970 it held 35,000 Communist prisoners of war.

8. While the Vietnamese Communists took over the South, the Cambodian Communists also established their regime in that country, on April 17, 1975, and named it the Democratic Kampuchea. From 1975 to 1979, the Khmer Rouge implemented radical policies that led to the deaths of some 1.7 million people from starvation, disease, overwork, and execution. The Khmer Rouge was driven from power by a Vietnamese invasion in 1979 and finally collapsed in 1999.

18. A Korean Captain and His Hospital

1. Interviews by the author in Bellingham, Washington, in September 2005.

2. The South Korea (Republic of Korea) government sent two infantry divisions, totaling 60,000 troops, to South Vietnam in 1967–1973.

3. For further reading on the South Korean troops in the Vietnam War, see Ahn Jung-hyo, "A Double Exposure of the War," in Philip West, Steven I. Levine, and Jackie Hiltz, eds., *America's Wars in Asia: A Cultural Approach to History and Memory* (Armonk, N.Y.: M. E. Sharpe, 1998); Robert M. Blackburn, *Mercenaries and Lyndon Johnson's "More Flags": The Hiring of Korean, Filipino and Thai Soldiers in the Vietnam War* (Jefferson, N.C.: McFarland, 1994); and Ahn Jung-hyo's wonderful historical novel, *White Badge* (New York: Soho Press, 1989).

4. The "White Horse Division" was the nickname of the ROK Ninth Infantry Division. The division operated in Vietnam from 1965 to 1973.

5. Tuy Hoa is a coastal city midway between Qui Nhon and Nha Trang. It had one of the few U.S. bases constructed by the U.S. Air Force under its own direction and with its own assets. The Korean Twenty-eighth Regiment had its headquarters next to the Ninth MASH unit.

6. During the 1965–1973 Vietnam War, 4,407 South Korean soldiers were killed.

7. After his tour in Vietnam in 1966–1967, Captain Jung served as the medical supply officer in the ROK Thirty-fifth Division in 1967–1969. For the last two years of his service, in 1969–1971, he taught military logistics at the South Korean Army Medical School for officers taking basic and advanced courses and training. As a captain, he petitioned his release from the ROK Army and obtained it in 1971.

19. "Loggie's" War

1. Interviews by Lt. Col. Terry May in June–July 2002, who contributed the story in 2003.

2. For further reading on U.S. support to the Vietnam War, see George C. Herring, *America's Longest War: The United States and Vietnam, 1950–1975*, 4th ed. (New York: McGraw-Hill, 2001); and Wallace Terry, ed., *Bloods: Black Veterans of the Vietnam War: An Oral History* (Novato, Calif.: Presidio Press, 1985).

3. Cam Ranh Bay, about 180 miles northeast of Saigon and 20 miles south of Nha Trang, was the site of a major U.S. port facility, including a U.S. Army complex and a major U.S. Air Force base. The army complex consisted of the main cantonment, two personnel replacement depots, the army logistics areas, and an army port (CP 050–155). For details, see Kelley, *Where We Were in Vietnam*, 5–83, 5–84.

4. According to Nelson, the position was normally held by a captain and not at all a typical situation for a lieutenant.

5. Phan Rang is about 160 miles northeast of Saigon and 25 miles southwest of Cam Ranh Bay. The U.S. Air Force had a jet-capable airfield about 3 miles from Phan Rang.

6. Bill Nelson was awarded the Bronze Star medal for meritorious service in Vietnam.

20. Support and Survival in Thailand

1. Interviews by the author with a graduate student research assistant in Moore, Oklahoma, in February 2004.

2. U Tapao is near the coast, about 130 kilometers southeast from Bangkok, Thailand, and 640 kilometers northwest of Saigon, South Vietnam. The U.S. Air Force built a major bomber/fighter-bomber base at U Tapao.

3. David Graves is still very proud of the awards he received, including the Good Conduct Medal, an Outstanding Unit Citation, a Vietnam Service Medal, and a Republic of Vietnam Service Medal.

21. Three Great Escapes

1. Interviews by the author and an undergraduate student research assistant in Dallas, Texas, in July 2002.

2. At that time, Vietnam and French Indochina were divided under three different colonial administrations: northern, middle, and southern.

3. Hoa Hung is a small town along the Song Tien River in the west of Tien Giang Province. See Tap Ban Do Hanh Chinh, *Viet Nam* (Vietnam Administrative Atlas), 69.

4. Gih Dinh was one of the provinces in the Republic of Vietnam in the South from 1955 to 1975. It was annexed by Ho Chi Minh City in 1976.

5. Long Binh is about twelve miles northeast Saigon. It was a strategic point in the war and had the largest U.S./ARVN military base in South Vietnam, including an airport, supply depot, heliport, hospital, and jails. The headquarters of the ARVN's II Corps was at Long Binh.

6. Thu Duc, north Ho Chi Minh City, was part of Gih Dinh Province before 1976. See Tap Ban Do Hanh Chinh, *Viet Nam* (Vietnam Administrative Atlas), 65.

7. Gen. Duong Van Minh became the RVN president in November 1963 after he and Gen. Tran Van Don led a military coup to overthrow the Diem regime.

8. Nguyen Vung was killed in a motorcycle accident in Bien Hoa, Vietnam, during his third trip back home in 2003. At that time, he had done the paperwork and was about to bring his wife and remaining children to the United States. They finally arrived in the United States a year later, according to his son Nguyen Hoang.

22. Chinese Railroad Engineering Operations

1. Li Ke and Hao Shengzhang, *Wenhua dageming zhong de renmin jiefangjun* (The PLA during the Cultural Revolution), 409.

2. Many veteran officers mentioned this report. Also, interview with Col. Yan Guitang (PLA, ret.) in Xi'an, Shaanxi, China, on July 29, 2006. He served as a staff member for the delegation and toured Vietnam five times between 1959 and 1966.

3. Interviews by the author in Changchun, Jilin Province, China, in July 2006.

4. For more details, see Qu Aiguo, "Military Operations of the Chinese Supporting Forces in Vietnam," in Li Danhui ed., *Zhongguo yu yindu zhina zhanzheng* (China and the Indochina Wars) (Hong Kong: Tiandi Tushu [Heavenly Earth Books], 2000), 47.

5. The CPVEF had established six divisions. Its Second Division, an engineering division, consisted of three engineering regiments, one hydrology brigade, one maritime transportation brigade, one communication engineering brigade, one truck transportation regiment, and a few antiaircraft artillery units, totaling 12,000 men. The Third Division was mainly comprised of PLA Air Force engineering troops for the construction of a large air base. The Fourth, Fifth, and Sixth Divisions of the CPVEF were all comprised of road construction engineering troops, including sixteen regiments with 80,000 men.

6. Li Ke and Hao Shengzhang, *Wenhua dageming zhong de renmin jiefangjun* (The PLA during the Cultural Revolution), 358, 362–363.

7. Also, interview with Col. Yan Guitang (PLA, ret.) in Xi'an, Shaanxi, China, on July 29, 2006.

8. For the statistics, see Li Ke and Hao Shengzhang, *Wenhua dageming zhong de renmin jiefangjun* (The PLA in the Cultural Revolution), 421.

9. For more detailed statistics, see Qu Aiguo, Bao Mingrong, and Xiao Zuyue,

eds., *Yuanyue kangmei: zhongguo zhiyuan budui zai yuenan* (Aid Vietnam and Resist America: China's Supporting Forces in Vietnam), 12.

10. For more details on U.S. bombing, see Li Qingde, "Unbreakable Railway Lines," in Qu Aiguo, Bao Mingrong, and Xiao Zuyue, eds., *Yuanyue kangmei: zhongguo zhiyuan budui zai yuenan* (Aid Vietnam and Resist America: China's Supporting Forces in Vietnam), 83–85.

11. Li Qingde, "Unbreakable Railway Lines," 91.

12. For more details about Long's story, see Long Guilin, "Show the Valor and Spirit Again," in Qu Aiguo, Bao Mingrong, and Xiao Zuyue, eds., *Yuanyue kangmei: zhongguo zhiyuan budui zai yuenan* (Aid Vietnam and Resist America: China's Supporting Forces in Vietnam), 76–77.

Conclusion

1. Director of Central Intelligence, "SNIE 10-11-65: Probable Communist Reactions to a U.S. Course of Action, September 22, 1965," in National Intelligence Council (NIC), *Estimative Products on Vietnam, 1948–1975*, 304.

2. Moss, *Vietnam*, table C, 384.

3. I borrow the term "useful adversary" from Thomas J. Christensen's research on grand strategy in *Useful Adversaries: Grand Strategy, Domestic Mobilizations, and Sino-American Conflict, 1947–1958* (Princeton, N.J.: Princeton Univ. Press, 1996), 1–2.

4. Mao Zedong, "We Agree with Vietnam's Policy to both Fight and Negotiate," in Ministry of Foreign Affairs and Party Archives and Manuscript Research Center of the CCP Central Committee, comps., *Mao Zedong on Diplomacy*, 442–443.

5. Han Huaizhi, *Dangdai zhongguo jundui de junshi gongzuo* (Contemporary Chinese Military Affairs), 1:550.

6. Truong Nhu Tang, minister of justice of the Provisional Republican Revolutionary Government (PRRG), quoted in Tang with David Chanoff and Doan Van Toai, *Yu Hanoi fendao yangbiao* (Parting Company with Hanoi) (Beijing: Shijie zhishi chubanshe [World Knowledge Press], 1989), 229.

7. Moss, *Vietnam*, 361–363.

8. The U.S. Army actually began its rotation system in the Korean War of 1950–1953. The policy was based upon studies of World War II soldiers' experiences.

9. Moss, *Vietnam*, table C, 384.

10. Gaiduk, *The Soviet Union and the Vietnam War*, 215, 231.

Selected Bibliography

English Language

Addington, Larry H. *America's War in Vietnam: A Short Narrative History.* Bloomington: Indiana Univ. Press, 2000.

Ahn Jung-hyo. *White Badge.* New York: Soho Press, 1989.

Alexander, Ron, and Charles W. Sasser. *Taking Fire: The True Story of a Decorated Chopper Pilot.* New York: St. Martin's Press, 2001.

Allen, George. *None So Blind: A Personal Account of the Intelligence Failure in Vietnam.* Chicago: Ivan R. Dee, 2001.

Anderson, Christopher J. *Grunts: U.S. Infantry in Vietnam.* London, England: Greenhill Books, 1998.

Andrew, Christopher M., and Vasili Mitrokhin. *The Sword and the Shield: The Mitrokhin Archive and the Secret History of the KGB.* New York: Basic Books, 1999.

Angelucci, Enzo, and Pierluigi Pinto. *The American Combat Aircraft and Helicopters of the Vietnam War.* New York: Orion Books, 1987.

Appy, Christian G. *Patriots: The Vietnam War Remembered from All Sides.* New York: Viking, 2003.

———. *Working-Class War: American Combat Soldiers and Vietnam.* Chapel Hill: Univ. of North Carolina Press, 1993.

Atkinson, Rick. *The Long Gray Line.* New York: Henry Holt, 1999.

Bailey, Mark. *Aspects of the Australian Army Intelligence System during the Confrontation in Vietnam.* Canberra, Australia: Australian Defense Force Academy, 1994.

Baker, Mark. *Nam: The Vietnam War in the Words of the Men and Women Who Fought There.* New York: Morrow, 1981.

Ball, George W. *The Past Has Another Pattern.* New York: W. W. Norton, 1982.

Ball, Phil. *Ghosts and Shadows: A Marine in Vietnam, 1968–1969.* Jefferson, N.C.: McFarland, 1998.

Bao Ninh. *The Sorrow of War.* New York: Riverhead, imprint of Penguin Group, 1996.

Barr, Marshall. *Surgery, Sand and Saigon Tea: An Australian Army Doctor in Viet Nam.* Crows Nest, Australia: Allen and Unwin, 2001.

Basel, Gene I. *Pak Six: A Story of the War in the Skies of North Vietnam.* New York: Jove, 1987.

Bell, Kenneth H. *100 Missions North.* Washington, D.C.: Brassey's, 1993.

Bendell, Don. *Snake-Eater: Characters in and Stories about the U.S. Army Special Forces in the Vietnam War.* New York: Dell, 1994.

Berger, Carl, and Jack S. Ballard. *The United States Air Force in Southeast Asia,*

1961–1973: An Illustrated Account. Washington, D.C.: Office of Air Force History, U.S. Air Force, 1984.

Bergerud, Eric M. *Red Thunder, Tropic Lightning: The World of Combat Division in Vietnam.* Boulder, Colo.: Westview, 1993.

Biedermann, Narelle. *Tears on My Pillow: Australian Nurses in Vietnam.* Milsons Point, Australia: Random House, 2004.

Bigler, Philip. *Hostile Fire: The Life and Death of First Lieutenant Sharon Lane.* Arlington, Va.: Vandamere Press, 1996.

Bilton, Michael, and Kevin Sim. *Four Hours in My Lai: The Soldiers of Charlie Company.* New York: Viking, 1992.

Bird, Kai. *The Color of the Truth: McGeorge Bundy and William Bundy: Brothers in Arms.* New York: Simon and Schuster, 2001.

Birdwell, Dwight W., and Keith William Nolan. *A Hundred Miles of Bad Road: An Armored Cavalryman in Vietnam, 1967–68.* Novato, Calif.: Presidio Press, 1997.

Blackburn, Robert M. *Mercenaries and Lyndon Johnson's "More Flags": The Hiring of Korean, Filipino, and Thai Soldiers in the Vietnam War.* Jefferson, N.C.: McFarland, 1994.

Blaxland, John Charles. *Revisiting Counterinsurgency: A Manoeuvrist Response to the 'War on Terror' for the Australian Army.* Duntroon, Australia: Land Warfare Studies Centre, 2006.

Blout, Harry D., and Melvin F. Porter. *Air Operations in Northern Laos, 1 Nov. 1970–1 Apr 1971.* Christiansburg, Va.: Dalley Book, 1997.

Bowman, John. *The Vietnam War Almanac.* New York: Barnes and Noble, 2005.

Boyle, Richard. *The Flower of the Dragon: The Breakdown of the U.S. Army in Vietnam.* San Francisco: Ramparts Press, 1972.

Bradfield, Carl. *The Blue Spaders: Vietnam.* Lakeland, Fla.: ASDA Publication, 1992.

Bradford, Alfred S. *Some Even Volunteered: The First Wolfhounds Pacify Vietnam.* Westport, Conn.: Praeger, 1994.

Bradley, Mark, and Robert Brigham. "Vietnamese Archives and Scholarship on the Cold War." *Cold War International History Project,* Work Paper 7. Washington, D.C.: Wilson International Center for Scholars, 1993.

Brant, Toby L. *Journal of a Combat Tanker: Vietnam, 1969.* New York: Vantage Press, 1988.

Brennan, Matthew. *Brennan's War: Vietnam 1965–69.* Novato, Calif.: Presidio Press, 1985.

———. *Headhunters: Stories from the 1st Squadron, 9th Cavalry in Vietnam, 1965–1971.* Novato, Calif.: Presidio, 1987.

———. *Hunter-Killer Squadron: Aero-Weapons, Aero-Scouts, Aero-Rifles, Vietnam 1965–1972.* Novato, Calif.: Presidio, 1990.

Brigham, Robert K. *ARVN: Life and Death in the South Vietnamese Army.* Lawrence: Univ. Press of Kansas, 2006.

Broughton, Jack. *Thud Ridge*. Friendswood, Tex.: Baxter Press, 1996.

Buckingham, William A., Jr. *Operation Ranch Hand: The Air Force and Herbicides in Southeast Asia, 1961–1971*. Washington, D.C.: Government Printing Office, 1982.

Bushby, Richard Nicholas. *"Educating an Army": Australian Army Doctrinal Development and the Operational Experience in South Vietnam, 1965–72*. Canberra, Australia: Strategic and Defense Studies Centre, Australian National University, 1998.

Buzzanco, Robert. *Masters of War: Military Dissent and Politics in the Vietnam Era*. Cambridge, Mass.: Harvard Univ. Press, 1996.

Calley, William Laws, and John Sack. *Lieutenant Calley: His Own Story*. New York: Viking Press, 1971.

Camp, Richard D., and Eric M. Hammel. *Lima-6: A Marine Company Commander in Vietnam*. New York: Pocket Books, 1989.

Carlock, Chuck. *Firebirds: The Best First-Person Account of Helicopter Combat in Vietnam Ever Written*. Arlington, Tex.: Summit Publishing Group, 1995.

Castle, Timothy. *One Day Too Long: Top Secret Site 85 and the Bombing of North Vietnam*. New York: Columbia Univ. Press, 1999.

Catton, Philip E. *Diem's Final Failure: Prelude to America's War in Vietnam*. Lawrence: Univ. Press of Kansas, 2002.

Chambers, Larry. *Death in the A Shau Valley: L Company LRRPs in Vietnam, 1969–70*. New York: Ivy Books, 1998.

Chang, Gordon H. *Friends and Enemies: The United States, China, and the Soviet Union*. Stanford, Calif.: Stanford Univ. Press, 1990.

Chang, Jung, and Jon Halliday. *Mao: The Unknown Story*. New York: Knopf, 2005.

Chanoff, David, and Doan Van Toai. *Portrait of the Enemy*. New York: Random House, 1986.

Chen Jian. *Mao's China and the Cold War*. Chapel Hill: Univ. of North Carolina Press, 2001.

Chen Jian, and Xiaobing Li. "China and the End of the Cold War." In *From Détente to the Soviet Collapse: The Cold War from 1975 to 1991*, edited by Malcolm Muir Jr., 120–131. Lexington: Virginia Military Institute, 2005.

Chinnery, Philip D. *Life on the Line: Stories of Vietnam Air Combat*. New York: St. Martin's Press, 1988.

Christian, David, and William Hoffer. *Victor Six: The Saga of America's Youngest, Most Decorated Officer in Vietnam*. New York: McGraw-Hill, 1990.

Christensen, Thomas J. *Useful Adversaries: Grand Strategy, Domestic Mobilizations, and Sino-American Conflict, 1947–1958*. Princeton, N.J.: Princeton Univ. Press, 1996.

Clarke, Jeffery J. *Advice and Support: The Final Years, 1965–1973*. Washington, D.C.: Center for Military History, 1988.

Clay, Lucius D. *USAF Operations in Laos: 1 January 1970–30 June 1971*. Christiansburg, Va.: Dalley Book, 1994.

Clodfelter, Mark. *The Limits of Air Power: The American Bombing of North Vietnam.* New York: The Free Press, 1989.

———. *Vietnam in Military Statistics.* Jefferson, N.C.: McFarland, 1993.

Colby, William Egan, and James McCargar. *Lost Victory: A Firsthand Account of America's Sixteen-Year Involvement in Vietnam.* Chicago: Contemporary Books, 1989.

Colvin, John. *Volcano under Snow: Vo Nguyen Giap.* London, England: Quartet Books, 1996.

Conboy, Kenneth J., Don Greer, and Tom Tullis. *War in Laos, 1954–1975.* Carrollton, Tex.: Squadron/Signal Publishing, 1994.

Cook, John. *The Advisor: Phoenix Program in Vietnam, A U.S. Advisor's Personal Narrative.* Atglen, Pa.: Schiffer Publishing, 2000.

Coulthard-Clark, Christopher David. *Hit My Smoke: Targeting the Enemy in Vietnam.* St. Leonards, Australia: Allen and Unwin, 1997.

Cowley, Robert, ed. *The Cold War: A Military History.* New York: Random House, 2005.

Culbertson, John J. *13 Cent Killers: The 5th Marine Snipers in Vietnam.* New York: Ballantine Books, 2003.

Daly, James A., and Lee Bergman. *Black Prisoner of War: A Conscientious Objector's Vietnam Memoir.* Lawrence: Univ. Press of Kansas, 2000.

Dang Thuy Tram. *Last Night I Dreamed of Peace.* Trans. by Andrew X. Pham. New York: Harmony Books, 2007.

Dennis, Peter, and Jeffrey Grey. *The Australian Army and the Vietnam War, 1962–1972: Proceedings of the Australian Army History Conference.* Canberra, Australia: Department of Defense, 2002.

———. *From Past to Future: The Australian Experience of Land/Air Operations: Proceedings of the Australian Army History Conference.* Campbell, Australia: Department of History, University of New South Wales, 1995.

———. *Serving Vital Interests: Australia's Strategic Planning in Peace and War: Proceedings of the Australian Army History Conference.* New South Wales, Australia: Australian Defense Force Academy, 1996.

Devanter, Lynda Van. *Home before Morning: The Story of an Army Nurse in Vietnam.* Boston: Massachusetts Univ. Press, 2001.

Dinh Thi Van, Col. *I Engaged in Intelligence Work.* Hanoi, Vietnam: Gioi Publishers, 2006.

Dorr, Robert F. *Marine Air: The History of the Flying Leathernecks in Words and Photos.* New York: Berkley Caliber Books, 2005.

Donahue, James C. *Blackjack-34.* New York: Ballantine Books, 2000.

Doss, Gary. *Tales of an Ugly Angel.* Farmington, Mo.: River Road Press, 2006.

Downs, Frederick. *The Killing Zone: My Life in the Vietnam War.* New York: Norton, 1993.

Doyle, Jeff, Jeffrey Grey, and Peter Pierce. *Australia's Vietnam War.* College Station, Tex.: Texas A&M Univ. Press, 2002.

Drew, Paul. *After the Storm: A Vietnam Veteran's Reflection.* Central Point, Oreg.: Hellgate Press, 1999.

Duiker, William J. *Vietnam: Revolution in Transition,* 2nd ed. Boulder, Colo.: Westview, 1995.

Dunnigan, James F., and Albert A. Nofi. *Dirty Little Secrets of the Vietnam War.* New York: St. Martin's Press, 1999.

Duong Thu Huong. *Novel Without a Name.* New York: Penguin, 1996.

Ebert, James R. *A Life in a Year: The American Infantryman in Vietnam, 1965–1972.* Novato, Calif.: Presidio Press, 1993.

Edelman, Bernard, ed. *Dear America: Letters Home from Vietnam.* New York: Pocket Books, 1985.

Edwards, Fred L. *The Bridges of Vietnam: From the Journals of a U.S. Marine Intelligence Officer.* Denton, Tex.: Univ. of North Texas Press, 2000.

Eilert, Rick. *For Self and Country: For the Wounded in Vietnam the Journey Home Took More Courage Than Going into Battle: A True Story.* New York: Morrow, 1983.

Elkins, Frank Callihan, and Marilyn Roberson Elkins. *The Heart of a Man: A Naval Pilot's Vietnam Diary.* Annapolis, Md.: Naval Institute Press, 1991.

Elliott, David W. P. *The Vietnamese War: Revolution and Social Change in the Mekong Delta, 1930–1975,* concise ed. New York: M. E. Sharpe, 2007.

Estep, James L. *Comanche Six: Company Commander, Vietnam.* Novato, Calif.: Presidio, 1991.

Eun Ho and Yong Soon Yim Lee. *Politics of Military Civic Action: The Case of South Korean and South Vietnamese Forces in the Vietnamese War.* Hong Kong: Asian Research Service, 1980.

Evans, Michael. *Forward from the Past: The Development of Australian Army Doctrine, 1972–Present.* Duntroon, Australia: Land Warfare Studies Centre, 1999.

Fairbank, John K., and Merle Goldman. *China: A New History,* enlarged ed. Cambridge, Mass.: Harvard Univ. Press, 1998.

Fallows, Carol. *Love and War: Stories of War Brides from the Great War to Vietnam.* Sydney, New South Wales, Australia: Bantam Books, 2002.

Fawcett, Bill. *Hunters and Shooters: An Oral History of the U.S. Navy SEALs in Vietnam.* New York: Morrow, 1995.

Ford, Harold P. *CIA and the Vietnam Policymakers: Three Episodes, 1962–1968.* Springfield, Va.: Center for the Study of Intelligence, Central Intelligence Agency, 1998.

Foster, Wynn F. *Captain Hook: A Pilot's Tragedy and Triumph in the Vietnam War.* Annapolis, Md.: Naval Institute Press, 1992.

Frankum, Ronald B., Jr. *Like Rolling Thunder: The Air War in Vietnam, 1964–1975.* Lanham, Md.: Rowman and Littlefield, 2005.

Freedman, Dan, and Jacqueline Rhoads, eds. *Nurses in Vietnam: The Forgotten Veterans.* Austin, Tex.: Texas Monthly Press, 1987.

Frey-Wouters, Ellen, and Robert S Laufer. *Legacy of a War: The American Soldier in Vietnam.* Armonk, New York: M. E. Sharpe, 1986.

Gadd, Charles. *Line Doggie: Foot Soldier in Vietnam.* Novato, Calif.: Presidio, 1987.

Gaiduk, Ilya V. *The Soviet Union and the Vietnam War.* Chicago: Univ. of Chicago Press, 1996.

Gallucci, Robert L. *Neither Peace nor Honor: The Politics of American Military Policy in Vietnam.* Baltimore: Johns Hopkins Univ. Press, 1975.

Garland, Albert N. *Infantry in Vietnam.* New York: Ballantine Books, 1985.

Gettleman, Marvin, et al. *Vietnam and America: A Documented History.* New York: Grove Press, 1995.

Gibson, James William. *The Perfect War: Techno-War in Vietnam.* New York: Atlantic Monthly, 1987.

Gilbert, James L. *The Most Secret War: Army Signals Intelligence in Vietnam.* Washington, D.C.: Government Printing Office, 2003.

Gillcrist, Paul T. *Crusader: Last of the Gunfighters.* Atglen, Pa.: Schiffer Publishing, 1995.

Goff, Stanley, and Robert Sanders. *Brothers: Black Soldiers in Nam.* New York: Berkley Books, 1986.

Goldsmith, Wynn. *Papa Bravo Romeo: U.S. Navy Patrol Boats at War in Vietnam.* New York: Ballantine Books, 2001.

Goodman, Rupert Douglas. *Queensland Nurses: Boer War to Vietnam.* Brisbane, Queensland, Australia: Boolarong Publications, 1985.

Goodson, Barry L. *CAP Mot: The Story of a Marine Special Forces Unit in Vietnam, 1968–1969.* Denton, Tex.: Univ. of North Texas Press, 1997.

Grant, Zalin. *Over the Beach: The Air War in Vietnam.* New York: Norton, 1986.

Grey, Jeffrey. *Up Top: The Royal Australian Navy and Southeast Asian Conflicts, 1955–1972.* St. Leonards, Australia: Allen and Unwin, 1998.

Grey, Jeffrey, and Jeff Doyle. *Vietnam: War, Myth and Mystery: Comparative Perspectives on Australia's War in Vietnam.* North Sydney, Australia: Allen and Unwin, 1992.

Gruhzit-Hoyt, Olga. *A Time Remembered: American Women in the Vietnam War.* Novato, Calif.: Presidio Press, 1999.

Guan, Ang Chen. *Vietnamese Communists' Relations with China and the Second Indochina Conflict, 1956–1962.* Jefferson, N.C.: McFarland, 1997.

———. *The Vietnam War from the Other Side: The Vietnamese Communists' Perspective.* London, England: RoutledgeCurzon, 2002.

Guiden, Timothy Alan. *Defending America's Cambodian Incursion.* Charlottesville: Univ. of Virginia Press, 1993.

Gunston, Bill. *Aircraft of the Vietnam War.* San Bernardino, Calif.: Borgo Press, 1989.

Halberstadt, Hans. *War Stories of the Green Berets: The Viet Nam Experience.* Osceola, Wisc.: Motorbooks International, 1994.

Hall, Don C., and Annette R. Hall. *I Served.* Bellevue, Wash.: Hall Publishing, 2001.

Hamblen, Donald N., and B. H. Norton. *One Tough Marine: The Autobiography of First Sergeant Donald N. Hamblen, USMC.* New York: Ballantine Books, 1993.

Hammel, Eric. *KheSanh: Siege in the Clouds: An Oral History.* New York: Crown, 1989.

Hammond, William M. *Public Affairs: The Military and the Media, 1962–1968.* Washington, D.C.: U.S. Army Center of Military History, 1988.

———. *Public Affairs: The Military and the Media, 1968–1973.* Washington, D.C.: U.S. Army Center of Military History, 1996.

Hampton, Lynn. *The Fighting Strength: Memoirs of a Combat Nurse in Vietnam.* New York: Warner Books, 1992.

Hannah, Craig C. *Striving for Air Superiority: The Tactical Air Command in Vietnam.* College Station, Tex.: Texas A&M Univ. Press, 2002.

Hanson, Victor Davis. *Carnage and Culture.* New York: Anchor Books, 2001.

Heckman, Charles W. *The Phnom Penh Airlift: Confessions of a Pig Pilot in the Early 1970s.* Jefferson, N.C.: McFarland, 1990.

Hemingway, Albert. *Our Way Was Different: Marine Combined Action Platoons in Vietnam.* Annapolis, Md.: Naval Institute Press, 1994.

Hemphill, Robert. *Platoon: Bravo Company.* Fredericksburg, Va.: Sergeant Kirkland's Press, 1999.

Hendin, Herbert, and Ann Pollinger Haas. *Wounds of War: The Psychological Aftermath of Combat in Vietnam.* New York: Basic Books, 1984.

Herring, George C. *America's Longest War: The United States and Vietnam, 1950–1975,* 4th ed. New York: McGraw-Hill, 2001.

Hiam, Michael. *Who the Hell Are We Fighting? The Story of Sam Adams and the Vietnam Intelligence Wars.* Hanover, N.H.: Steerforth, 2006.

Hoang Khoi. *The Ho Chi Minh Trail.* Hanoi, Vietnam: Gioi Publishers, 2002.

Hoang Ngoc Thanh and Than Thi Nhan Duc. *Why the Vietnam War? President Ngo Dinh Diem and the U.S.: His Overthrow and Assassination.* Tuan-Yen and Quan-Viet, Vietnam: Mai-Nam Publishers, 2001.

Hoang Van Thai, Gen. *How South Viet Nam Was Liberated.* Hanoi, Vietnam: Gioi Publishers, 2005.

Hong, Kyudok. "Unequal Partners: ROK-US Relations during the Vietnam War." Ph.D. diss., University of South Carolina, 1991.

Howes, Craig. *Voices of the Vietnam POWs: Witnesses to Their Fight.* New York: Oxford Univ. Press, 1993.

Humphries, James F. *Through the Valley: Vietnam, 1967–1968.* Boulder, Colo.: Rienner, 1999.

Hunt, Richard A. *Pacification: The American Struggle for Vietnam's Hearts and Minds.* Boulder, Colo.: Westview, 1995.

Hutchens, James M. *Beyond Combat.* Great Falls, Va.: Shepherd's Press, 1986.

Hutchins, Joel. *Swimmers among the Trees: SEALs in the Vietnam War.* Novato, Calif.: Presidio Press, 1996.

Ieng Sary. *Cambodia 1972.* Phnom Penh, Cambodia: Royal Government of the National Union of Cambodia, 1972.

Institute of Medicine. *Veterans and Agent Orange: Health Effects of Herbicides Used in Vietnam.* Washington, D.C.: National Academy Press, 1994.

Johnson, James D. *Combat Chaplain: A Thirty-Year Vietnam Battle.* Denton, Tex.: Univ. of North Texas Press, 2001.

Johnson, Lawrence H. *Winged Sabers: The Air Cavalry in Vietnam, 1965–1973.* Harrisburg, Pa.: Stackpole Books, 1990.

Johnson, Sam, and Jan Winebrenner. *Captive Warriors: A Vietnam POW's Story.* College Station, Tex.: Texas A&M Univ. Press, 1992.

Jorgenson, Kregg P. J. *The Ghosts of the Highlands: 1st Cav LRRPs in Vietnam, 1966–67.* New York: Ivy Books, 1999.

Kaiser, David. *American Tragedy: Kennedy, Johnson, and the Origins of the Vietnam War.* Cambridge, Mass.: Harvard Univ. Press, 2000.

Kelley, Michael P. *Where We Were in Vietnam: A Comprehensive Guide to the Firebases, Military Installations and Naval Vessels of the Vietnam War, 1945–75.* Central Point, Oreg.: Hellgate Press, 2002.

Kugler, Ed. *Dead Center: A Marine Sniper's Two-Year Odyssey in the Vietnam War.* New York: Ivy Books, 1999.

Lacombe, Tom. *Light Ruck: Vietnam 1969.* Fort Valley, Va.: Loft Press, 2002.

Lake, Bruce R. *1500 Feet Over Vietnam: A Marine Helicopter Pilot's Diary.* Haverhill, N.H.: Almine Library, 1990.

Lang, Daniel. *Casualties of War.* New York: Pocket Books, 1989.

Lanning, Michael Lee. *Inside the Crosshairs: Snipers in Vietnam.* New York: Ivy Books, 1998.

Lanning, Michael, and Dan Cragg. *Inside the VC and the NVA.* New York: Ballantine Books, 1992.

Larzelere, Alex. *The Coast Guard at War: Vietnam, 1965–1975.* Annapolis, Md.: Naval Institute Press, 1997.

Lavell, Kit. *Flying Black Ponies: The Navy's Close Air Support Squadron in Vietnam.* Annapolis, Md.: Naval Institute Press, 2000.

Lawrence, Mark Atwood. *Assuming the Burden: Europe and the American Commitment to War in Vietnam.* Berkeley: Univ. of California Press, 2005.

———. *The Vietnam War: A Concise International History.* New York: Oxford Univ. Press, 2008.

Lee, Alex. *Force Recon Command: A Special Marine Unit in Vietnam, 1969–1970.* Annapolis, Md.: Naval Institute Press, 1995.

Lee, Chan-Shik, and Sae-ho Lee. *Korean Forces in Vietnam: Six Years for Peace and Construction.* Seoul, South Korea: HQs ROKF-V, 1971.

Leppelman, John. *Blood on the Risers: An Airborne Soldier's Thirty-Five Months in Vietnam.* New York: Ivy Books, 1991.

Lehrack, Otto J. *No Shining Armor: The Marines at War in Vietnam: An Oral History.* Lawrence: Univ. Press of Kansas, 1992.

Lester, Robert. *Vietnam Documents and Research Notes Series: Translation and Analysis of Significant Viet Cong/North Vietnamese Documents* (Microfilmed from the Holdings of the Library of the U.S. Army Military History Institute). Bethesda, Md.: University Publications of America, 1991.

Levant, Victor. *Quiet Complicity: Canadian Involvement in the Vietnam War.* Toronto, Canada: Between the Lines, 1986.

Lewis, Lloyd B. *The Tainted War: Culture and Identity in Vietnam War Narratives.* Westport, Conn.: Greenwood Press, 1985.

Li, Xiaobing. *A History of the Modern Chinese Army.* Lexington: Univ. Press of Kentucky, 2007.

Li, Xiaobing, and Richard Peters. *Voices from the Korean War: Personal Stories of American, Korean, and Chinese Soldiers.* Lexington: Univ. Press of Kentucky, 2004.

Li, Xiaobing, Allan R. Millett, and Bin Yu, trans. and eds. *Mao's Generals Remember Korea.* Lawrence: Univ. Press of Kansas, 2001.

Li, Xiaobing, and Hongshan Li, eds. *China and the United States: A New Cold War History.* New York: Univ. Press of America, 1998.

Linderer, Gary A. *Eyes Behind the Lines.* New York: Ivy Books, 1991.

Linnett, Richard, and Roberto Loiederman. *The Eagle Mutiny.* Annapolis, Md.: Naval Institute Press, 2001.

Lodge, Henry Cabot, Jr. *The Storm Has Many Eyes: A Personal Narrative.* New York: Kensington, 1981.

Lofgren, William W., and Richard R. Sexton. *Air War in Northern Laos: 1 April–30 June 1971.* Christiansburg, Va.: Dalley Book, 1993.

Logevall, Fredrik. "Bringing in the 'Other Side': New Scholarship on the Vietnam War." *Journal of Cold War Studies* 3, no. 3 (fall 2001): 77–93.

Lowry, Timothy S. *And Brave Men, Too.* New York: Crown, 1985.

MacLeod, Joan B. F., and Pamela Ann Barlow. *The Longest Mile: A Nurse in the Vietnam War, 1968–69.* Arcadia, Australia: P.A. Barlow, 2006.

Maneki, Sharon. *The Quiet Heroes of the Southwest Pacific Theater: An Oral History of the Men and Women of CBB and FRUMEL.* Washington, D.C.: Center for Cryptology History, National Security Agency, 1996.

Marolda, Edward J. *By Sea, Air, and Land: An Illustrated History of the U.S. Navy and the War in Southeast Asia.* Washington, D.C.: Naval Historical Center, 1994.

Marolda, Edward J., and Oscar P. Fitzgerald. *The U.S. Navy and Vietnam Conflict: From Military Assistance to Combat, 1959–1965.* Washington, D.C.: Government Printing Office, 1986.

Marshall, Kathryn. *In the Combat Zone: An Oral History of American Women in Vietnam, 1966–1975.* Boston, Mass.: Little, Brown, 1987.

Mason, Robert. *Chickenhawk.* New York: Viking, 1983.

Maurer, Harry. *Strange Ground: Americans in Vietnam, 1945–1975, An Oral History.* New York: Henry Holt, 1989.

McCarthy, A. J. *The Bay of Chaleur at War: From Vimy Ridge to Vietnam.* Halifax, Canada: Nimbus, 1998.

McGarvey, Patrick H. *Visions of Victory: Selected Vietnamese Communist Military Writings, 1964–1968.* Stanford, Calif.: Hoover Institution on War, 1969.

McMahon, Robert J., ed. *Major Problems in the History of the Vietnam War: Documents and Essays,* 3rd ed. Lexington, Mass.: D. C. Heath, 2003.

McNamara, Francis Terry, and Adrian Hill. *Escape with Honor: My Last Hours in Vietnam.* Washington D.C.: Brassey's, 1997.

Merrell, Betty J., and Priscilla Tunnell. *Stories That Won't Go Away: Women in Vietnam, 1959–1975.* Birmingham, Ala.: New Hope, 1995.

Mersky, Peter B. *F-8 Crusader Units of the Vietnam War.* London, England: Osprey, 1998.

Mersky, Peter B., and Norman Polmar. *The Naval Air War in Vietnam.* New York: Kensington, 1981.

Mertel, Kenneth D. *Year of the Horse: Vietnam, 1st Air Cavalry in the Highlands, 1965–1967.* Atglen, Pa.: Schiffer Publishing, 1997.

Mesko, Jim. *Airmobile: The Helicopter War in Vietnam.* Carrollton, Tex.: Squadron/Signal Publications, 1984.

Michel, Marshall. *Clashes: Air Combat over North Vietnam, 1965–1972.* Annapolis, Md.: Naval Institute Press, 1997.

———. *The Eleven Days of Christmas: America's Last Vietnam Battle.* San Francisco, Calif.: Encounter Books, 2002.

Mikesh, Robert C. *Flying Dragons: The South Vietnamese Air Force.* Atglen, Pa.: Schiffer Publishing, 2005.

Mills, Hugh, L., and Robert A. Anderson. *Low Level Hell: A Scout Pilot in the Big Red One.* Novato, Calif.: Presidio Press, 1992.

Ministry of Foreign Affairs and Party Archives and Manuscript Research Center of the CCP Central Committee, comps. *Mao Zedong on Diplomacy.* Beijing: Foreign Languages Press, 1998.

Moore, Harold G., and Joseph L. Galloway. *We Were Soldiers Once . . . and Young: Ia Drang—The Battle That Changed the War in Vietnam.* New York: Harper-Collins, 1992.

Moreau, Donna. *Waiting Wives.* New York: Atria, 2005.

Morgan, Paul B. *K-9 Soldiers: Vietnam and After.* Central Point, Oreg.: Hellgate Press, 1999.

Moriarty, J. M. *Ground Attack—Vietnam: The Marines Who Controlled the Skies.* New York: Ivy Books, 1993.

Moss, George Donelson. *Vietnam: An American Ordeal,* 6th ed. Upper Saddle River, N.J.: Prentice Hall, 2010.

Moyar, Mark. *Triumph Forsaken: The Vietnam War, 1954–1965.* New York: Cambridge Univ. Press, 2006.

Muir, Malcolm, Jr., and Mark F. Wilkinson, eds. *The Most Dangerous Years: The Cold War, 1953–1975.* Lexington: Virginia Military Institute, 2005.

Mullen, Robert W. *Blacks in Vietnam.* Washington, D.C.: Univ. Press of America, 1981.

Myers, Thomas. *Walking Point: American Narratives of Vietnam.* New York: Oxford Univ. Press, 1988.

Nagl, John A. *Learning to Eat Soup with a Knife: Counterinsurgency Lessons from Malaya and Vietnam.* Chicago: Univ. of Chicago Press, 2005.

National Guard Bureau. "Guard Aero Med Team Meets Unexpected Crisis." *The National Guardsman* (March 1967): 11–14.

National Intelligence Council. *Estimative Products on Vietnam, 1948–1975.* Washington, D.C.: Government Printing Office, 2005.

———. *Tracking the Dragon: National Intelligence Estimates on China during the Era of Mao, 1948–1976.* Washington, D.C.: Government Printing Office, 2004.

National United Front of Cambodia. *The Armed Struggle and Life of the Khmer People in the Liberated Areas in Pictures.* Cambodia: NUFC Press (National United Front of Cambodia), 1971.

———. *The Military Situation in Cambodia at the End of October 1970.* Cambodia: Office of Samdech Norodom Sihanouk, 1970.

———. *Reality of the NUF and Its Armed Forces in Cambodia.* Cambodia: Office of Samdech Norodom Sihanouk, 1970.

Nichols, J. B., and B. Tillman. *On Yankee Station: The Naval Air War over Vietnam.* Annapolis, Md.: Naval Institute Press, 1987.

Nolan, Keith William. *Death Valley: The Summer Offensive, I Corps, August 1969.* Novato, Calif.: Presidio, 1999.

Norman, Elizabeth. *Women at War: The Story of Fifty Military Nurses Who Served in Vietnam.* Philadelphia: Univ. of Pennsylvania Press, 1990.

Norman, Geoffrey. *Bouncing Back: How a Heroic Band of POWs Survived Vietnam.* Boston, Mass.: Houghton Mifflin, 1990.

O'Brien, Tim. *If I Die in a Combat Zone: Box Me Up and Ship Me Home.* New York: Delacorte Press/Seymour Lawrence, 1973.

O'Keefe, Brendan G., and F. B. Smith. *Medicine at War: Medical Aspects of Australia's Involvement in Southeast Asia, 1950–1972.* St. Leonards, Australia: Allen and Unwin, 1994.

Olsen, Howard. *Issues of the Heart: Memoirs of an Artilleryman in Vietnam.* Jefferson, N.C.: McFarland, 1990.

Palazzo, Albert. *Australian Military Operations in Vietnam.* Canberra, Australia: Army History Unit, 2006.

Palek, Charlie. *Tattletale: A Two-Tour Vietnam Veteran's Combat Experiences on the Ground and in the Air.* Columbia, Mo.: Softlight Photography, 2001.

Palmer, Laura. *Shrapnel in the Heart: Letters and Remembrances from the Vietnam Veterans Hospital.* New York: Vintage, 1987.

Pape, Robert A. *Bombing to Win: Air Power and Coercion in War.* Ithaca, N.Y.: Cornell Univ. Press, 1996.

Parrish, Robert D. *Combat Recon: My Year with the ARVN.* New York: St. Martin's Press, 1991.

Peterson, Michael E. *The Combined Actions Platoons: The U.S. Marines' Other War in Vietnam.* New York: Praeger, 1989.

Phạm, Kim Vinh. *In Their Defense: U.S. Soldiers in the Vietnam War.* Phoenix, Ariz.: Sphinx Publishing, 1985.

Phung The Tai, Gen. *Remembering Uncle Ho: Memories in War Years.* Hanoi, Vietnam: Gioi Publishers, 2005.

Pike, Douglas. *PAVN: People's Army of Vietnam.* Novato, Calif.: Presidio Press, 1986.

———. *Vietnam and the Soviet Union: Anatomy of an Alliance.* Boulder, Colo.: Westview, 1987.

Pisor, Robert. *The End of the Line: The Siege of Khe Sanh.* New York: Ballantine Books, 1983.

Plaster, John L. *SOG: A Photo History of the Secret Wars.* Boulder, Colo.: Paladin Press, 2000.

Powell, John, ed. *Magill's Guide to Military History.* 6 vols. Pasadena, Calif.: Salem Press, 2001.

Prados, John. *Safe for Democracy: The Secret Wars of the CIA.* Chicago: Ivan R. Dee, 2006.

———. *Vietnam: The History of an Unwinnable War, 1945–1975.* Lawrence: Univ. Press of Kansas, 2009.

Prashker, Ivan. *Duty, Honor, Vietnam: Twelve Men of West Point Tell Their Stories.* New York: William Morrow, 1988.

Pribbenow, Merle L., trans. *Victory in Vietnam: Official History of the PAVN.* Lawrence: Univ. Press of Kansas, 2002.

Redmond, Jessica. *A Year of Absence: Six Women's Stories of Courage, Hope and Love.* New York: Elva Resa, 2005.

Roberts, Priscilla, ed. *Behind the Bamboo Curtain: China, Vietnam, and the World beyond Asia.* Stanford, Calif.: Stanford Univ. Press, 2006.

Ronnau, Christopher. *Blood Trails: The Combat Diary of a Foot Soldier in Vietnam.* New York: Ballantine, 2006.

Ross, Angus. *The New Zealander at War.* Auckland, New Zealand: New Zealand Publishing Society, 1966.

Rotter, Andrew Jon. *Light at the End of the Tunnel: A Vietnam War Anthology.* Wilmington, Del.: SR Books, 1999.

Rottman, Gordon L. *Green Beret in Vietnam: 1957–73.* Oxford, England: Osprey, 2002.

Rowe, James G., and Gary Rowe Prescott. *Love to All, Jim: A Young Man's Letters from Vietnam.* San Francisco, Calif.: Strawberry Hill Press, 1989.

Ryan, Mark A., David M. Finkelstein, and Michael A. McDevitt, eds. *Chinese Warfighting: The PLA Experience since 1949.* New York: M. E. Sharpe, 2003.

SarDesai, D. R. *Southeast Asia: Past and Present.* Boulder, Colo.: Westview, 2003.

———. *Vietnam: Past and Present,* 4th ed. Boulder, Colo.: Westview, 2005.

Santoli, A., ed. *Everything We Had: An Oral History of the Vietnam War by*

Thirty-Three American Soldiers Who Fought It. New York: Random House, 1981.

Schild, James J. *For Garry Owen in Glory: The True Account of an Airmobile Platoon Leader in Vietnam, 1968–69*. Florissant, Mo.: Auto Review Publishing, 1989.

Schmid, Alex P., and Ellen Berends. *Soviet Military Interventions since 1945*. New Brunswick, N.J.: Transaction Books, 1985.

Schneider, Donald K. *Air Force Heroes in Vietnam*. Washington, D.C.: Office of Air Force History, U.S. Air Force, 1986.

Schreadley, R. L. *From the Rivers to the Sea: The United States Navy in Vietnam*. Annapolis, Md.: Naval Institute Press, 1992.

Scotti, Paul C. *Coast Guard Action in Vietnam: Stories of Those Who Served*. Central Point, Oreg.: Hellgate Press, 2000.

Senich, Peter R. *The Long-Range War: Sniping in Vietnam*. Boulder, Colo.: Paladin Press, 1994.

———. *The One-Round War: USMC Scout-Snipers in Vietnam*. Boulder, Colo.: Paladin Press, 1996.

Shellenbarger, Jean. *The 9th Engineer Battalion, First Marine Division, in Vietnam: 35 Personal Accounts*. Jefferson, N.C.: McFarland, 2000.

Sherwood, John Darrell. *Fast Movers: America's Jet Pilots and the Vietnam Experience*. New York: Free Press, 2000.

Shulimson, Jack. *U.S. Marines in Vietnam: The Landing and the Buildup, 1965*. Nashville, Tenn.: Battery Press, 1996.

———. *U.S. Marines in Vietnam: 1966*. Washington, D.C.: U.S. Marine Corps, 1982.

Silvey, Michael W. *Knives of the United States Military in Vietnam*. Sacramento, Calif.: M. W. Silvey, 1997.

Simpson, Howard R. *Tiger in the Barbed Wire: An American in Vietnam, 1952–1991*. Washington, D.C.: Brassey's, 1992.

Smith, Eric. *Not by the Book: A Combat Intelligence Officer in Vietnam*. New York: Ivy Books, 1993.

Smith, R. B. *An International History of the Vietnam War: Revolution versus Containment, 1955–1961*. 2 vols. New York: Macmillan and Palgrave, 1987.

Smith, Tom. *Easy Target: The Long, Strange Trip of a Scout Pilot in Vietnam*. Novato, Calif.: Presidio Press, 1996.

Smith, Winnie. *American Daughter Gone to War: On the Front Lines with an Army Nurse in Vietnam*. New York: W. Morrow, 1992.

Spector, Ronald H. *After Tet: The Bloodiest Year in Vietnam*. New York: Free Press, 1993.

Spence, Jonathan D. *Advice and Support: The Early Year of the United States Army in Vietnam, 1941–1960*. Washington, D.C.: U.S. Army Center for Military History, 1984.

———. *The Search for Modern China*, 2nd ed. New York: Norton, 1999.

Stanton, Shelby L. *The 1st Calvary in Vietnam: Anatomy of a Division.* Novato, Calif.: Presidio Press, 1999.

———. *The Rise and Fall of an American Army: U.S. Ground Forces in Vietnam, 1965–1973.* Novato, Calif.: Presidio Press, 1985.

Stevens, Paul Drew. *The Navy Cross: Vietnam: Citations of Awards to Men of the U.S. Navy and the United States Marine Corps, 1964–1973.* Forest Ranch, Calif.: Sharp and Dunnigan Publications, 1987

Strayer, Robert. *The Communist Experiment: Revolution, Socialism, and Global Conflict in the Twentieth Century.* Boston, Mass.: McGraw Hill, 2007.

Summers, Harry G., Jr. *On Strategy: A Critical Analysis of the Vietnam War.* Washington, D.C.: Government Printing Office, 1981.

Sympson, Kenneth P. *Images from the Otherland: Memoir of a United States Marine Corps Artillery Officer in Vietnam.* Jefferson, N.C.: McFarland, 1995.

Taylor, John M. *General Maxwell Taylor: The Sword and the Pen.* New York: Doubleday, 1989.

Taylor, Sandra C. *Vietnamese Women at War: Fighting for Ho Chi Minh and the Revolution.* Lawrence: Univ. Press of Kansas, 2003.

TeCube, Leroy. *Year in Nam: A Native American Soldier's Story.* Lincoln: Univ. of Nebraska Press, 1999.

Terry, Wallace, ed. *Bloods: Black Veterans of the Vietnam War: An Oral History.* Novato, Calif.: Presidio Press, 1985.

Thayer, Thomas C. *War without Fronts: The American Experience in Vietnam.* Boulder, Colo.: Westview, 1985.

Tilford, Earl H., Jr. *Crosswinds: The Air Force's Setup in Vietnam.* College Station: Texas A&M Univ. Press, 1993.

———. *Setup: What the Air Force Did in Vietnam and Why.* Maxwell Air Force Base, Ala.: U.S. Air University Press, 1991.

Tran Van Tra. *Vietnam: History of the Bulwark B2 Theatre: The 30-Year War.* Ho Chi Minh City, Vietnam: Van Nghe Publishing House, 1982.

Trauschweizer, Ingo. *The Cold War U.S. Army: Building Deterrence for Limited War.* Lawrence: Univ. Press of Kansas, 2008.

Tripp, Nathaniel. *Father, Soldier, Son: Memoir of a Platoon Leader in Vietnam.* South Royalton, Vt.: Steerforth Press, 1996.

Trujillo, Charley, ed. *Soldados: Chicanos in Vietnam.* Albuquerque, N.Mex.: Chusma House, 1989.

Truong Nhu Tang. *A Viet Cong Memoir.* New York: Random House, 1985.

Tucker, Spencer C. *Vietnam.* Lexington: Univ. Press of Kentucky, 1999.

Tucker, Spencer C., ed. *The Encyclopedia of the Vietnam War: A Political, Social, and Military History.* Oxford, England: Oxford Univ. Press, 1998.

Turley, G. H. *The Easter Offensive, Vietnam, 1972.* Novato, Calif.: Presidio Press, 1985.

Van Devanter, Lynda. *Home before Morning: The Story of an Army Nurse in Vietnam.* Boston: Massachusetts Univ. Press, 2001.

Van Tien Dung. *Our Great Spring Victory.* New York: Monthly Review Press, 1977.

Vaughan, David Kirk. *Runway Visions: An American C-130 Pilot's Memoir of Combat Airlift Operations in Southeast Asia, 1967–1968*. Jefferson, N.C.: McFarland, 1998.

Veterans Administration. *Myths and Realities: A Study of Attitudes toward Vietnam Era Veterans*. Washington, D.C.: Government Printing Office, 1980.

Veith, George J. *Codename Bright Light: The Untold Story of U.S. POW Rescue Efforts during the Vietnam War*. New York: Free Press, 1998.

Vo Nguyen Giap, Gen. *Big Victory, Great Task*. New York: Praeger, 1963.

———. *People's War, People's Army*. New York: Bantam, 1962.

Vo Nguyen Giap and Van Tien Dung. *How We Won the War*. Ypsilanti, Mich.: RECON Publications, 1976.

Walker, Keith. *A Piece of My Heart: The Stories of 26 American Women Who Served in Vietnam*. Novato, Calif.: Presidio Press, 1999.

Walker, Paul D. *Jungle Dragoon: The Memoir of an Armored Cav Platoon Leader in Vietnam*. Novato, Calif.: Presidio Press, 1999.

Walt, L. W. *Strange War, Strange Strategy: A General's Report on Vietnam*. New York: Funk and Wagnalls, 1970.

War Experience Recapitulation Committee of the Military Institute. *The Anti-U.S. Resistance War for National Salvation 1954–1975: Military Events*. Hanoi, Vietnam: People's Army Publishing House, 1980.

Ward, Joseph T. *Dear Mom: A Sniper's Vietnam*. New York: Ivy Books, 1991.

Warner, Roger. *Back Fire: The CIA's Secret War in Laos and Its Link to the War in Vietnam*. New York: Simon and Schuster, 1970.

Weldon, Charles. *Tragedy in Paradise: A Country Doctor at War in Laos*. Bangkok, Thailand: Asia Books, 1999.

West, Philip, Steven I. Levine, and Jackie Hiltz, eds. *America's Wars in Asia: A Cultural Approach to History and Memory*. Armonk, N.Y.: M. E. Sharpe, 1998.

Westad, Odd Arne, ed. *Brothers in Arms: The Rise and Fall of the Sino-Soviet Alliance, 1945–1963*. Washington, D.C., and Stanford, Calif.: Woodrow Wilson Center Press and Stanford Univ. Press, 1998.

———. *The Global Cold War: Third World Interventions and the Making of Our Times*. Cambridge, England: Cambridge Univ. Press, 2007.

Westad, Odd Arne, Chen Jian, Stein Tonnesson, Nguyen Vu Tungand, and James G. Hershberg, eds. "77 Conversations between Chinese and Foreign Leaders on the Wars in Indochina, 1964–1977." Cold War International History Project, Working Paper No. 22. Washington, D.C.: Woodrow Wilson International Center for Scholars, 1998.

Westbrook, Lee. *The Broken Sword*. Grapevine, Tex.: Nissi Publishing, 1996.

Westheider, James E. *Fighting on Two Fronts: African Americans and the Vietnam War*. New York: New York Univ. Press, 1997.

Westmoreland, William C. *A Soldier Reports*. Garden City, N.Y.: Doubleday, 1976.

Whitlow, Robert H. *U.S. Marines in Vietnam: The Advisory and Combat Assistance Era, 1954–1964.* Washington, D.C.: Government Printing Office, 1977.

Wiest, Andrew, ed. *Rolling Thunder in a Gentle Land.* New York: Osprey, 2006.

————. *Vietnam's Forgotten Army: Heroism and Betrayal in the ARVN.* New York: New York Univ. Press, 2007.

Wilson, James R. *Landing Zones: Southern Veterans Remember Vietnam.* Durham, N.C.: Duke Univ. Press, 1990.

Willbanks, James H. *Abandoning Vietnam: How America Left and South Vietnam Lost Its War.* Lawrence: Univ. Press of Kansas, 2008.

Xinhua News Agency. *China's Foreign Relations: A Chronology of Events, 1949–88.* Beijing: Foreign Languages Press, 1989.

Yedinak, Steven M. *Hard to Forget: An American with the Mobile Guerrilla Force in Vietnam.* New York: Ivy Books, 1998.

Yi, Kil J. "Alliance in the Quagmire: The United States, South Korea, and the Vietnam War, 1964–1968." Ph.D. diss., Rutgers University, 1997.

Young, Darryl. *The Element of Surprise: Navy SEALs in Vietnam.* New York: Ivy Books, 1990.

Young, Marilyn B. *The Vietnam Wars, 1945–1990.* New York: HarperCollins, 1991.

Young, Rick. *Combat Police: U.S. Army Military Police in Vietnam.* Farmingdale, N.J.: Sendraak's Writings, 1997.

Zaffiri, S. *Westmoreland. A Biography of General William C. Westmoreland.* New York: Morrow, 1994.

————. *Hamburger Hill, May 11–20, 1969.* Novato, Calif.: Presidio Press, 1988.

Zeinert, Karen. *The Valiant Women of the Vietnam War.* Brookfield, Conn.: Millbrook Press, 2000.

Zhai, Qiang. *China and the Vietnam Wars, 1950–1975.* Chapel Hill: Univ. of North Carolina Press, 2000.

Zhu, Fang. *Gun Barrel Politics: Party-Army Relations in Mao's China.* Boulder, Colo.: Westview, 1998.

Vietnamese Language

Dang Cong San Viet Nam (Vietnamese Communist Party Committee). *Dang Vien Cao Nien Tuoi Dang* (Generals of the Vietnamese Communist Party). Long Xuyen, An Giang, Vietnam: Dang Bo Thanh Pho, 2002.

Kim Chin-sŏn, and Việt Hùng Phạm. *Ký úc Chiến Tranh: Sách Tham Khảo* (Narratives and Biographical Information on South Korean Generals during Vietnam War). Hà Nọî, Vietnam: Nhà xuát bản Chính trị quốc gia, 2002.

Lam Giang. *Chien Cong Cua Nhung Nguoi Ahn Hung* (My Story of the War). Ho Chi Minh City, Vietnam: Nha Xuat Ban Tre (Ban Tre Publishers), 2005.

Nguyen Nhi. *Con Gai Nguoi Gac Den Bien* (Daughter of the Service Man). Dallas, Tex.: Vhnt Publishing, 1999.

Nguyen Phuong Thao. *Cho Mot Ngay Hoa Binh* (For One Day Peace). Ho Chi Minh City, Vietnam: Nha Xuat Ban Tre (Ban Tre Publishers), 2004.

Nhieu Tac Gia (Composition Group). *Cuoc Khang Chien Chong My* (Fighting the American War). Ho Chi Minh City, Vietnam: Nha Xuat Ban Tre (Ban Tre Publishers), 2005.

Tap Ban Do Hanh Chinh, *Viet Nam* (Vietnam Administrative Atlas). Hanoi, Vietnam: Nha Xuat Ban Ban Do (Ban Do Cartographic Publishing House), 2005.

Vo Bam, Maj. Gen. *Viet Nam Di Tien Phong* (Fight for Vietnam). Ho Chi Minh City, Vietnam: Nha Xuat Ban Tre (Ban Tre Publishers), 2004.

Chinese Language

Chen Pai. *Yuezhan qinliji* (My Personal Experience in the Vietnam War). Zhengzhou: Henan renmin chubanshe (Henan People's Press), 1997.

Guo Ming. *Zhongyue guanxi yanbian sishinian* (Uncertain Relations between China and Vietnam, 1949-1989). Nanning: Guangxi renmin chubanshe (Guangxi People's Press), 1992.

Han Huaizhi. *Dangdai zhongguo jundui de junshi gongzuo* (Military Affairs of Contemporary China). 2 vols. Beijing: Zhongguo shehui kexue chubanshe (China Social Sciences Press), 1989.

Li Danhui, ed. "The Sino-Soviet Dispute over Assistance for Vietnam's Anti-American War, 1965-1972." http://www.shenzhihua.net/ynzz/000123.htm.

———. *Zhongguo yu yindu zhina zhanzheng* (China and the Indochina Wars). Hong Kong: Tiandi Tushu (Heavenly Earth Books), 2000.

Li Ke and Hao Shengzhang. *Wenhua dageming zhong de renmin jiefangjun* (The PLA in the Cultural Revolution). Beijing: Zhonggong dangshi ziliao chubanshe (CCP Historical Document Press), 1989.

Military History Research Division, China Academy of Military Science, ed. *Junqi piaopiao: xinzhongguo 50 nian junshi dashi shushi* (PLA Flag Fluttering; Facts of China's Major Military Events in the Past Fifty Years). 2 vols. Beijing: Jiefangjun chubanshe (PLA Press), 1999.

Qu Aiguo, Bao Mingrong, and Xiao Zuyue, eds. *Yuanyue kangmei: zhongguo zhiyuan budui zai yuenan* (Aid Vietnam and Resist America; China's Supporting Forces in Vietnam). Beijing: Junshi kexue chubanshe (Military Science Press), 1995.

Shang Like and Xing Zhiyuan, eds. *Xuesa yuenan: 60 niandai yuanyue kangmei zhandi caifang jishi* (Bleeding Vietnam: Our Trips to the Front during the Vietnam War in the 1960s). Beijing: Zhongguo renshi chubanshe (China Human Resources Press), 1993.

International Liaison Division Records, *PRC Ministry of Railway Administration Archives*.

Tang, Truong Nhu, with David Chanoff and Doan Van Toai. *Yu Hanoi fendao yangbiao* (Parting Company with Hanoi). Beijing: Shijie zhishi chubanshe (World Knowledge Press), 1989.

Tong Xiaopeng. *Fengyu sishinian* (Forty Years in the Storm of Struggle). 2 vols. Beijing: Zhongyang wenxian chubanshe (CCP Central Archives and Manuscript Press), 1996.

Wang Dinglie. *Dangdai zhongguo kongjun* (Contemporary Chinese Air Force). Beijing: Zhongguo shehui kexue chubanshe (China's Social Sciences Press), 1989.

Zhang Aiping et al. *Zhongguo renmin jiefangjun* (The Chinese People's Liberation Army). 2 vols. Beijing: Dangdai zhongguo chubanshe (Contemporary China Press), 1994.

Zhang Baijia and Niu Jun, eds. *Lengzhan yu zhongguo* (The Cold War and China). Beijing: Shijie zhishi chubanshe (World Knowledge Publishing), 2002.

Korean Language

Ch'ae, Myŏng-sin. *Pet'ŭnam Chŏnjaeng kwa Hangukkun* (History of South Korean Armed Forces in Vietnam). Sŏul, South Korea: Pet'ŭnam Ch'amjŏn Chŏnuhoe, 2002.

Kim, Chin-sŏn. *San cha ŭi Chŏnjaeng, Chugŭn cha ŭi Chŏnjaeng: 4-sŏng Changgun Kim Chin-sŏn ŭi Wŏllamjŏn Ch'amjŏn Kobaek Sugi* (Personal Narratives and Biographical Information on South Korean Generals during Vietnam War). Sŏul, South Korea: Chungang M & B, 2000.

Pak, Chŏng-hwan. *Nŭsi* (Korean Prisoners [during the Vietnam War]). Sŏul-si, South Korea: Munyedang, 2000.

P'awŏl Chŏnsa P'yŏnch'an Wiwŏnhoe. *Wŏllamjŏn kwa Koyŏpche: Wŏllam ch'amjŏn 33-yŏnsa* (South Korea in the Vietnam War: Chemical Warfare, Agent Orange, and Diseases of the Veterans). Sŏul T'ŭkpyŏlsi, South Korea: Chŏnu Sinmunsa, 1997.

P'awŏl Hangukkun Chonsa Sajinjip (Pictorial War History of ROK Forces to Vietnam). Seoul, South Korea: ROK Ministry of National Defense, 1970.

Taet'ongnyo'ng Sosok U'imunsa Chinsang Kyumyo'ng wiwo'nhow (A Hard Journey to Justice: Report by the Presidential Commission on Suspicious Deaths of the ROK Soldiers). Seoul, South Korea: Samin Books, 2004.

Yi, Tae-yong. *Saigong Ŏngnyugi* (Prisoners in Vietnam). Sŏul, South Korea: Hanjin Ch'ulp'ansa, 1981.

Index

aircraft, 6, 79, 81, 91, 115
  American, 71, 89, 93, 95
  B-52, 70, 117, 201
  Boeing 707, 113
  C-130, 158–59, 160
  C-135, 159
  C-141, 155–56
  Chinese, 215
  F-4C, 88
  F-105, 79, 88, 89
  F-105F, 88
  F-105G, 88
  F-111, 71
  jet engine, 82
  KC-135, 201
Alaska Barge and Transport, 193
Allen, Richard, 124
ammunition, 191, 193, 196, 215
An Giang, 16, 55, 60, 62
An Hoa, 114
An Khe, 52
Annam Cordillera, 44
Army of the Republic of Vietnam (ARVN;
    South Vietnam), 15, 17, 19, 20, 23, 32,
    61, 107, 111, 118, 210, 223, 225–26
  Airborne Division, 23–24, 27–28
  air force of, 167
  casualties of, 20, 21, 24, 25
  corruption in, 17, 26, 35–36
  desertion, 20, 24, 26
  drafting, 17, 24, 165, 168, 207
  First Battalion, Third Regiment (An
      Giang Command), 16, 19–20
  Fourth Tactical Zone, 19, 166, 171
  Giang Doan Naval Base, 32, 34
  Ham Doi Naval Base, 32, 34
  high command, 23, 27
  national force of, 24
  nationalism of, 15, 23
  navy of, 31–32, 33–34, 233–34n8, 234n9
  offensives, 51, 52
  officers, 19, 20, 26, 34–36, 165
  operations, 17, 19, 20, 25, 31, 35, 45, 46

  organization of, 16, 24, 195, 232n8
  popular force, 20, 24
  popularity of, 17, 19
  postwar prison, 1, 11, 37, 210, 246n2
  replenishment, 26, 27
  Second Tactical Zone, 171
  Seventy-fourth Medical Group, 171
  training, 17, 19, 20–21, 23, 24–25, 27, 31,
      33–34
  Twenty-third Infantry Division, 24, 25,
      27
  U.S. aid to, 16, 167
artillery, 44, 113, 115, 117, 127, 134, 174,
    180
  55 mm AAA, 87
  57 mm AAA, 75, 86
  60 mm mortar, 57, 62, 174
  75 mm recoilless, 57, 59
  76 mm AAA, 75, 79, 87
  80 mm, 57
  82 mm, 57
  85 mm AAA, 86, 92
  100 mm AAA, 75, 76, 79, 86, 90
  105 mm, 51
  120 mm, 60
  155 mm, 60, 106
  175 mm, 106
  AAA fix of, 89
  AAA rocket, 43
  Chinese AAA guns, 87–88
  Chinese imitation of Russians, 87
  Chinese made, 57, 92, 215
  French made, 58
  French technology, 58
  NVA, 55, 56, 57–59, 60, 61
  NVA training center in China, 57
  projectiles of, 193
  Russian made, 60, 76, 86
  shells from China, 215
  six-rocket launchers, 57
  support, 52
  technology, 55, 56
  U.S. air-defense artillery, 102

artillery *(cont.)*
 U.S. Army Field Artillery Center, 112
 U.S. troops of, 60, 102, 117
 Viet Cong, 55, 56, 60, 194
Asia, 177
Astana, 6
attrition warfare, 5

B., Mr. (pseud.; KGB agent), 93–94
Bac Ninh, 91
Bangkok, 200
Bao Dai, Emperor, 166
Bao Thang, 218
Beijing, 3, 5, 7, 77, 85, 86, 97, 98, 215, 217,
 223
 Regional Command, 79
 Vietnamese leaders in, 225, 239n9
Bien Hoa, 103, 104, 132, 133
Brezhnev, Leonid, 2, 3
Buddhists, 15, 17, 19, 20, 22, 232n6

Cai Dau, 19, 20
Ca Mau, 19
Ca Mau River, 60
Cambodia, 40, 49, 54, 77, 103, 106, 136,
 166, 174
 border of, 53, 54, 60, 174, 175
 "killing fields" of, 174, 247n8
 U.S. incursion of, 54
Cam Rahn Bay, 104, 192, 193, 194, 195, 196
Can Tho, 19, 159, 166, 169, 171, 174
Catholic, 15, 232n6
 ARVN officer, 15, 19
 church, 207, 213
 college, 56
 priest, 207
Central Highlands (South Vietnam), 40,
 45, 47, 48, 51, 53, 103
Central Intelligence Agency (CIA), 131, 132
Cham Lan, 28
Chang, Jung, 5
Cha Rang Valley, 103
Chen Jian, 3
China, People's Republic of (PRC), 1, 3, 6,
 7, 9, 73–74, 82, 97
 aid to Vietnam, 3, 73, 74, 215, 223,
 230n13

air space of, 79
alliance with the Soviet Union, 3
border with Vietnam, 78
counterattack war against Vietnam, 7, 73
defense of, 77
engineering schools for Vietnamese, 57
Great Proletariat Cultural Revolution
 (1966–1976), 3, 74, 88, 97
leaders of, 85, 86, 223
northern, 81
northeastern, 74, 78, 83
NVA officer academy in, 57
railroad construction agreement with
 Vietnam, 217–18
rapprochement with the U.S., 228
relations with Vietnam, 7, 73, 77, 174
sending Chinese troops, 5, 7, 73
southwestern, 78, 87
Chinese Civil War (1946–1949), 86, 216
Chinese Communist Party (CCP), 76, 228
 Central Military Commission of, 217
 members of, 76, 77
Chinese Nationalist Army, 86
Chosin Reservoir, 216
Christianity, 15, 19, 136, 206
Chu Lai, 125
Cluff, Greg, 115
cold war, 3, 7, 223, 228
Communist, 1, 145
 ideology, 76, 121, 145, 165
 international aid to Vietnam, 6, 230n13
 international revolution, 3, 184, 206
 leadership, 8
 movements in Asia, 2, 5, 223
Con Dao, 171
Crea, Dominick, 108
Cuba, 67

Da Nang, 27, 47, 119, 143, 144, 145, 147,
 148, 150, 158, 167
Dang Thanh, 27
decoration awarded
 ARVN Courageous Combatant Medal,
 168
 ARVN Honor Medal, 171
 U.S. Army commendation medal
 (ARCOM), 104

U.S. Navy-Marine Corps Medal, 115
U.S. Silver Star, 124
Deo Nong Nuoc, 27
Deo Phu Da, 27
Dien Bien Phu, Battle of (1954), 41, 59, 167
DMZ (Demilitarized Zone), 113
Doss, Gary, 123–24
Dung Tao, 28
Duong Van Minh, 28

education, 192
    American, 102, 112, 120, 143, 144, 151,
        154, 199
    American college, 177, 191, 213
    Chinese, 74–75, 76
    French, 166, 206
    North Vietnamese, 42, 62
    North Vietnamese college, 207
    Russian, 66
    South Vietnamese, 16, 31, 32, 56, 166–
        67, 206–7
    South Vietnamese college, 209
18th parallel, 44

family, 108, 149, 199
    American, 102, 108, 109, 117, 119, 137,
        138, 139, 143, 158, 161, 163, 197
    Chinese, 74–75
    North Vietnamese, 41, 48, 59
    Russian, 66, 67
    South Vietnamese, 9, 16–17, 24, 32–33,
        56, 136, 166, 167, 173, 174, 206–8,
        210–13
    Viet Cong, 61–62
firepower, 49, 53, 81
forward observer (FO), 113, 117
French, 73, 134
    colonial policy, 56
    defeat, 59, 167
    government, 166, 167, 206
    Indochinese Union, 206
    military force, 56, 166, 167, 224
    occupation of Indochina, 166
    railroads built by, 220, 221
French Indochina War (1946–1954), 1, 16,
    39, 41, 43, 55, 56, 57, 59, 66, 67, 73,
    165, 206, 224

Geneva Convention on POWs, 183
Geneva Settlement of Indochina (1954),
    42, 55, 167, 207
Gih Dinh, 206, 207
Glasnost Foundation, 94
Go Quao River, 35
Graham, Annie Ruth, 159
Graves, David, 199–200
Green, Wallace M., 123
Grigoryantz, Sergei, 94
Guam, 199
Guangxi, 78, 218
guerrilla, 46, 49, 145
    campaign, 73
    force, 32, 46
    NVA and, 45, 49, 60
    tactics, 86, 91, 92, 145
    Viet Cong and, 46
    warfare, 8, 61
Gulf War, 111
Guo Haiyun, 6, 85–86
Guo Yenlin, 217

Hai Phong, 207
Halliday, Jon, 5
Hamilton, Judy Crausbay, 153–54, 156
Hanoi, 7, 8, 39, 40, 43, 54, 55, 59, 60, 62,
    65, 69, 73, 77, 91, 96, 97, 98, 172, 206,
    207, 215, 217, 223, 228
    Capital Division from, 43
    Medical University of, 166
    Russian spies in, 93, 94
    Soviet embassy in, 94
    Soviet leaders in, 2
    University of, 207
Hao Binh, 79
Harbin, 73, 84
Harris, James, 124
Ha Tinh, 71
Heilongjiang, 73, 84
Hekou, 218
helicopter, 28, 52, 123
    CH-46, 114
    crash, 168
    gunship, 180
    Huey, 128
    ARVN, 27, 28, 52, 168

helicopter *(cont.)*
  Seahorse, 123
  Sikorsky, 123
  UH-34D, 123, 125
  U.S., 52, 53, 168, 244n7
Heston, Charlton, 147
Hoa Hung, 207, 210
Ho Chi Minh, 5, 43, 48, 56, 59–60, 67, 73,
    77, 103, 216, 225
  death of, 98, 234n5
  on air defense, 56
Ho Chi Minh City, 1, 8, 15, 47, 62, 174
Ho Chi Minh Trail, 40, 44, 47, 48, 103, 106,
    107
Homba Mountain, 180
Hong Kong, 6
hospitals, 81, 157
  in America, 143, 154, 157, 158
  of ARVN, 165, 169–70
  at Fort Ord (U.S. Army), 157
  at Fort Sam Houston (U.S. Army), 159
  Can Tho General Hospital, 171
  captured Communist patients in, 182
  Charlie Med (C-Med), 146
  Chinese, 79, 81, 82
  facilities of, 178
  of the Fourth Army (U.S. Army), 166
  military administration of, 170
  Ninety-first Evacuation, 153, 159
  Ninth Mobile Army Surgical Hospital
    (M.A.S.H.), 178
  of NVA, 53, 54
  problems in, 170
  supply to, 185
  two-in-one, 170
  in Vietnam, 11, 169, 178, 181, 182, 183
Hou Zhenlu, 215–16
Hue, 27, 159, 166, 167
Hue Phu Bai, 158
humanitarian organizations, 11, 37
Hunter, Tab, 150
Huynh Thu Truong, 55–56
Huynh Van No, 1, 15–16, 232n10

Ia Drang, Battle of, 47, 48, 51–54, 235n9
intelligence,
  ARVN, 31, 33, 34–35

Chinese, 93, 97, 215–16
  Communist system, 94–95, 96, 97
  international conference of, 93
  NVA, 56
  Russian, 94–95, 96
  U.S., 66, 85, 131, 132, 133, 134, 135, 136,
    223
Ivanovo, Yepher, 94

Jackson, Phillip, 125–26, 128, 130
Japan, 98, 103, 144, 145, 155, 157, 159, 160
  occupation of China, 216
  U.S. forces in, 199
  war with Vietnam, 41, 206, 224
Johnson, Lyndon, 5, 16, 111, 163
Jung, Walter Byong I., 177–78

Karatsupa, Nikita, 98, 242n7
Kazakhstan, 6, 65
Kennedy, John F., 16, 111
Kep, 220, 221
KGB, 2, 6
  agents, 93, 94, 95, 96
  assisting China, 93
  Counterintelligence School, 94
  headquarters, 94
  internal control, 96
  officer, 94
  recruiting, 93, 94
  Sixth Department of, 94
  spying on China, 93, 94, 96–97
  training, 93, 94, 97
  "war of twins," 93, 94
Khe Sanh Mountains, 113, 114, 119
Khrushchev, Nikita, 2, 3
Kim, Col., 181
Kim, Lt., 179
Kim, Pt., 185–86
Kirk, Rusty, 124
Kissinger, Henry, 121
Korea, 1, 77, 86, 177, 178, 192
Korea, Republic of (ROK; South Korea),
    177, 178
  army of, 178, 180, 183, 184, 187
  Bachelor Officers' Quarters (BOQ), 181
  Capital Infantry Division, 177
  Field Engineering Group, 178

landing zone of ROK Army, 181
logistics battalion, 186
Logistics Command Headquarters, 178
marine brigade of, 118, 177
military police, 185, 186
Ninth Infantry Division, 177, 178
Ninth Mobile Army Surgical Hospital
    (M.A.S.H.), 178
Second Army Corps, 178
Twenty-eighth Regiment, White Horse
    Infantry Division, 179, 181, 183
White Horse Infantry Division, 178, 179
Korean War (1950–1953), 5, 75, 86, 87, 89,
    111, 126, 138, 159, 167, 178, 199, 216,
    219, 220
Kosygin, Alekei, 2
Krulak, Victor H., 123
Ky Ha, 124, 125–26
Kyiv, 7, 65

Lai Chau, 41, 43, 44
Lang Son, 78, 79
Lao Cai, 88, 218
Laos, 40, 44, 49, 77, 103, 106
    border of, 45, 60
    U.S. incursion of, 46
LARC (lighter, amphibious, resupply,
    cargo), 193, 196
LCU (large, military cargo water craft), 193
Le Duan, 85
Li Danhui, 3
Linh Cam, 44
Li Qingde, 217
logistics, 11, 178
    American, 191
    ARVN, 26, 27–28
    Chinese, 78, 215, 218
    NVA, 40, 44
    officer, 65
    supply depot, 79
    Viet Cong, 44–45
Long Bien Bridge (Paul Dewey Bridge),
    221–22
Long Binh, 207
Long Guilin, 217, 222
Long Khang, 27, 28
Long Xuyen, 16, 17, 19, 21

LST, 193
Lubyanka, 97

Mahoney, Tom, 104
Malaysia, 212, 213
Mao Zedong, 73, 76, 83, 86, 216, 224
Mau Than, 170
May, Terry Lynn, 131–32, 143, 191
McCray, David E., 101–2
McNamara, Robert, 121
McQuinn, Col., 196
medical, 62, 72, 167, 175, 215
    equipment, 167
    field surgery, 167
    French curriculum, 166
    NVA school in China, 62
    sanitary inspection of ARVN, 168
    supply, 170, 178, 215
    technology, 167
    U.S. instructors, 167
    U.S. service, 170
    Wisconsin Medical Center, 175
medics, 11, 128, 146, 148, 149, 160, 161,
    163
    ARVN, 26
    Chinese, 78
    combat of, 143, 144
    corpsman, 143
    doctor, 11, 165, 166, 169–70, 185
    medevac, 127, 148
    officer, 165, 168
    nurse, 11, 153, 156
    U.S. Army Nurse Corps, 157
Mekong Delta, 168
Mekong River, 45, 159, 174
Minsk, 94
missiles, 67, 70, 71, 92, 94
    Chinese, 5, 92, 215
    NVA officers, 67, 69–70
    NVA regiments, 67–68, 71
    NVA Technology Academy, 71
    Russian instructors, 66, 67, 68, 69–70
    Russian operations, 65, 66, 67–68, 70, 90
    Russian technology, 67, 70, 71, 85, 95
    SAM, 67
    SAM-2, 69
    SAM-3, 69

missiles *(cont.)*
SAM-6, 71
SAM-75M, 95
SAM-125, 95
Shrike (U.S.), 88, 89, 90
Morris, Bob, 116
Moscow, 3, 6, 7, 65, 68, 93, 94, 96, 98, 223, 228
Munson, Curt, 111–12
Muse, Stephen, 108
My Tho, 37

Nam Giao, 27
National Liberation Front (NLF), 45.
See also Viet Cong; PLAF (People's
Liberation Armed Force)
Nelson, Bill, 191–92
Ngo Dinh Diem, 15, 16, 17, 19
anti-Communism, 55, 59–60
areas controlled by, 60
assassination of, 20, 209
Ngo Quang Truong, 170
Nguyen Canh Minh, 165–66
Nguyen Khang, 206
Nguyen Khoa Nam, 170
Nguyen Nhieu, 31–32
Nguyen Vung, 205–6
Nguyen Yen Xuan, 1, 23–24
Nha Trang, 33, 103, 178
Ningming City, 78
North Korea, 178
North Vietnam (Democratic Republic of
Vietnam; DRV), 2, 42, 67, 70, 71, 73–
74, 78, 85, 94, 121, 131, 136, 153, 159,
160, 207, 223
Black Thai in, 41, 42–43, 44, 45, 46
border with China, 57, 62, 73, 171
China and, 2, 4–5, 73, 77, 215
founding of, 56
government of, 42, 43, 86, 96, 171
militia, 42
minorities, 41–42
neutrality in Sino-Soviet rivalry, 5, 224
prisoner camp, 165, 171, 246n2
Russian spies in, 93
sending officers to the South, 55
service system, 48
Soviet Union and, 2–3, 67

North Vietnam railroads, 68, 77, 215, 216, 217
bridges of, 220, 221, 222
bypass links, 221
capacity of, 68, 215–16, 220
Chinese construction and repair of, 217–
18, 220, 222
protection of, 220
tunnels, 221, 222
U.S. bombing of, 218–19, 221
North Vietnamese Army (NVA; or People's
Army of Vietnam, PAVN), 2, 6, 16, 77,
90, 111, 119, 145, 166, 170, 172
305th Division, 47
308th Division, 43
316th Division, 40, 43
325th Division, 47
351st Division, 57, 59
air defense, 56, 61, 70, 71, 79, 85, 95
air force of, 39
casualties of, 40, 46, 51, 53, 223, 224
Chinese aid to, 2, 3
command in the South, 45, 49, 235n7
drafting, 40, 42–43, 47, 165
high command, 55, 62, 87, 222, 224
infiltration of the South, 40, 43, 224
minority units, 43
navy of, 39
organization and formation of, 39–40,
43, 44, 51
operation in the South, 21, 27–28, 40,
45–46, 47, 49, 51, 86
prisoners of, 182
replenishment, 51
self-defense force, 42
special force, 96
training, 8, 40, 43, 48
transformation of, 8, 224

Okinawa, 199

Pacific Alaska Columbia (PAC), 193, 196
pacification, 49
Pacific war, 206
Paris, 120
Accord, 228
peace talks, 121, 225
University of, 206

Pechernikov, Georgiy, 95
Pentagon, 23
People's Liberation Armed Forces (PLAF), 2, 16, 111, 170, 171
  casualties of, 40
  joint command, 45, 49
  transformation of, 224
  officer of, 60
  Soviet aid to, 60
  training camps of, 60–61
  See also Viet Cong
People's Liberation Army (PLA; China), 2, 57, 77, 87, 111
  air force of, 79, 87, 92
  Chinese Military Advisory Group (CMAG), 57
  cooperation with NVA, 78, 91
  high command, 6, 77, 85, 86, 87, 88, 217, 238–39n6
  in Cultural Revolution, 83–84
  navy of, 36, 87
  Ninth Army Corps, 216
  officers, 85, 87, 216, 224
  operation in Vietnam, 77, 249n5
  party committees in, 76
  recruitment, 75
  songs of, 73
  training NVA troops, 8
People's Liberation Army (PLA) AAA (antiaircraft artillery) force, 73, 74, 78, 92, 225
  First Division, Shenyang Regional Command, 75, 77, 79
  Thirty-first Division, 74, 78, 80–82
  Sixty-fourth Division, 85–86, 87, 88, 92
  Sixty-fifth Division, 87, 88
  air-defense tactics, 91, 92
  battles of, 6, 79, 81, 82, 88, 89, 92, 241n15
  casualties, 82, 92
  divisions in Vietnam, 5, 6, 7, 73–74, 78, 225
  officers, 5, 7, 78
  reorganization, 87, 92
  rotation of, 5, 77, 79, 83, 86, 239n10
People's Liberation Army (PLA), Railroad Engineering Corps (REC), 217, 218, 220

casualties of, 222
First Division, 216, 217, 218, 221, 222
  operation in Vietnam, 5, 215
people's war, 47, 232n9, 235
Peterson, Ron, 143–44
Pham Van Dong, 225
Phan Rang, 193, 195
Philippines, 199
Phuoc Ty, 28
Phu Quoc Island, 171
Phu Tho, 209, 210
Phu Tuc, 27
Pleiku, 52, 103, 108
Plei Me, 51
Poland, 6, 67
Ponder, Darrell L., 107
post-traumatic stress disorder (PTSD), 119, 120
Poulo Candae Island, 171
Preobrazhensky, George, 98
prisoners of war (POW)
  American, 228
  camps in Vietnam, 90, 165, 171, 172
  Communist prisoners, 171, 182, 183
  health condition of, 171
  injured or killed, 172, 173
  medicine for, 172
  U.S. programs for, 213
  Viet Cong, 178

Qin Chaoying, 85
Quang Tri, 158
Quin Nhon, 104

Rach Gia, 35
radar, 86, 88
  air defense, 65
  antenna, 89
  Chinese system, 215
  fire-control, 87, 92
  gun-laying, 88
  long-range, 36
  medium-range, 91
  Model-405, 92
  Model-572, 92
  Model-586, 92
  Model-589, 92

radar *(cont.)*
  operation, 33
  NVA regiments, 71
  Russian operators, 72
  Russian system, 70
Red Cross, 175, 182
Red River, 45, 59
roads in Vietnam
  Route 1, 79, 222
  Route 9, 19
  Route 21, 52
Robertson, Dale, 119
Romania, 6

Sadehip, 200, 201
Saigon, 9, 11, 27, 32, 33, 56, 57, 59, 103,
    133, 134, 135, 136, 167, 171, 174, 184,
    207
  commando of, 137
  fall of, 228
  Medical University of, 167
  River, 133, 134
searchlight, 78
17th parallel, 55, 167
Shandong, 216
Shanghai, 216
Shenyang, 86
  AAA Academy (PLA), 86
  Regional Command (PLA), 75, 83, 87
Sino-Soviet rivalry, 3, 93, 97–98, 223,
    224–25
  polemic debate, 3
  in Vietnam, 5
Smith, George, 124
Son La, 44
Son Loc, 28
South China Sea, 36, 126, 178, 179, 183,
    186, 193, 211
Southeast Asia, 3, 23, 174
  Communist movement in, 5
  countries, 9
  U.S. forces in, 199
South Vietnam (Republic of Vietnam;
    ROV), 77, 101, 102, 103, 106, 111,
    113, 123, 125, 134, 135, 136, 137, 145,
    153, 158, 165, 171, 177, 183, 187
  against Communists, 167, 226

army of, 118
"boat people," 9, 55, 175, 211–12
Communist takeover of, 165, 225
corruption in, 205, 207–9, 210
founding of, 167, 207
government, 59–60, 205
minorities, 45
nationalism in, 15, 23
National Police Academy, 167
refugees from, 9, 125, 175, 212, 213
Soviet Union (Union of Soviet Socialist
    Republics; USSR), 2, 5–6, 7, 8, 9, 11,
    65, 66, 71, 72, 86, 88, 97, 121, 224,
    225, 228, 230
  aid to Vietnam, 2–3, 230n13
  border with China, 68
  collapse of, 65, 121
  embassy at Hanoi, 94, 95
  government of, 65, 71, 72
  policy toward Vietnam, 2–3, 6, 7, 93,
    237n5, 237n9
Soviet Union armed forces, 8, 66, 68, 71,
    76, 95
  AAA Technology Academy, 66
  Detachment #31920, 68
  experience, 8, 70
  Foreign Military Intelligence Directorate,
    General Staff, 96
  military missionary, 95
  officer, 67, 68, 71
  recruits, 66
  training of NVA, 8, 65, 66, 69–70
  troops in Vietnam, 65, 66, 68, 69, 71, 72,
    90, 237n7
Spry, Ed, 119
Stalin, Joseph, 93
Strategic Hamlet Program, 16, 20, 49,
    232n9
Stuchilov, Alexander, 68, 70

T., Major (pseud.; Russian missile
    instructor), 65–66
Ta Duc Hao, 47–48
Taiwan, 77, 199
Tet Offensive (1968), 16, 40, 47, 51, 111,
    162, 170, 187, 224
Thailand, 71, 77, 166, 174, 201

people of, 201–2
U.S. forces in, 199, 200, 201
Thai Nguyen, 79, 220–21
Thanh Noi, 27
Thu Duc, 207
Thuong Duc, 27
Tin Can, 106
Tonkin Gulf Incident, 43
Tran Lai Li, 9, 11, 15, 55
Tran Thanh, 39–40
Truong Son mountain range, 44
Tucker, Don, 116
Tucker, Spencer C., 5
Tung Son, 27
tunnels, 1, 45, 46, 51
Tuy Hoa, 103–4, 158, 159, 179

Ukraine, 6, 7, 65, 66
UN Truce Supervision Officer, 111
uniform, 68, 78, 215, 218
United States (U.S.), 1–2, 5, 6, 7, 10–11, 15,
    20–21, 32, 43, 77, 117, 136, 155, 157,
    159, 161, 163, 165, 166, 175, 177, 223
advisers to South Vietnam, 165
aid to South Vietnam, 15, 16, 23, 24, 31,
    32, 101, 102, 111, 112, 123, 124, 132,
    167, 226
antiwar movement in, 227
Defense Intelligence Agency (DIA), 96
Federal Aviation Administration (FAA),
    200
imperialism of, 43, 184
normalization with Vietnam, 228
people of, 37, 67, 77, 79, 87, 121, 145,
    148, 149, 154, 164, 193
policy toward Vietnam, 15–16, 23
Vietnamese refugees in, 29, 31, 37, 41,
    46, 136
war in Vietnam, 1, 2, 26
United States Air Force (USAF), 11, 71, 77,
    157, 192, 200, 218–19
air evacuation, 159
air force base, 71, 179, 199
Air National Guard, 153–54, 157
aviation technology, 90
Bien Hoa USAF Base, 103, 104, 132, 133
Brooks USAF Base, 154

Clark USAF Base, 155, 200
Da Nang USAF Base, 149
FAC (forward air controller), 162
Hickam USAF Base, 156
Keesler USAF Base, 200
Lackland USAF Base, 206
137th Air Medical Evacuation Squadron,
    155
pilots, 77, 90–91, 96
Scott USAF Base, 200
Tinker USAF Base, 203
Ton Son Nhut USAF Base, 134, 136
training, 200
Travis USAF Base, 102, 138, 157
Tuy Hoa USAF Base, 158
U Tapao USAF Base (Thailand), 199,
    200, 201
United States armed forces, 6, 137, 153,
    156–57, 164, 223–24
I Corps Tactical Zone, 123
advisors in ARVN, 15, 19, 20, 24, 26,
    165, 167, 168–70, 195
casualties, 227, 228
drafting, 102
estimated time of separation (ETS), 108
Green Berets, 162
ground force in South Vietnam, 1, 5, 27,
    48
Military Affiliate Radio System (MARS),
    161–62
Military Assistance Command, South
    Vietnam (MACV), 107, 194, 195
operation, 177, 178
rotation to the States (DEROS), 193, 226
ROTC, 131
R&R, 149, 160, 163
special force, 162
"useful adversary," 224
withdrawal from Vietnam, 27, 86, 210
United States Army, 102, 135, 154, 156,
    181, 192
advanced individual training (AIT), 107,
    157
Camp Evans, 158
Charlie Battery, 103, 104, 105
Charlie Company, 102
Fire Direction Center (FDC), 105

United States Army *(cont.)*
First Log (logistical command), 194
Fort Bliss, 105
Fort Bragg, 132
Fort Eustis, 192
Fort Lewis, 108, 197
Fort Ord, 157
Fort Polk, 102
Forty-fifth Military Intelligence
Company, 192
Forty-first Artillery, 102–4
Fourth Army Corps, 170–71
GI, 149, 156, 158
inactive reserve, 108
Lambert Field, 132
landing zone (LZ), 102–3, 105–6, 114,
115
Ninety-first Evac, 153
Non-Commissioned Officer Candidate
School (NCOCS), 102, 107, 108, 109
Oakland Army Base, 102, 104, 108
101st Airborne Division, 159–60
173rd Airborne Division, 102, 105
officers, 118, 193
Parker Compound, 134, 135, 137
ROTC, 132, 178, 192
soldiers of, 118, 193, 194
Staging Battalion, 113, 116
training, 102
United States Marines, 21, 111, 113–14,
118, 120, 121, 123, 124, 125, 146, 148,
160
Basic Infantry Training School (BITS),
112
cooperation with navy, 134
First Marine Air Wing (1st MAW), 124,
125, 143–44
First Marine Division, 113, 216
H&S Company, 113
Infantry Regiment Training (IRT), 112,
124
Marine Air Group (MAG), 16, 17, 125,
147
Marine Corps Command and Staff
College, 112
Marine Corps Recruit Depot, 112
Mike Company, 113

National Aviation Technology Training
Center (NATTC), 124
operations, 26, 27
Third Battalion, 113
"Ugly Angel" Squadron, 123
United States Navy, 31, 33–34, 134
boot camp, 199
medical support for the marines, 143
Naval War Academy, 33
reserves, 143, 144, 199
United States Rolling Thunder campaign,
47, 67, 70, 71, 74, 79, 85–87, 95, 215,
221, 223
bombing, 81, 88, 94, 96, 217, 218–19, 221
results of, 82, 215, 218–19, 221
time-delay bombs, 222
Urumqi, 6
USO, 147
USSR (Union of Soviet Socialist Republics).
See Soviet Union

vehicle, 16, 215
ARVN armored, 51, 52
Chinese armored, 215
Chinese tanks, 215
jeep, 137
Russian, 91
truck, 44, 48, 52, 78, 108, 192, 193, 194
truck company, 194
Verkhoturov, Boris, 72
vessels, 32, 33, 35, 36, 37
Chinese warship, 35, 36, 215
of Panama, 212
reconnaissance boat, 34
Soviet, 212
supply ship, 36
U.S. warship, 33
veterans
American, 1, 9, 10, 108, 109, 112, 119,
121, 143, 153, 191, 197
ARVN, 1, 10–11, 15, 23, 29, 31, 226
Chinese, 7, 73–74, 84, 89, 92, 220
homecoming, 197
Korean, 10
NVA, 7–8, 39, 47, 54, 121
Russian, 65, 71–72
Veterans Administration (U.S.), 143, 144

Viet Cong, 7–8
Vietnam Veterans against the War
    (VVAW; U.S.), 120
Viet Cong (VC), 2, 17, 101, 106, 118, 119,
    121, 133, 134, 145, 150, 159, 162, 168,
    170, 171, 174, 177, 179, 180, 182, 184,
    187, 196, 224
  agent of, 32, 35
  aid to, 2, 47
  attack by, 24, 25
  cooperation with NVA, 44–45
  high command, 45
  insurgents, 16
  operation of, 46
  punishing the former ARVN soldiers, 28
  transformation of, 224
  See also People's Liberation Armed
    Forces (PLAF)
Viet Minh, 39, 41, 56, 58, 166
  agent of, 206
  anti-French movement, 206
  assassination by, 207
  Chinese aid, 57
  high command, 57
  training programs, 57–59
Vietnam, 2, 3, 6, 7, 9, 41, 67, 68, 72, 73, 77,
    82, 85, 88, 101–2, 104, 108, 113, 117,
    121, 123, 125, 131, 132, 133, 135, 145,
    147, 150, 152, 154, 155, 156, 157, 158,
    160, 161, 163, 165, 177, 200
  Americans in, 191, 192
  civilian casualties, 1, 20
  climate, 49, 81, 86, 101, 135, 146, 149
  culture, 206
  language of, 57–58, 69, 72, 82, 94, 95
  Memorial, 116
  Nationalist Army of, 166, 167
  people of, 77, 78, 134, 148, 151, 152, 163,
    165, 168
  terrain, 87, 163, 226
Vietnamese Communist Party, 38, 39, 41,
    43, 85
  in South Vietnam, 45, 56
  party committee, 57, 234n5
Vietnam War, 1, 2, 5, 9, 16, 41, 55, 76, 77,
    90, 93, 112, 121, 123, 131, 139, 153,
    163, 165, 177, 223

  Americans in, 191
  Chinese in, 72, 74, 216
  history of, 7, 9, 10, 84, 92, 123, 178
  Russians in, 65, 67–68, 72
Vo Nguyen Giap, 39

Washington, D.C., 7, 34, 101–2, 109, 228
weapons, 49, 166
  .38 caliber, 130
  37 mm antiaircraft machine gun, 75, 76,
    79, 80, 81–82, 90, 92
  AK-47, 119
  antitank rockets, 43
  automatic rifles, 43
  Chinese made, 40, 73, 215
  grenade, 185, 194
  M-16, 107
  machine gun, 21, 43, 194
  Russian made, 40, 86–87
  small arms, 33, 48, 193, 194
  U.S. made, 48, 167
Weber, Major General, 156
Westmoreland, William C., 111
West Point, 9, 108
White House, 23, 26, 135
World War II, 39, 41, 56, 87, 111, 112, 117,
    119, 123, 138, 159, 166, 199, 206, 216,
    227

Xinjiang, 6

Yen Bai, 88, 89
Youyiguan (Friendship Pass), 78, 218, 220,
    221
Yugoslavia, 6
Yunnan, 218

Zhang Aiping, 5
Zhang Shuguang, 5
Zhao Shunfen, 73–74